Chicago

Comparative American Cities

A series edited by Joe T. Darden

Chicago

Race, Class, and the Response to Urban Decline

Gregory D. Squires
Larry Bennett
Kathleen McCourt
Philip Nyden

Temple University Press · Philadelphia

Temple University Press, Philadelphia 19122

Copyright © 1987 by Temple University. All rights reserved

Published 1987

Printed in the United States of America

∞ The paper used in this publication meets the minimum
requirements of American National Standard for Information
Sciences—Permanence of paper for Printed Library Materials,
ANSI Z39.48-1984

Library of Congress Cataloging-in-Publication Data

Chicago: race, class, and the response to urban decline.

  (Comparative American cities)

  Includes index.

  1. Chicago (Ill.)—Social conditions.

2. Chicago (Ill.)—Economic conditions.

3. Community organization—Illinois—Chicago.

4. Chicago (Ill.)—Race relations.

5. Urban renewal—Illinois—Chicago.

I. Squires, Gregory D.

II. Series.

HN80.C5C54   1987   306'.09773'11   87-1876

ISBN 0-87722-487-0 (alk. paper)

Contents

vi   Contents

List of Maps, Figures, and Tables

Maps

Figures

Tables

Acknowledgments

Many people contributed in invaluable ways to this book. Joe Darden got us into this project and provided helpful guidance throughout. Doris B. Braendel, our editor, did a magnificent job of turning our occasionally illiterate prose into comprehensible text and creating what we believe is now a most readable book. We also wish to thank the several colleagues in our respective departments and universities who read and commented on earlier drafts of the manuscript, as well as DePaul University's College of Liberal Arts and Sciences, which assisted Larry Bennett with a summer research grant. The many Chicagoans who shared their thoughts with us during our research, and the scholars, journalists, organizers, and others whose work inspired us are too numerous to mention. Nevertheless, we are indebted to them all. Our greatest appreciation goes to the many people who have struggled for decades to make Chicago a livable community. Finally, we want to acknowledge the support, intellectual, emotional, and otherwise, of Margot Squires, Warren Friedman, and Gwen Nyden.

SERIES PREFACE

The Comparative American Cities series grew out of a need for more comparative scholarly works on America's urban areas in the post-World War II era. American cities are storehouses of potential assets and liabilities for their residents and for society as a whole. It is important that scholars examine the nation's metropolitan areas to assess trends that may affect economic and political decision-making in the future.

The books have a contemporary approach, with the post-World War II period providing historical antecedents for current concerns. Each book generally addresses the same issues, although the peculiarities of the local environments necessarily shape each account. The major areas of concern include uneven regional development, white middle-class suburbanization, residential segregation of races and classes, and central-city issues such as economic disinvestment, black political power, and the concentration of blacks, Hispanics, and the poor. Each city in the series is viewed within the context of its metropolitan area as a whole. Taken together, these studies describe the spatial redistribution of wealth within the metropolises—the economic decline of central cities and the economic rise of the suburbs—a redistribution facilitated by the massive construction of interstate highways in the 1950s, 1960s, and 1970s.

Since World War II the metropolitan areas included in this series have been increasingly affected by uneven economic and social development and by conflict between cities and suburbs and between the white majority and the growing nonwhite minority. The central cities of each metropolitan area have also been losing jobs to the suburbs. There has been a tendency toward growing income inequality between cities and suburbs and between blacks and whites. Economic growth and decline have followed closely the racial composition of neighborhoods—that is, black neighborhoods have declined, while white neighborhoods have generally grown.

All of these studies assess the ways central-city governments have responded to these issues. In recent years most central-city elected officials have attempted to provide services and employment opportunities on a more equitable basis and to implement a more balanced and progressive economic development agenda. Most central-city mayors have been elected with the strong support of minorities, and the mayors have often cooperated with the business elite in attempts to stimulate more economic growth and to save the cities from further economic decline. Since this decline is related to structural changes in the economy within the context of uneven development, however, attempts at preventing the flow of jobs to the suburbs have largely failed, and the economic and social gap continues to widen.

There are no quick solutions to the economic, racial, and political problems of the cities in these studies. Though high-technology industries may play a part in each city's future, it is unlikely that they will produce as many jobs as are needed, or reduce the racial differences in unemployment rates. Blacks and other minorities who have limited spatial access to the areas of high-tech industries may not receive a fair share of their benefits.

Each city's plight is deeply rooted in America's problems of free-market economic investment, racial prejudice and discrimination, and the outmoded political structure that continues to separate the city from the suburbs, one suburb from another, the rich from the poor, and blacks from whites. As long as this structure remains, there is a strong probability that the situation will worsen, as population mobility continues to reinforce patterns of economic, social, and racial inequality, contributing to more racial and class conflict.

The problems of urban America require the immediate attention of government officials and the citizenry of this nation. New solutions involving changes in the political structure are long overdue. Our hope is that comparative studies such as these might provide the impetus for informed decisions and policies that will address the underlying problems besetting America's major urban areas.

Joe T. Darden, Series Editor
Comparative American Cities

Chicago

1

Introduction: The Chicago Growth Machine

"What can I do for you?" still means "What can you do for me?"

Nelson Algren[1]

As the Daley era fades further into history and Chicago has experienced life under its first black mayor, the city confronts many new problems along with the changing contours of troubles that have long plagued the nation's Second City. During the mid-fifties and sixties Richard J. Daley ruled a growing and prosperous city. Over the past twenty years, however, Chicago has experienced a steady loss of jobs, fiscal crises affecting virtually all public services, and exacerbation of tensions along racial, ethnic, and class lines that have historically divided this city of neighborhoods.

In an all too typical headline the *Chicago Tribune* announced in the summer of 1983: "City Loses 123,500 Jobs."[2] The study cited by the *Tribune* found that, while the city lost 123,500, or 10 percent, of its private sector jobs between 1972 and 1981, the metropolitan area experienced a 25 percent increase. One significant trend cut across the city-suburban line: on both sides of the city limits, black and racially mixed neighborhoods lost jobs while predominantly white communities experienced net gains.

The loss of jobs in the city has had several adverse consequences. Subsequent revenue shortfalls have been translated into declining municipal services and widening cleavages in city council. In recent years Chicagoans have endured strikes by their fire fighters, county hospital workers, transit workers, and teachers. And the question of whether or not the schools will have enough money to open on time has become an annual fall drama.

Chicago's declining economic fortunes have been accompanied by many lacerations in the community's social and political fabric. If Chicago earned its reputation as the nation's most segregated city in decades past, little in the 1980s has served to dispel the notion.[3] That Harold Washington became the mayor in 1983 does not deny the significance of his opponent's most persuasive campaign slogan, "Epton, before it's too late." The subsequent "Council Wars" between Mayor Washington's supporters and an opposition faction in the city council offered vivid daily reminders of the continuing significance of race in Chicago and the detrimental economic and social impact citywide of that racial conflict. In what is both a cause and a consequence of the deterioration of the Daley machine, Chicago is simply not the political force it was just a decade ago. As the suburbs grow, at the expense of the city, Chicago is losing its influence locally. Consequently, Chicago has less power in the state capital. For similar reasons, it is doubtful that Chicago's mayor will ever again be the kingmaker in national politics that Mayor Daley was a few years ago.

This book explores the dynamics of economic change in Chicago, the concomitant racial and ethnic strife and class conflict, and the evolving political structure of the city and the metropolitan area since World War II. Chicago has aged in the last 40 years. It is no longer the "Hog Butcher for the World" that Carl Sandburg portrayed in his romantic vision of the city 70 years ago; the stockyards left Chicago more than a decade ago. Neither is Chicago the "Tool Maker" or "Player with Railroads" that it used to be. The smokestacks certainly have not disappeared, but the loss to the city of 25 percent of its factories during the 1970s represents a trend that is not likely to be reversed in the near future.[4] In addition, despite some recent slight gains in population between 1980 and 1985, the city has lost population in past decades. Between 1970 and 1980, for example, the city's population dropped from 3,363,000 to 3,005,000.[5] Chicago is undergoing a transition that will affect all city neighborhoods and every dimension of life in the metropolitan area. The precise trajectory of ongoing changes is, however, uncertain.

While the city has aged, in many respects it has also matured. As Chicago confronts many problems, both new and old, it does so equipped with many strengths, some of which have long been part of the city's landscape and some of which have been cultivated only in recent years. The following chapters examine these advantages and identify the tools available to the city for building a prosperous future. Whether that potentiality becomes a reality depends largely on the outcome of the political struggles that are described in the following chapters. If "Chicago ain't ready for reform," as the famed saloon keeper and alderman Paddy Bauler reputedly proclaimed after Daley's election in 1955,[6] it does appear in the 1980s that, ready or not, the city is at least getting a dose of it.

Chicago: The Machine and the Muckrakers

The city of Chicago has been the subject for writers of every stripe. Poets and novelists, social scientists and journalists, public officials and private citizens over the years have produced volumes about this small plot of land that Yankee traders hustled from the Pottawattomies almost 200 years ago. The mounds of material tend to coalesce around four types of literature, described below. Despite the knowledge that has accumulated, there are critical blind spots in the literature on Chicago.

Chicago may be best known for its legendary political machine, which has provided the grist for one of Chicago's literary mills. The machine, most notably under Richard J. Daley, has been the subject of many journalistic and scholarly books, particularly in the 1970s, when the machine appeared to be weakening and Daley's power was on the decline.[7] Invaluable insights about the city's political and social life have been revealed. Scandals are often exposed and the guilty excoriated. Yet this literature tends to glorify the machine and its constituent parts. Such perverse celebration of corruption has served to mystify as well as unveil the workings of the political structure, thus inadvertently perpetuating that corruption. According to Chicago folklore, it is the presumed efficiency of the machine that has made Chicago the city that works. After all, it is often stated, look what democracy under Lindsay did to New York. Of course about the only thing the machine has done efficiently is to reward its members and their friends. Daley himself has generally been portrayed as a deeply religious and committed family man. Indeed he may have been. But this image, along with the presumed efficiency of the "organization," enabled the Chicago machine to perpetuate itself long after other big city machines had disappeared.

A second enduring literature is represented by the "Chicago School of Sociology," particularly its community studies tradition beginning in the 1920s and continuing today.[8] Ecological analyses from Florian Znaniecki and Robert Park to Gerald Suttles and Albert Hunter provide detailed descriptions of Chicago's cultural mosaic. But description is not explanation. If the ordered segmentation of age, sex, ethnic, and territorial groupings found by Suttles in a near West Side neighborhood in the 1960s is "impelled by a far more basic task of finding an order within which [the residents] can secure themselves against common apprehensions,"[9] questions arise as to what the fundamental causes of those apprehensions are, why the "defended neighborhood" takes the shape that it does, who benefits, who loses, and how changes in the order (or disorder) can be explained.

Political pamphleteering by the city's civic organizations and activist community groups constitutes a third genre. This tradition goes back at least to the turn of the century in the work of Jane Addams, Upton Sinclair, and many other social reformers. Among the better-known organizations today are the Chicago Urban League, the Illinois Public Action Council, the Community Renewal Society, the Latino Institute, the Leadership Council for Metropolitan Open Communities, the League of Women Voters, the Metropolitan Housing and Planning Council, the Midwest Community Council, the Organization of the Northeast, and TRUST, Inc. The interests of such organizations cover a wide range including civil rights, neighborhood empowerment, clean elections, jobs, transportation, culture, and architecture. The number of such organizations is in the thousands. A 1983 directory of groups involved in economic development alone includes over 130 organizations.[10]

The reports published by these organizations are generally reform-motivated and liberal-oriented. While occasionally those reports reach statewide or even nationwide audiences, they are generally prepared for a particular group of public officials or prominent private citizens—the "movers and shakers"—as well as other political activists within Chicago. They tend to be narrowly focused, usually on one issue, and directed to a specific target (for example, city and state government, banks, school boards). At the same time, these documents are frequently disseminated through the media to the general public. Often they achieve the intended results. For example, as part of the anti-redlining campaign spearheaded by Gale Cincotta in 1979, the National Training and Information Center (NTIC) released two reports documenting the refusal of major insurance companies to write homeowners insurance in older urban communities: "Insurance Redlining: Profits vs. Policyholders" and "Insurance Redlining: Organizing to Win." The state of Illinois proceeded to enact several laws prohibiting redlining practices. At the same time major insurers (including Aetna, Allstate, and Travelers) signed written agreements with NTIC and a number of community organizations to increase their underwriting and investment activities in Chicago and other urban communities around the nation.[11]

Unfortunately, a more typical response of city officials to the disclosure of impropriety was Mayor Daley's statement in 1972 after he was criticized for transferring city insurance business to a company in suburban Evanston that his son John had just joined. An angry Daley said, about his critics, "If I can't help my sons . . . then they can kiss my ass. . . . I make no apologies to anyone. There are many men in this room whose fathers helped them and they went on to become fine public officials. . . . If a man can't put his arms around his sons, then what kind of world are we living in?"[12] One outcome of these events was to improve the mayor's image as a good family man.

Among the schools of Chicago literature, the novelists have probably come closest to explaining the essence of the city. Sixty years ago H. L. Mencken stated that, with few exceptions, all the important writers came from Chicago. Nelson Algren, Sherwood Anderson, Saul Bellow, Theodore Dreiser, James Farrell, Studs Terkel, and Richard Wright are just some of the writers associated most closely with Chicago who have emerged since Mencken offered one of his rare compliments to the Midwest. Such fictional characters as Frank Cowperwood, Studs Lonigan, and Bigger Thomas provided a more sophisticated understanding of race relations, ethnic neighborhoods, and the intimately connected worlds of business and politics than the most carefully designed empirical study or the most dogged journalistic investigation could reveal.[13] Yet, if these artists have dramatically articulated the conflicts that are continually played out in Chicago, they offer little concrete guidance for the well-meaning (and the not so well-meaning) mortals who struggle with these concerns daily.

Each Chicago school of literature has contributed immensely to the store of knowledge about this community. Each also has its limitations. Even when viewed collectively, critical blind spots remain. At least two key shortcomings are frequently manifested. First, vital connections that link the city with the national and international communities, as well as connections among neighborhoods within the city and between wealth and poverty generally, are inadequately treated. Second, most analysts (be they apologists or advocates) are unwittingly blinded by a growth ideology.

Chicago Connections: The Missing Links

It has become obvious in recent years that the fate of Chicago is inextricably tied to the fate of the industrial Midwest and the dynamics of national and international economies. But even today, the implications of these relationships for developments within the Chicago metropolitan area are underestimated, and sometimes ignored altogether.

Chicago, the Nation, and the World

Clearly, the growth and prosperity Chicago enjoyed in the 1950s and the 1960s was rooted in the postwar boom that benefited many sections of the country. Several heavy manufacturing industries that profited handsomely had operations in Chicago. The city was, and remains, a transportation hub and regional headquarters for many businesses. But such structural dimensions of the city's life are invisible to the purveyors of Chicago folklore. Chicagoans prefer to think of their town as the "City of Broad Shoulders," as if there is something in the spirit and sinew of the residents, identified by Sandburg 70 years ago, that accounts for the wealth of the city. Mayor Jane Byrne frequently defended her administration by proclaiming that Chicago was not a Cleveland, in a manner that suggested the differences were attributable to the personal qualities of the respective public officials. Despite differences in the history of the two cities, conveniently forgotten were the many similarities in the structural forces shaping their evolution.

If the dynamics of regional, national, and international economics are ignored by many observers, economics is dispensed with altogether in some efforts to explain Chicago. In his attempt to explain the Daley years through personal interviews with the era's major political actors, political scientist Milton Rakove stated up front in 1979, "I decided at the beginning that I would only ask questions about the political side of politics, and would ignore the economic side, since no politician would talk about such matters on a tape recorder."[14] But reality can be elusive; it does not always reveal itself in a manner that coincides with the personal convenience of the researcher. If we are to understand fully the evolution of Chicago, any of its neighborhoods, or any other community, economics and the linkages with the "outside world" must be confronted.

Conglomerate-merger activity is an illustrative case. Many insurance companies, for example, have been taken over by conglomerates and used as "cash cows" by the parent. By draining the reserves of what is now an insurance subsidiary for the non-insurance investment priorities of the parent, the firm must restrict the amount of insurance it writes. Older urban communities—particularly their minority areas—are the first to suffer. As *Business Week* editor Gelvin Stevenson concluded in his analysis of the ITT takeover of the Hartford Insurance Company, "Suddenly, when the survival of Hartford's North End or Chicago's Logan Square depends on what is best for ITT, Chile does not seem so far away."[15]

None of this is meant to deny the very real difference that individuals can make. Chicago may well have been able to forestall municipal employee strikes, keep several businesses from leaving the city, and secure an inordinate share of federal dollars over a longer period of time on the strength of Mayor Daley's handshake and persuasive powers. But the latitude Daley and others had to maneuver and negotiate was framed by many structural constraints.

No Neighborhood Is an Island

Relationships among Chicago communities constitute a second set of all too often missing links in the Chicago literature. Yet connections among neighborhoods within the Chicago metropolitan area must also be explored to understand why some areas thrive while others barely survive. That differences exist among the city's neighborhoods is, of course, quite evident to all residents. Such unanimity does not prevail, however, in efforts to explain those differences. Again, many are quick to point to individual or personal traits in lauding the virtues of their community while at the same time characterizing individuals from other neighborhoods according to derogatory group stereotypes. Many Chicagoans "know" what will happen to property values if "they" move in.

Many institutional practices are predicated on, and reinforce, these prejudices. As the Code of Ethics of the National Real Estate Board said until 1950: "A realtor should never be instrumental in introducing into a neighborhood a character of property or occupancy, members of any race or nationality, or any individuals whose presence will clearly be detrimental to property values in that neighborhood."[16] Often, the mere fact that a neighborhood is integrated is sufficient for appraisers to downgrade the property value, no matter what the condition of the physical structures or the financial status of the families may be.[17] Once the appraisers speak, the lenders listen, and a self-fulfilling prophecy is well under way.[18]

Despite the seemingly universal tendency to view human behavior in individualistic terms, these real estate practices illustrate the variety of institutional and structural linkages that play primary roles in shaping the uneven development of any city. One factor that certainly influences the overall health of a community is money. Without money, or more precisely investment capital, people cannot operate businesses, build or renovate homes, or provide any of the essential (or even non-essential) services for a liveable community. Among the major sources of capital are banks, savings and loans, insurance companies, and government. Yet research has demonstrated that in their mortgage lending and investment activities, Chicago financial institutions have exhibited a clear preference for predominantly white and suburban communities even after conventional financial considerations of risk are taken into account.[19] That is, a racial bias exists that cannot be accounted for in terms of strictly economic criteria. And city expenditures for planning and economic development mirror these patterns of private investment. Public dollars generally go where private dollars have gone as the city strives to attract middle-class white families to its residential neighborhoods.[20]

Competition and conflict do exist among Chicago's many communities —geographic and others. While these struggles for investment capital and other resources do not necessarily constitute a zero-sum game, some groups in the city do benefit at the expense of others. These adversarial, if not exploitative, relationships may go a long way toward explaining the apprehensions that give rise to the defended neighborhood.

Wealth and Poverty

A third and most important set of connections that must be understood to explain Chicago, or any other metropolitan area, are the linkages between wealth and poverty. Symbols of Chicago's wealth abound on the lakefront from the mansions in the North Shore suburbs, the luxury apartments in Water Tower Place, North Michigan Avenue's Magnificent Mile, the Gold Coast, to the parks and museums that run the length of the city. But Marshall Field (I, II, III, IV, or V) never lifted a brick to construct any of the family's department stores. Just a few blocks west of Lake Michigan are the Robert Taylor and Cabrini-Green public housing projects and Haymarket Square, concrete reminders that poverty continues to be as much a part of Chicago as the lakefront. Chicago's wealth has not come cheap. As Charles Bowden and Lew Kreinberg observed:

> Human misery and the waste of human lives was as much the product of the economy as the tall towers, the railroads, the factories, the boulevards. It was a payment, a charge avoided, ignored, largely denied. The city—the City That Works—worked by pyramiding debt in the form of diminished men, women, and children, terrible housing, unfit working conditions.
>
> The initial thing to note is that Chicago at its prime, the Chicago that became the global pattern for the industrial city, never paid these bills, never operated with these costs figured into its budget. The city that said I Will, was not willing to take up every task, meet every obligation.[21]

John H. Perkins, chairman of the Chicago Economic Development Commission and former president of Continental Bank boasted, "If you objectively analyze the assets and advantages of Chicago, you will come to one conclusion. It is simply one of the best cities in the world for business." [22] He proceeded to point to the city's location, its supply of resources and people, the fact that every business in Chicago has a friend in city hall, and the many recreational and cultural opportunities including the symphony, opera, museums, theatre, and educational institutions. Perkins concluded, "The city that works, lives well too."

But the opportunity to live well frequently comes at the expense of those who Nelson Algren claimed form the heart of the city:

> And all the stately halls of science, the newest Broadway hit, the endowed art galleries, are not for their cold pavement-colored eyes. For the masses who do the city's labor also keep the city's heart. And they think there's something fishy about someone giving them a museum for nothing and free admission on Saturday afternoon.
>
> They sense somebody got a bargain, and they are right. The city's arts are built upon the uneasy consciences that milked the city of millions on the grain exchange, in traction and utilities and sausage-stuffing and then bought conscience-ease with a minute fraction of the profits. A museum for a traction system, an opera building for a utilities empire. Therefore the arts themselves here, like the acres of Lorado Taft's deadly handiwork, are largely statuary. Mere monuments to the luckier brokers of the past. So the people shy away from their gifts, they're never sure quite why. [23]

Growth Ideology as an Obstacle to Growth

If these critical connections frequently go unnoticed, the facts that Chicago has serious economic problems, that these problems affect virtually all dimensions of the community's social life, and that the political structure is changing dramatically are widely recognized. More recent scenarios for Chicago's future are beginning to recognize that the city is not immune to problems facing the Midwest or even the nation. [24] That Chicago's industrial mix is shifting from heavy manufacturing to service and high-technology industries is noted, along with the conviction that the city should encourage such developments to take advantage of emerging growth industries. Yet more fundamental structural and particularly exploitative dimensions inherent in the process of uneven development are either ignored or viewed as issues that can only be addressed after higher-priority concerns—generating economic growth—have been resolved. If it is widely understood that the city's economic and social problems will not be resolved simply by the next upturn in the business cycle, with perhaps a few exceptions nobody is demanding fundamental changes in the city's and nation's basic institutional structure either.

Almost three decades ago Daniel Bell proclaimed the end of ideology, asserting that conflicts over fundamental values had virtually disappeared, leaving the technical question of how we can produce "more" as the central challenge of American society.[25] What in fact occurred was not the end of ideology but the onset of the growth ideology. And cities increasingly became growth machines—centers for private capital accumulation—with civic leaders in both the private and public sectors viewing their role as primarily one of "preparing the ground" for capital.[26] Such a perspective has blinded policymakers to ongoing ideological struggles and served to retard the very growth it endorses.

The essence of the growth ideology can be stated succinctly: none of the nation's urban social problems can be resolved until greater economic growth occurs, and the way to stimulate that growth is by providing financial incentives to private investors. Other legitimate concerns must simply take a back seat, according to this perspective, which has been advocated by public officials at all levels of government and by prominent private citizens throughout the nation, including Chicago.

As *Business Week* argued in 1980:

Stated plainly, all social groups in the U.S. today must understand that their common interest in returning the country to a path of strong economic growth overrides other conflicting interests. . . . In the U.S. during the past 20 years, policy has emphasized improving the quality of life, particularly attempts to redistribute income to low income groups and minorities and to create an egalitarian society. Now it is clear that the government cannot achieve such goals no matter how admirable, without economic growth. . . . Special interest groups must recognize that their own unique goals cannot be satisfied if the U.S. cannot compete in world markets. The drawing of a social contract must take precedence over the aspirations of the poor, the minorities, and the environmentalists. Without such a consensus, all are doomed to lower levels of living, fewer rights, and increasingly dirty water.[27]

In order to create the necessary economic wealth, money must be redirected from social programs to capital investment. Congressional acquiesence to virtually every component of the economic program that President Reagan introduced in 1981 illustrates the extent to which this perspective permeated the hearts and minds of the nation's policymakers, at least at that time.

Reagan identified four key elements in his 1981 proposal: reductions in personal tax rates and business taxes; social spending cuts and other measures to reduce the federal budget deficit; reductions in federal regulations; and a stable monetary policy.[28] In anticipation of some of the President's critics economic advisor Michael J. Boskin observed, "The group in the population with the greatest stake in a pro-growth set of economic policies, even if that means temporary sacrifice by slowing social spending, is blacks."[29]

The austerity measures Reagan called for in the area of social services had already been accepted by leading urban experts as the first step for resolving the many crises facing large cities. In reference to the New York City fiscal crisis former presidential economic advisor Herbert Stein surmised, "I think that the prescription of New York cutting down its services, cutting down its expenses, and learning to live within its income is the only prescription."[30] Expressing similar sentiments in more colorful language Milton Friedman said New York would have to "tighten its belt, pay off its debt, live within its means and become an honest city again."[31] A key to reducing the city's expenditures, from this perspective, is to reduce labor costs. As Nathan Glazer asserted, "There has to be a serious confrontation with the trade unions. . . . There are presumably hundreds of thousands of people ready to do jobs that city employees are doing—for one-half to two-thirds the salary."[32]

These observations are not restricted to New York. In reference to Chicago, First National Bank vice-president Nina Klarich stated, "What we need is control on the city's spending and a control on patronage."[33] In discussing what business views as the disadvantages of doing business in Chicago, a 1983 report concluded, "Unions are a constant source of problems for industries."[34] Though couched in neutral terms, efforts to control spending or eliminate union problems have generally not been neutral in their impact, as will be illustrated in subsequent chapters.

As John H. Perkins acknowledged, Chicago businesses have long had a friend in city hall. In a typical brochure entitled "Chicago's Economic Incentives for Business," the Economic Development Commission states that it "provides economic incentives to encourage local industrial development" and proceeds to describe 11 of them.[35] And it is not just the owners of businesses or sympathetic public officials who have adopted this perspective on the nature of urban problems and what the appropriate response of government should be. Janet Malone, director of the civic organization TRUST, Inc., maintained, "It's the responsibility of governments to create a climate that is advantageous for private investors."[36] James Compton, director of the Chicago Urban League, stated, "Economic activity is not simply the central preoccupation of the city, it is the reason the city exists."[37] Put even more bluntly, former Independent Democratic alderman William Singer concluded, "The future of the City of Chicago, then, depends quite simply upon its ability to grow."[38]

As Alan Wolfe demonstrated in his book *America's Impasse*, the United States has consistently attempted to resolve its internal conflicts through a politics of growth: expand the pie and the lid can be kept in place. Reaganomics may have represented a different approach to growth, but its fundamental philosophical underpinnings diverged little from either Republican or Democratic administrations during the past 40 years.[39] Unfortunately, as Wolfe observed, the politics of growth has encountered the economics of decline. The elixer is not working. The notion that economic growth is essential before virtually any other social problems can be seriously addressed, and that giving incentives to the private sector is the key that will unlock that growth, is problematic in at least three respects.

Misguided Diagnosis

First, this perspective simply misdiagnoses the causes of current economic maladies, principally because of its uncritical devotion to market forces. High taxes, costly governmental regulations, excessive wage demands by unions, and an overly generous welfare state are viewed as the primary culprits. Yet this perspective is unable to explain why Sweden, Japan, and virtually all of the U.S. major trading partners in Western Europe have enjoyed greater levels of productivity growth than the United States despite higher taxes, greater government and union involvement in management, more generous welfare policies, and more equal distributions of income.[40] And by advocating financial incentives to private investors, this perspective seeks salvation in the very forces that caused nationwide decline and disinvestment of older urban communities. The deindustrialization of America is real and the fundamental cause is market-based investment activity predicated on maximum private enrichment. By appealing to those forces, growth advocates are unwittingly exacerbating the conditions they hope to ameliorate.

Perhaps the most direct illustration of the destructive nature of market-based investment occurs when a business is shut down or relocated. Such management decisions may be in the best interest of the stockholders, but for the far larger number of people who lose their jobs the benefits are few. Barry Bluestone and Bennett Harrison estimate that during the 1970s the United States lost between 32 and 38 million jobs due to such investment decisions.[41] A more recent study in the Chicago area found that between 1977 and 1981 the SMSA experienced a net loss of 436,172, or 14.3 percent of all jobs. This represented a loss of 1.9 jobs through closings, relocations, and contractions for every new job created due to startups, in-migration, and expansion.[42]

It is argued, of course, that a job loss for one community is often a job gain in another. The appropriate response from this perspective is to facilitate the relocation of people to where the jobs are. As the President's Commission for a National Agenda for the Eighties concluded, "Contrary to conventional wisdom, cities are not permanent."[43] Yet jobs are not simply moving from cities to suburbs or from the snowbelt to the sunbelt. Jobs are also going overseas. Bluestone and Harrison report that foreign investment between 1950 and 1980 increased at more than twice the rate of domestic investment.[44] In an age of labor concessions, the question arises as to whether Chicago steelworkers making $15 an hour should be expected to accept $2 or $3 per day in order to be more "competitive" with the Third World countries currently attracting U.S. capital. Or perhaps a Presidential Commission for an Agenda for the Nineties will provide the answer when it observes that "contrary to conventional wisdom, nations are not permanent."

Ironically, many of the facilities that have been closed were profitable at the time of the shutdown. And in other cases profitable facilities were turned into losers by management decisions to utilize available cash for investment in other businesses rather than to maintain the facility generating that cash. This has been particularly prevalent where conglomerate mergers have occurred and the parent has milked a subsidiary for the benefit of the conglomerate's stockholders, but at the expense of the workers and communities of that subsidiary.[45]

Conglomerate merger activity has increased substantially in the 1980s. In 1981 $82 billion was spent on 2,395 mergers, almost 50 percent more than the previous year.[46] Not only are many jobs destroyed in the process, but vast sums of capital that could be used for productive, job-generating investment are utilized instead simply for asset rearrangement. Such financial transactions illustrate what Harvard University business professor Robert B. Reich calls "paper entrepreneurialism," which has become increasingly prevalent among the managers of U.S. corporations. According to Reich, "The outcome of all these actions is certain in only two respects: Some money will change hands, and no new wealth will be created."[47]

"Paper entrepreneurialism" reflects a broader trend in current management practice identified by two of Reich's colleagues at Harvard. According to Robert H. Hayes and William J. Abernathy the decline in U.S. productivity growth is attributable more to a prevailing emphasis on short-term profits at the expense of long-term research and development than to conventionally assumed factors like high taxes or government interference.[48]

Management practices that are unquestionably legal, and are taught in all major business schools, constitute a major force behind U.S. economic troubles. But illegal or quasi-legal practices cannot be discounted altogether, particularly in understanding the immediate fiscal crises of major cities. New York journalists Jack Newfield and Paul A. DuBrul have demonstrated how specific bankers, politicians, and developers formed a "permanent government" in that city with the assistance of the Mafia and a small number of unions. They institutionalized a system of legal graft that enabled them to profit personally while bringing the city to the verge of bankruptcy. (Unfortunately, these were not the kinds of practices Milton Friedman had in mind when he made his plea for honesty.) Ironically, the austerity measures that "saved" the city forced even greater sacrifices on those already victimized by the clubhouse system, but protected the interests of the financial community.[49] Clearly, New York is not the only city plagued by graft and corruption. If the phrase "clubhouse system" is replaced by "machine," Newfield's and Dubrul's thesis could serve as a guide to Chicago politics.

Another clear indicator of the misguided diagnosis of the growth advocates is the failure of the many incentive programs that have been implemented throughout the country. Tax abatements, low-interest loans, industrial revenue bonds, and a variety of other financial incentives have become favorite tools for economic development officials in Chicago and around the nation. But available research shows that these tactics are simply not effective in attracting or creating jobs.[50] For example, a 1986 study of Chicago's industrial revenue bond program found that one-third of the recipients of this subsidy experienced a net loss in total employment, despite the fact that job creation and retention is the primary objective of the program.[51] Companies exploit the competition for these subsidies, of course, when they plan an expansion or relocation in order to negotiate the best deal for themselves.

As municipalities and states attempt to outbid each other with such incentives businesses benefit by receiving an ill-conceived subsidy. But no net gain in jobs occurs, tax revenues and public services decline, and as a result some communities find the business climate is even less attractive than before the unaffordable incentives were offered. Further, the net financial impact is a shift in wealth from lower- and middle-income workers to upper-income stockholders.[52]

Avoidance of Social Costs

If the first fundamental problem with the growth ideology is its flawed diagnosis of the causes of prevailing economic ills, the second shortcoming is that, when market criteria and private enrichment are accepted as the basis of investment, a host of social costs are either ignored or treated as inevitable. Unemployment has obvious implications for the financial health of workers who find themselves out of a job. Job loss is also linked to a variety of physical, psychological, and social ills. Johns Hopkins University researcher Harvey Brenner has demonstrated that each one percent increase in the national unemployment rate is associated with an increase of 650 homicides, 3,300 admissions to state mental hospitals, 500 deaths from cirrhosis of the liver, and 20,000 deaths from heart disease.[53] Sudden job losses that occur when a plant shuts down lead to a higher incidence of depression, hypertension, ulcers, high blood pressure, and alcoholism. In turn these personal troubles lead to higher divorce rates, spouse and child abuse, and other family problems.[54] One study found that suicide rates among workers laid off because of a plant closing is 30 times the national average.[55]

At the community level social costs due to disinvestment include reduced tax revenues and subsequent declines in municipal services, lower property values, and fewer charitable donations.[56] Racial inequalities are exacerbated. A study of a sample of Chicago-area firms that relocated from the central city to the surrounding suburbs in the late 1970s found that the number of minority employees decreased by 25 percent, but white employment fell less than 10 percent.[57] Women are also adversely affected. One case study found that among workers terminated as a result of a shutdown, the male/female wage gap increased, since women were more likely to be tracked into lower-wage jobs. Women tended to be unemployed for longer spells and to depend more on savings and government support. One consequence was that women, particularly those who were single and had children, were more demoralized by the economic and social consequences of their plight.[58]

In some cases where austerity measures are introduced to "save" struggling cities, political power is usurped and democracy itself is undermined as in the case of New York when a group of bankers and businessmen formed a "temporary" coalition to stave off bankruptcy.[59] The damage done by the growth ideology was succinctly stated by political scientist William E. Connolly:

> At every turn barriers to growth become occasions to tighten social control, to build new hedges around citizens rights, to insulate bureaucracies from popular pressures while opening them to corporate influence, to rationalize work processes, to impose austerity on vulnerable constituencies, to delay programs for environmental safety, to legitimize military adventures abroad. Growth, previously seen as the means to realization of the good life, has become a system imperative to which elements of the good life are sacrificed.[60]

Ironically, many boomtowns, those communities presumably benefiting from capital mobility, experience similar costs as a direct result of the massive disruption that sudden growth can bring.[61]

These costs are not incidental or accidental. They are not "externalities." Though they do not show up on any corporate balance sheet, they are very real. They can even be quantified and predicted. The social costs of private enterprise—the charge avoided in the city that said I Will (and elsewhere)—are inherent features of an economy predicated on market-based investment geared to private enrichment.

Alternatives Ignored

The third problem with the growth ideology is that its widespread acceptance virtually forecloses serious consideration of alternatives that offer promise for ameliorating these social costs and for generating economic growth as well. For example, employee-owned and managed firms report higher profits, greater worker satisfaction with the job, and better labor relations between supervisors and workers than conventionally structured firms within the same industries.[62] Cooperatives and community development corporations have demonstrated an ability to provide products and services ranging from food and clothing to credit and real estate management in areas where the normal private market either cannot or will not.[63] At least some communities have negotiated explicit commitments from those private firms receiving public dollars, instead of simply providing incentives and then passively accepting vague promises of some undefined public benefit that may or may not occur.[64]

Two unifying elements are apparent in these approaches. First decision-making or management within the organizations is opened up to include all the participants. Second, they strive to meet specific social needs (for example, jobs, food, clothing, shelter) directly, rather than indirectly through the accumulation of private wealth in hope that enough will trickle down to address the public concerns.

In fact, there is no inherent conflict between the pursuit of growth and the satisfaction of essential social needs. As Reich stated, "A social organization premised on equity, security, and participation will generate greater productivity than one premised on greed and fear."[65] However, another common element of these approaches is that such structural alternatives will never emerge on a large scale as long as public policy is predicated on the need to create financial incentives to private investors.

The fundamental limitation of the growth ideology is its blindness to what C. Wright Mills termed the sociological imagination: the ability to grasp the connections between personal troubles and public issues and to perceive the interplay between individual behavior and the increasingly complex interaction of evolving social institutions within contemporary society.[66] Mills cogently argued that what many people believe to be individual problems resulting from their own personal failings are in fact public issues that are consequences of structural contradictions that have emerged over time. For example, he noted that when one person in a community is unable to find a job, that may well be an individual problem. But when 10 or 20 percent are unemployed, the structure of opportunity has collapsed.

This book reflects an ongoing effort to revive the sociological imagination. The problems many individuals in Chicago confront in finding decent jobs, overcoming racial prejudice, and securing decent services from both the public and private sectors are examined within the context of the larger social, political, and economic forces that shape their lives. The following chapters explore the historical evolution of these institutions, the contours of conflict and change within Chicago as well as between Chicago and other communities, and how these dynamics intrude—perhaps unconsciously in many cases—into the personal lives of Chicagoans. Vast segments of the community have paid great costs as a result of the failure to recognize these critical linkages. The sociological imagination enables us to remove these ideological blinders, worn by many leaders and followers alike, and to begin to eliminate those costs.

The following chapter traces the evolution of Chicago's regional economy since World War II. Uneven development has characterized the shifting sands of economic fortune and misfortune. Manufacturing industries have declined while service industries have been on the rise. The city has lost jobs and people while the suburbs have grown, though select city neighborhoods have prospered while some older inner-ring suburbs have suffered. Racial groups have not all been equally affected, nor have all segments of Chicago's diverse work force. The major forces, at the local, national, and international levels, that have shaped Chicago's economy are examined. Clearly, there have been winners and losers. However, in recent years, some of the city's traditional losers are struggling to alter the terms of economic development. Their success will be discussed in this and subsequent chapters.

The evolution of Chicago's legendary political machine from its beginnings in the early years of this century to the zenith of the Daley years and through the Washington ascendancy is the focus of Chapter 3. Racial and ethnic divisions, within the broader context of class conflict, have long shaped Chicago's political culture. A supreme irony may rest in Harold Washington's advocacy of a politics that, in fact, has coincided with the interests of Chicago's white working-class and middle-class neighborhoods. Yet hostilities from these very same communities may well impede the majority of the city's white and black residents from implementing a political agenda that can effectively serve their mutual interests.

Chapter 4 surveys the spatial patterns of the racial and ethnic mix of Chicago and its suburbs. Focusing on housing, this chapter reviews the institutional forces that have both generated and managed the historical conflicts among Chicago's diverse population and, subsequently, have given rise to those patterns. Pre-eminent among those forces are the Loop business interests, the real estate and financial industries, and their allies in city hall.

Challenges to that alliance have arisen, however. Chapter 5 describes the efforts of some community organizations to assert their interests in the face of powerful assaults on the part of the city's machine-supported business establishment. Racial divisions among these groups have traditionally mitigated economic or social progress in the city. But at least in recent years some groups have been able to recognize and act on their mutual interests, despite continuing racial antagonisms. The greater openness of city government to neighborhood organizations in recent years may enhance progress along these lines.

Chapter 6 reviews post-World War II redevelopment efforts in Chicago, which have reflected significant national trends while having been responsive to cultural and political developments unique to Chicago. Historically, leading downtown or Loop businesses have been the major force in shaping redevelopment, generally with the consent of local officials. For most of the past 40 years public dollars have followed the flow of private investment, in a manner wholly consistent with the growth ideology. In recent years, however, a second track of redevelopment has emerged; one that is characterized by neighborhood participation and an emphasis on equity issues within the community. Serious barriers to the expansion of this track prevail, however, and its long-term significance for the city remains unclear.

The final chapter identifies those issues and struggles that will shape the future of Chicago. It suggests directions in which the community must move, and in some ways is moving, to create a brighter future. But it also acknowledges the impediments that threaten the realization of that future.

A City in Transition

There are commonalities in the forces that have shaped Chicago and other communities in the snowbelt and around the nation. Chicago has taken many actions that mirror those of its neighbors. At the same time Chicago's response to similar developments has been unique in certain respects. No city can extricate itself from its history, geography, or culture. Yet the future is not fatalistically pre-determined.

Chicago has many strengths it can exploit to provide for a prosperous future. Geographically it is well situated to continue as a regional headquarters city. Given its location and existing transportation networks, Chicago offers ready access to many markets. The community enjoys an abundant supply of water, power, and both skilled and unskilled workers. The entrepreneurial spirit is alive.

But prosperity is not automatically around the corner. If Chicago is to take advantage of its strengths, the community must act in ways that diverge sharply from previous policy. Two basic principles must become the foundation for such action. First, whatever decisions are made or programs are implemented should be responsive to democratically identified social need, not just market signals. The concept of the public balance sheet, whereby private benefits and public costs are explicitly taken into consideration in any expenditure, should guide the development of public policy and private investment.[67] Second, in order to implement the public balance sheet, wherever feasible activities should be governed and operated through participatory processes and structures rather than by elite or expert control of bureaucratic hierarchies, public or private. None of this precludes financial incentives to private businesses, public-private partnerships, or reliance on market forces when the benefits—public and private —outweigh the costs and are equitably distributed. What is suggested, however, are fundamentally different priorities and tactics to achieve a more affluent and more just community.

There is at least fragmentary evidence that these principles are already serving as the basis of community activity on a variety of fronts. Many public and private sector organizations with diverse and sometimes competing agendas have incorporated these populist principles—in some cases explicitly but in most cases by implication. On such issues as economic development, housing, and community organization generally, at least the outlines of an alternative Chicago can be discerned.

This admittedly inchoate vision of an alternative Chicago includes neighborhood groups trying to preserve their homes and businesses, coalitions seeking to make affordable mortgages available to central city residents, civic and labor groups attempting to stem the flow of jobs and investment capital to the suburbs, citizens fighting utility rate increases, and many others. These are not just protest groups. They know what they are fighting for and in many cases they are ready to deliver the goods themselves. This is not a cohesive or well-organized movement, but it is a movement nevertheless that has evolved over decades. Its most visible symbol in recent years may be the Washington victory, but that electoral triumph constitutes more of a continuation than a culmination of this ongoing struggle.

If an alternative Chicago is struggling to be born and to flourish, many barriers stand in the way. Time will tell the future of Chicago, but not merely the passage of time. The dynamics of future conflicts will shape the impact, if any, of an alternative Chicago.

Chicago's broad shoulders are sagging. For many people the city does not, and never did, work at all. But the scent of reform is in the air. If Paddy Bauler's famed dictum should become simply part of the city's history, rather than the eternal truth it has appeared to be, a more prosperous Chicago might not be far behind.

2

Chicago's Economy

Struggling Up the Down Escalator

The fires are out, the mills breathe clean.
The child is sick, the steel sits cold.
The child lay dying, the steel decays.
No time for us, no need for us, no promise for us.
It is done, they took our bodies, they stole our minds.
They took our bodies, they stole our minds.
Anthony Massaro[1]

In the 1980s, a number of people point to Chicago's diversified economy in arguing that this Midwestern metropolitan area has not and will not experience the economic crises of other cities in America's industrial heartland. The steelworkers, automobile workers, machinists, electrical workers, and other industrial employees who used to jam the roads leading to factory gates at the break of dawn seem to be giving way to office workers racing to their offices before 9 A.M. The boosters of Chicago see the smoke, grime, and noise of Chicago's heavy industry being replaced by modern office buildings housing workers in new or expanded service industries such as banking, finance, real estate, and insurance. They also see the region's "smokestack industries" being replaced by more sophisticated high-tech and service industries. The optimistic forecasters see a Chicago work force no longer dominated by the stereotypical sweaty, grimy, male factory worker. Instead they see a metropolitan labor force in which men and women don white collars and business suits, work in 9-to-5 jobs, and live in the suburbs. Yes, there are some problems of what to do with the displaced factory workers and growing minority population in the city, but that is the price of progress, so they say.

Although diversity is one of the pluses of Chicago's regional economy, this picture of a thriving economy with happily employed workers obscures the increasingly apparent inequality within the work force, the overall uneven development of the region's economy, and many of the social costs of that development.[2] The 1980 census revealed that Chicago has 10 of the 16 poorest neighborhoods in the country. At the same time, its corporate bedroom suburbs are thriving. Unemployment rates in the city have soared above the national average, while many of the newer and more affluent suburbs have kept their unemployment rates well below the average. The steel communities of Chicago's Southeast Side and contiguous Northwest Indiana are now watching banks, food stores, and small shopping malls close for lack of business. A casual visit to once neat and well-maintained blue-collar communities reveals that home repairs and improvements are being deferred as family income suffers from layoffs or reduced wages. Not far away in other suburbs, newspaper headlines announce the expansion of shopping malls or the opening of new office complexes.

In many ways there are two communities moving in divergent directions in this urban area. On the one hand are the city's central business district, the gentrified city neighborhoods such as Lincoln Park, old affluent neighborhoods such as the Gold Coast, and the more prosperous suburbs such as those on the North Shore. On the other hand are the low-income black and Hispanic communities like the West Side and Logan Square, struggling white ethnic neighborhoods like Chicago Lawn, and the older suburban industrial communities like East Chicago and Hammond, Indiana. Propelled by the Chicago growth machine, one group is accelerating while the other is running on empty. This chapter focuses on who the winners and losers have been in the evolution of Chicago's post-World War II economy.

Specifically, the following pages examine how economic shifts—shifts as much a product of national and international changes as they are a product of local planning—have shaped the social and economic character of the metropolitan area. The first part of the chapter looks at economic trends since World War II: the rise and fall of smokestack Chicago. The second part focuses on both the pro-growth policies that have guided Chicago's economic development and the alternative approaches that have emerged to challenge the dominant ideology.

Many questions are raised. Is Chicago still the "City of Broad Shoulders" or is it a city on its knees begging for jobs? How has the economic base—particularly the central business district—diversified in recent years? Has this diversification made up for decline in the manufacturing sector? What is the relationship between city and suburb? How has the work force changed? Does organized labor still exercise strong influence? Has Chicago discovered any innovative solutions to the urban economic crisis of the 1980s, a crisis shared with other industrial cities like Detroit,

Cleveland, Milwaukee, and Pittsburgh? To what extent has the changing political scene—most notably the shift in voting patterns that brought about the election of Harold Washington—challenged or altered the growth ideology in Chicago? Are "new" ideas such as the establishment of enterprise zones and the creation of high-tech industrial parks merely solutions developed out of the very growth ideology that has produced current economic crises? This chapter will look at why Chicago's economy is in its current condition and where it may be headed.

The Rise and Fall of Smokestack Chicago

The metropolitan area is a region of contrasts. Driving into the city from the west, at first you may pass through areas of DuPage County that are undergoing residential and commercial construction booms. As you travel through older suburbs closer to the city, however, fewer new housing developments and shining stainless steel office building facades are to be found. Instead the typical view includes older wood-frame houses in working-class neighborhoods and deteriorating factory buildings. When you enter the metropolitan area from neighboring Northwest Indiana, the industrial heritage of Chicago is even more apparent.

From the east, you run a gauntlet of industrial development that rivals any heavy industrial concentration in the United States. Passing through Gary, East Chicago, and Hammond, Indiana, you are stung by the acrid smoke from the coke ovens and furnaces of steel mills owned by USX (formerly U.S. Steel), Inland Steel, and LTV Corporation. At night the burn-off flames at the Standard Oil of Indiana Whiting refinery cast an eerie glow onto the road. The Lever Brothers and American Maize plants in the northwest corner of Hammond produce as many smells as they do products—soap, corn oil, margarine, and candy.

Entering Chicago and climbing the Chicago Skyway bridge, you get a bird's eye view of Chicago's industrial backyard. You pass over the entrance to Calumet Harbor, which is relatively quiet compared to earlier years when Great Lakes ships carrying anything from grain to iron ore could be seen entering and leaving. The modest bungalows and two-flats in the surrounding blue-collar neighborhoods are framed by industry. USX's South Works dominates the lakefront and a few smaller factories dot the grid of streets. It is hard to tell if the reddish color of the mill buildings is due to years of ferric oxide dust spewed out by the furnaces or to the rust of decaying corrugated steel mill buildings. Signs of the heyday

Table 2.1   Manufacturing employment in
the Chicago region, 1947–1982

Area	1947		1982	
	Number	Percent	Number	Percent
Chicago	668,000	70.6	277,000	34.2
Rest of Cook Co.	121,000	12.8	279,000	34.4
Rest of SMSA	64,000	6.8	189,000	23.4
Lake Co. (Ind.)	93,000	9.8	64,000	7.9
Total	946,000	100.0	808,000	100.0

Source: For 1947 figures, John F. McDonald, *Employment Location and Industrial Land Use in Metropolitan Chicago* (Champaign, Ill.: Stipes Publishing Co., 1984), table 1.4, p. 10; for 1982 figures, U.S. Bureau of the Census, *1982 Census of Manufactures*, Geographic Area Series, Illinois (MC82-A-14) and Indiana (MC82-A-15) (Washington, D.C.: U.S. Government Printing Office, 1985).

of America's industrial heartland now blend in with monuments to what has become our country's "rust bowl."

As the railroad hub of the country, Chicago's economy was fueled by the United States westward expansion in the late nineteenth and early twentieth centuries. The railroad, steel, and meatpacking industries, made famous by novelists, poets, and muckrakers, blossomed and flourished during this period. Except during the Depression, manufacturing employment steadily increased in Chicago from 1900 through the late 1940s.[3]

The region also benefited from the postwar economic boom. The local and national boom in construction, major appliance sales, and automobile production fed Chicago's industrial core. Even as early as 1947, however, one could see changes on the horizon. These changes were geographical; Chicago's manufacturing base was starting to move from the city to the suburbs. The changes were also sectoral; Chicago's economy was beginning to shift away from manufacturing toward the service sector. The locational shift was already quite apparent in the 1950s, although the sectoral shift did not become obvious until the following decades.

Plotting post-World War II manufacturing employment opportunities in various parts of the Chicago region produces a patchwork quilt of growth and decline. As shown in Table 2.1, between 1947 and 1982 manufacturing employment in the Chicago SMSA (standard metropolitan statistical area) and Lake County, Indiana experienced a decline from 946,000 to 808,000. Employment in this sector had been increasing up to 1977, when the comparable figure was 952,000, but declined sharply between 1977 and 1982.[4] However, the real story was the massive decline in the older industrial

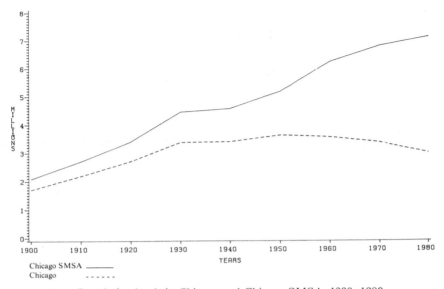

Figure 2.1   Population levels in Chicago and Chicago SMSA, 1900–1980
Source: Commercial Club of Chicago, "Economic Plan: Jobs for Metropolitan Chicago, Economic Scan," data prepared by Federal Reserve Bank of Chicago for a subsequent report: Commercial Club of Chicago, *Make No Little Plans: Jobs for Metropolitan Chicago* (Chicago: The Club, 1984).

area's portion of this total. In 1947, Chicago accounted for 70.6 percent of the total; by 1982 its share had eroded to 34.2 percent.[5] Between 1947 and 1982, factory employment in Chicago dropped from a twentieth-century high of 688,000 to 277,000 factory jobs—a decline of 59 percent. At the same time, suburban Cook County manufacturing jobs increased from 121,000 to 279,000 (a 131 percent increase), and factory jobs in the other SMSA counties jumped from 64,000 to 189,000 (a 195 percent increase).[6] According to University of Illinois economist John F. McDonald, "From 1947 to the present the record is one of almost continuous decline of manufacturing employment in the city," the only exception being a slight increase in jobs during the national industrial boom period from 1963 to 1967.[7]

This employment shift follows a pattern of disinvestment and plant relocation, marking Chicago as the loser and the suburbs as the winners.[8] According to a 1961 study by the Chicago Department of City Planning, many of the firms leaving the city were relocating to the suburbs.[9] This was the beginning of a trend paralleling the suburbanization of residential populations in most U.S. metropolitan areas. The exodus of population and businesses from America's cities to its suburbs has been well docu-

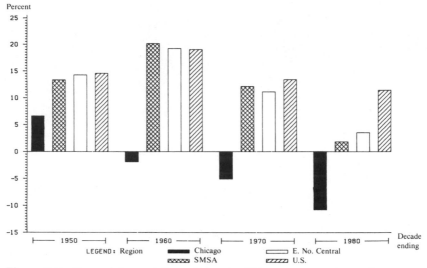

Figure 2.2 Decennial population change in Chicago compared to other areas, 1950–1980

Source: Commercial Club of Chicago, "Economic Plan: Jobs for Metropolitan Chicago, Economic Scan," data prepared by Federal Reserve Bank of Chicago for a subsequent report: Commercial Club of Chicago, *Make No Little Plans: Jobs for Metropolitan Chicago* (Chicago: The Club, 1984).

mented.[10] Figures 2.1 and 2.2 chart the shift in population from Chicago to the surrounding suburban areas. Shifts in business location and the concomitant shift in employment followed this pattern. Lower land costs, a growing labor pool, a greatly expanded expressway system, a lower unionization rate, as well as the shifting consumer market, were all reasons why manufacturers and other businesses relocated to the new suburbs.

More recently, there has been a shift of business firms from the metropolitan area to other areas of the country and the world. An Illinois Labor Market Information Service study of corporate disinvestment in the Chicago SMSA found that "non-independent" Chicago businesses—branches, headquarters, or subsidiaries of larger corporations—were often closed down at the same time as parent companies diversified into other industries outside the Chicago region.[11] In a sample of Chicago SMSA businesses, the researchers found that approximately 65 percent of total job loss—due to firm "deaths" or "contractions"—was attributable to this form of corporate disinvestment. The study estimates that, of 203,700 manufacturing jobs lost through closures and contractions in the Chicago SMSA between 1977 and 1981, approximately 132,400 were lost due to corporate decisions to shift investments outside the region.[12]

Disinvestment is, in part, the cause of the declining number of businesses and jobs in many sectors of Chicago's economy. In 1981 Chicago had one-quarter fewer factories than it had in 1970: 6,127 in contrast to 8,087. Also, between 1970 and 1978, the city lost 4,500 of its 30,000 retail stores.[13] According to a study completed for Continental Bank, the entire metropolitan area lost 14 percent of its manufacturing jobs through plant closings and relocations. The city experienced a more serious 27 percent decline in jobs due to the same factors.[14] Chicago's lifeblood has been manufacturing employment. Deindustrialization has bled much of the city dry. In a sense a transfusion has taken place; the metropolitan area is moving from an economy heavily based on manufacturing to one increasingly oriented to non-manufacturing sectors, for example, banking, finance, retail sales, insurance, and transportation. It is important, however, to look at exactly who has been affected by recent shifts in the Chicago-area economy.

Anatomy of Recent Economic Shifts

Large industrial operations that have employed thousands of blue-collar workers in many parts of the city and older suburbs now stand virtually empty; they have become silent witnesses of the industrial decline and lost jobs. Major closures in the 1980s have included Campbell's Soup, Johnson & Johnson, Schwinn Bicycle Company, Western Electric's Hawthorne plant, Wisconsin Steel, and a large portion of USX's South Works. In their industrial prime, these seven plants alone employed a total of more than 30,000 workers. Within Chicago, the steel communities of the Southeast Side as well as the predominantly black West Side and South Side have experienced dramatic losses in manufacturing employment opportunities. Among the suburbs, the hardest hit have been those older industrial communities immediately to the west, south, and southeast of the city. To the west, Bridgeview, Cicero, Justice, Maywood, and Summit have been adversely affected. Far to the southwest Joliet and Romeoville experienced high unemployment due to manufacturing declines. The longest list of industrial communities suffering from manufacturing declines includes southern suburbs in Illinois—Calumet City, Chicago Heights, Harvey, and Sauk Village—and the Northwest Indiana communities of East Chicago, Gary, and Hammond.

Black workers have borne much of the brunt of Chicago's job losses. For example, between 1963 and 1977, while the city as a whole was experiencing a 29 percent decline in jobs, available factory jobs in predominantly black West Central and near South Side neighborhoods dropped by 45 and 47 percent respectively.[15] Many of the working-class suburbs experiencing job loss are predominantly black; most notable among these are Harvey, Maywood, and Gary, all of which are more than two-thirds black. As noted earlier, the Illinois Advisory Committee to the U.S. Commission on Civil Rights found that plant closures have a disproportionate adverse effect on minority workers.[16]

In those areas hard hit by plant shutdowns, a ripple effect has ultimately caused other businesses to fold because they were suppliers for the closed firms or because they relied on consumer dollars from local workers. *Chicago Tribune* reporter R. C. Longworth explains:

> As the jobs and factories went, so did the other businesses they supported—the distributors, the shops that supplied the factories, the groceries where their employees shopped, and the restaurants where they ate. In 1973, Chicago had a total of 103,148 businesses; by mid-1983 this was down to 90,317. Almost all the loss was in small businesses.[17]

Economist Joe Persky estimated that the loss of 20,000 steelworker jobs in 1979 in the Gary-Hammond-East Chicago area produced an additional 10,000 jobless within the next year. Persky found that the loss of relatively high-paying jobs in basic industry had a ripple effect, severely cutting consumer demand in the region's service, transportation, manufacturing, and government sectors. He further concluded that within another four years an *additional* 24,000 jobs would be lost due to this ripple effect.[18]

While the workers and their communities in industrial areas may be hurting, there are signs that some manufacturing firms may actually be coming out ahead. Stockholders in some of the large manufacturing firms are not always taking the bruises that their workers are taking. In his study of economic development, James Greer found that, between 1954 and 1972, value added by manufacture and new capital expenditures in the manufacturing sector increased for both Chicago and its Illinois suburbs.[19] Automation, closure of older facilities, and a trimmed and more productive work force can benefit some manufacturing firms.[20]

Also, as is becoming so apparent, large corporations have a life that transcends the ups and downs of regional economies. USX's closure of most of its South Works (leaving fewer than 1,000 workers in a plant that had employed close to 10,000 steelworkers in the past) and cutbacks elsewhere in the metropolitan area did not necessarily bode poorly for the giant corporation. USX's purchase of Marathon Oil, along with earlier diversification into chemical production, insulation manufacturing, retailing, and mortgage services, made it a stronger company   a diverse multinational with greater potential for higher profits. Through its name change from U.S. Steel to USX, the corporation itself recognized its move out of steelmaking. Community leaders and union activists have shown that USX's acquisition diversification plan was carried out at the expense of steelworkers and their communities.[21] They observe that the conglomerate's reshaping was only made possible through milking old steel plants. This was done by using federal government import quotas and tax breaks to protect steel profitability while at the same time pumping funds into non-steel investments rather than back into the steel plants that produced that profit. The diversification effort helped USX to turn around its earnings record dramatically; after losing over $1.5 billion in 1982 and 1983, the number one steel maker reported a profit in 1984.[22]

The record corporate profits do not comfort former workers of USX's Chicago South Works plant. A major study of workers displaced by the phasing out of the Chicago facility shows that, while USX may have eliminated less productive operations, its former employees are bearing the brunt of the multi-national's cost-cutting and diversification. The Hull House Association in conjunction with United Steelworkers of America Local 65 found that, compared to the time when they were employed at the steel mill, former USX employees were much worse off. Among the 900 workers responding to a survey of displaced workers, the median income had dropped from $20,000–24,000 to $10,000–14,000; current unemployment was 47 percent (30 percent for whites and 60 percent for blacks); 62 percent of the former employees had either been forced to move or had fallen behind in monthly housing payments because of reduced income; and 30 percent had sought emergency food assistance.[23] One former steelworker responded: "I lost my wife, my apartment and my self-respect. Plans for my three young girls have gone to pieces. We live with my parents with no car, no privacy, no job, no health insurance, no hope."[24]

The companies and their stockholders appear to be the big winners in this conglomerate growth trend, while the displaced workers and their communities are the big losers. USX is certainly not the only conglomerate that has put corporate priorities above regional priorities; Ford Motor Company, International Harvester, Johnson & Johnson, just to name a few, have followed similar strategies.

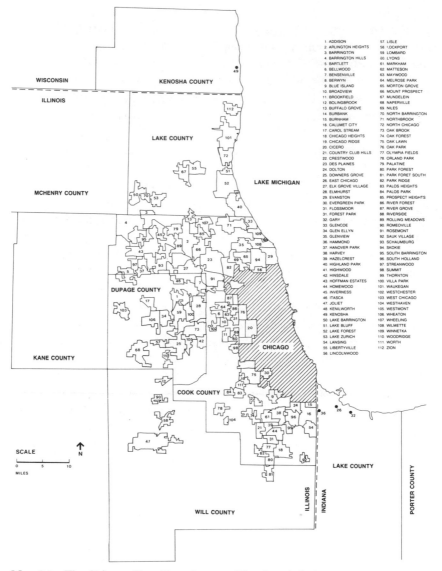

1. ADDISON	57. LISLE
2. ARLINGTON HEIGHTS	58. LOCKPORT
3. BARRINGTON	59. LOMBARD
4. BARRINGTON HILLS	60. LYONS
5. BARTLETT	61. MARKHAM
6. BELLWOOD	62. MATTESON
7. BENSENVILLE	63. MAYWOOD
8. BERWYN	64. MELROSE PARK
9. BLUE ISLAND	65. MORTON GROVE
10. BROADVIEW	66. MOUNT PROSPECT
11. BROOKFIELD	67. MUNDELEIN
12. BOLINGBROOK	68. NAPERVILLE
13. BUFFALO GROVE	69. NILES
14. BURBANK	70. NORTH BARRINGTON
15. BURNHAM	71. NORTHBROOK
16. CALUMET CITY	72. NORTH CHICAGO
17. CAROL STREAM	73. OAK BROOK
18. CHICAGO HEIGHTS	74. OAK FOREST
19. CHICAGO RIDGE	75. OAK LAWN
20. CICERO	76. OAK PARK
21. COUNTRY CLUB HILLS	77. OLYMPIA FIELDS
22. CRESTWOOD	78. ORLAND PARK
23. DES PLAINES	79. PALATINE
24. DOLTON	80. PARK FOREST
25. DOWNERS GROVE	81. PARK FOREST SOUTH
26. EAST CHICAGO	82. PARK RIDGE
27. ELK GROVE VILLAGE	83. PALOS HEIGHTS
28. ELMHURST	84. PALOS PARK
29. EVANSTON	85. PROSPECT HEIGHTS
30. EVERGREEN PARK	86. RIVER FOREST
31. FLOSSMOOR	87. RIVER GROVE
32. GARY	88. RIVERSIDE
33. GLENCOE	89. ROLLING MEADOWS
34. GLEN ELLYN	90. ROMEOVILLE
35. GLENVIEW	91. ROSEMONT
36. HAMMOND	92. SAUK VILLAGE
37. HANOVER PARK	93. SCHAUMBURG
38. HARVEY	94. SKOKIE
39. HAZELCREST	95. SOUTH BARRINGTON
40. HIGHLAND PARK	96. SOUTH HOLLAND
41. HIGHWOOD	97. STREAMWOOD
42. HINSDALE	98. SUMMIT
43. HOFFMAN ESTATES	99. THORNTON
44. HOMEWOOD	100. VILLA PARK
45. INVERNESS	101. WAUKEGAN
46. ITASCA	102. WESTCHESTER
47. JOLIET	103. WEST CHICAGO
48. KENILWORTH	104. WESTHAVEN
49. KENOSHA	105. WESTMONT
50. LAKE BARRINGTON	106. WHEATON
51. LAKE BLUFF	107. WHEELING
52. LAKE FOREST	108. WILMETTE
53. LAKE ZURICH	109. WINNETKA
54. LANSING	110. WOODRIDGE
55. LIBERTYVILLE	111. WORTH
56. LINCOLNWOOD	112. ZION

Map 2.1   The Chicago-Gary-Kenosha consolidated statistical area
Source: Loyola University of Chicago Media Services

Suburban and Central Business District Growth

In addition to the corporate winners in the disinvestment game, there have
been particular areas within the metropolitan region that have benefited
from shifts in capital investment and employment opportunities.

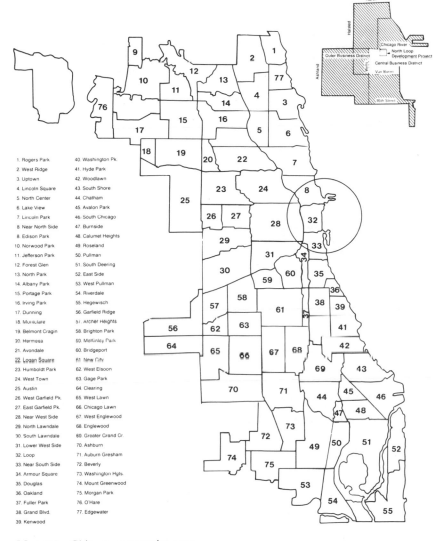

1. Rogers Park
2. West Ridge
3. Uptown
4. Lincoln Square
5. North Center
6. Lake View
7. Lincoln Park
8. Near North Side
9. Edison Park
10. Norwood Park
11. Jefferson Park
12. Forest Glen
13. North Park
14. Albany Park
15. Portage Park
16. Irving Park
17. Dunning
18. Montclare
19. Belmont Cragin
20. Hermosa
21. Avondale
22. Logan Square
23. Humboldt Park
24. West Town
25. Austin
26. West Garfield Pk.
27. East Garfield Pk.
28. Near West Side
29. North Lawndale
30. South Lawndale
31. Lower West Side
32. Loop
33. Near South Side
34. Armour Square
35. Douglas
36. Oakland
37. Fuller Park
38. Grand Blvd.
39. Kenwood
40. Washington Pk.
41. Hyde Park
42. Woodlawn
43. South Shore
44. Chatham
45. Avalon Park
46. South Chicago
47. Burnside
48. Calumet Heights
49. Roseland
50. Pullman
51. South Deering
52. East Side
53. West Pullman
54. Riverdale
55. Hegewisch
56. Garfield Ridge
57. Archer Heights
58. Brighton Park
59. McKinley Park
60. Bridgeport
61. New City
62. West Elsdon
63. Gage Park
64. Clearing
65. West Lawn
66. Chicago Lawn
67. West Englewood
68. Englewood
69. Greater Grand Cr.
70. Ashburn
71. Auburn Gresham
72. Beverly
73. Washington Hgts.
74. Mount Greenwood
75. Morgan Park
76. O'Hare
77. Edgewater

Map 2.2   Chicago community areas

Source: Chicago Fact Book Consortium, Department of Sociology, University of Illinois at Chicago (eds.), *Local Community Fact Book: Chicago Metropolitan Area, 1980* (Chicago: The Consortium, 1980).

While older industrial communities have been losing jobs and businesses, some suburbs and Chicago's central business district (see Maps 2.1 and 2.2) appear to have been gaining jobs and employers. Both the suburbs and the central business district (CBD) have seen increases in employment

Table 2.2 Chicago region employment , 1970–1980

County	1970	1980	Percent change
Cook	2,525,350	2,578,700	2.1
Chicago	1,752,400	1,506,500	−14.0
Suburban Cook	772,950	1,072,250	38.7
DuPage	134,050	274,200	104.6
Kane	95,100	122,100	28.4
Lake (Ill.)	105,450	154,500	46.5
McHenry	31,850	44,700	41.0
Will	75,500	95,150	20.7
Total Ill. suburbs	1,214,900	1,758,900	44.8
Total	2,967,300	3,265,400	10.0
Lake and Porter (Ind.)	224,000	253,200	13.0

Source: Northeastern Illinois Planning Commission, *Spatial Distribution of Employment*, Chicago: The Commission, 1981, table 2C, p. 15. Indiana data are from Indiana Employment Security Division, "Labor Force Summary and Establishment Employment," report, 1970 and 1980.

in the past decade. Chicago's suburbs account for most of the region's employment growth between 1970 and 1980. In that decade, SMSA employment grew from 2,967,000 to 3,265,000. However, in this ten-year period, suburban jobs increased by 44.8 percent while Chicago employment dropped by 14 percent (see Table 2.2). In absolute numbers, Chicago lost over 245,000 jobs in this decade while the suburbs gained more than 540,000 employment slots.[25] There was also job growth in Northwest Indiana between 1970 and 1980, but this employment picture changed dramatically between 1980 and 1985. In this period, marked by layoffs and factory shutdowns in the steel and other basic manufacturing industries, employment dropped from 253,200 in 1980 to 211,000 in 1985 in Lake and Porter counties. This represents a 16.7 percent decline in jobs.[26]

However, this masks some modest job growth in the Chicago central business district. Between 1972 and 1982 employment in the CBD rose from 222,600 to 240,200—an increase of 7.9 percent.[27] Job growth in the Loop is largely the result of the construction of new office space. In the past decade, the CBD has been characterized by a growth and vitality that has been absent in most other areas of Chicago. Nevertheless, the growth of the CBD relative to suburban growth is very small.

A closer look at suburban job trends shows two key growth areas. DuPage County and northwestern Cook County both shine brightly in reports on recent employment gains and economic development in the

Table 2.3 Changes in number of jobs
in Chicago and Illinois suburbs, 1972–1982

Area	Number of jobs		Percent change
	1972	1982	
Chicago (outside CBD)	1,066,924	880,910	−17.4
Chicago CBD	222,668	240,188	7.9
Cook Co. (excluding Chicago)	690,586	815,922	18.1
Northwest Cook Co.	181,216	260,492	43.7
Southwest Cook Co.	153,691	159,150	3.6
West Cook Co.	142,003	133,699	−5.8
North Cook Co.	124,278	151,458	21.9
South Cook Co.	89,398	111,123	24.3
DuPage Co.	117,481	193,946	65.1
Kane Co.	78,473	86,039	9.6
Lake Co.	91,256	109,553	20.0
Will Co.	53,893	56,680	5.2
McHenry Co.	27,423	34,363	25.3

Source: Compiled from data from Illinois Department of Employment Security, *Where Workers Work, 1982* (Springfield, Ill.: Department of Employment Security, 1983).

region. As shown in Table 2.3, these two areas experienced substantial job growth in the ten-year period. Already the largest source of jobs outside Cook County in 1972, DuPage County employment grew by 65 percent in the following ten years. Northwestern Cook County employment grew by almost 44 percent in this same period. While there was also significant job growth in northern and southern Cook County, and in Lake and McHenry counties, growth in these areas was considerably less. What factors contributed to the growth of DuPage County and northwestern Cook County?

If Chicago has an equivalent to a high-tech Route 128 or Silicon Valley, it is the band of research facilities and high-tech companies located in DuPage County, particularly along Route 5, the East-West Tollway. Although the concentration of firms is considerably less than the rival high-tech concentrations in either California or Massachusetts, it is sizeable for the Chicago metropolitan area. Among the research facilities are AT&T/Bell Labs, Amoco Research Center, Argonne National Laboratory, and Fermi National Accelerator Laboratory. These research facilities alone employ close to 10,000 workers.

DuPage has also become a mecca for corporations seeking to set up regional and national offices in the Midwest. Among the prominent corporate employers are CBI (construction), Ceco (building products), Interlake (steel), McDonald's Corporation, Nalco Chemical, the Wall Street Journal (printing plant), and Waste Management. Robert Palmer, a staff member of the DuPage County Development Department, explains that much of this growth was stimulated by AT&T's decision to locate their research facility in Naperville in the 1970s.[28] Amoco Oil's relocation of their research and development facilities from Whiting, Indiana to Naperville in the mid-1970s added to DuPage County's claim to high-tech fame. Amoco moved to Illinois despite the option of building a new facility in Indiana, where corporate taxes are lower than in Illinois.[29]

DuPage County has benefited from the business community's growth ideology. When corporate planners at Toyota Corporation's California headquarters were seeking a location for its regional operations, they looked through a list of the fastest-growing counties in the Midwest. Consequently, DuPage County was the automobile company's choice for a new facility.[30] This attractiveness of a growth area, along with the county's own efforts to facilitate economic development, has contributed to the 230 percent increase in business establishments in DuPage County from 1965 to 1982. No other Chicago SMSA county comes close to this growth rate.[31]

The other significant suburban growth area is the "Golden Corridor"—the northwestern section of Cook County along the Northwest Tollway between O'Hare Airport and Elgin. This includes the communities of Elk Grove Village, Schaumburg, Rolling Meadows, Arlington Heights, Palatine, and Hoffman Estates. After DuPage County, this section of Cook County had the greatest increase in employment between 1972 and 1982 (see Table 2.3). While it does not have the high-tech research base of DuPage County, it is becoming the suburban equivalent of Chicago's central business district. Office buildings are mushrooming in the area. Its proximity to one of the largest airports in the country, as well as its location along an excellent interstate road system, has fed its growth. A sign of the shift of this area from bedroom suburb to semi-autonomous business center is the shift in its residents' commuting patterns. In 1970 an estimated three-fourths of the residents commuted outside of the northwest Cook County area for jobs; by 1980 that figure had dropped to 25 percent.[32] Among the major employers in this area are Honeywell, Motorola, Northrup Defense Systems, Pfizer (distribution center), Square D Corporation (electrical equipment), Union Oil of California, Western Electric, and Zurich American Insurance.

Like DuPage County, growth in northwestern Cook County can be likened to an economic chain reaction. Corporate planners are attracted by growth already apparent. On top of this, local, regional, and state government agencies have facilitated corporate growth in this area. Don Klein, executive director of the Greater Barrington Area Council of Governments —a government unit that has battled nearby growth to protect affluent residential communities—has been amazed by the "machinations of state and regional agencies" that have "subordinated everything else to economic development." He observes that past concerns about the future adequacy of the infrastructure, such as roads, water supply, and sewers, as well as concerns about the quality of life, have been "thrown out" in recent pro-development government decision-making.[33]

Although DuPage and northwestern Cook counties are the preferred locations for corporations seeking to expand within the metropolitan area, there has been some economic development in southern and eastern Lake County, north of the city. This area serves as home for Abbott Labs (medical products), Baxter Travenol Labs (medical products), Sara Lee (food products), and Walgreen corporate offices (retail drug stores), but it has not matched the development in the two areas already discussed.

Much of the growth in corporate facilities in Lake, DuPage, and northwestern Cook County has come from other communities within Cook County. For example, Beth Benoit, a senior economic development specialist for Lake County, observed that most of the new employment in her county and other growing county regions has come from suburban Cook County, not from the city of Chicago.[34] The post-World War II growth pattern, which saw businesses abandoning the central city for the suburbs, is now evolving into a new pattern in which older suburbs are losing to new suburbs. Suburbs in southwestern and western Cook County are the new victims of the growth ideology; these include Cicero, McCook, Bedford Park, Bellwood, Maywood, Melrose Park, Northlake, and River Grove.

Chicago as a Regional Capital

Employment stability in Chicago's central business district, employment expansion in key suburban areas, and diversification of Chicago's economy into more service sector employment are, in part, due to Chicago's status as a regional capital. It has served as the headquarters region for many large corporations and has provided many of the ancillary banking, real estate, and insurance services required by businesses in the Midwest.

Therefore, as heavy manufacturing declines, Chicago has been increasingly relying on its diversified economic base. Headquarters of 26 Fortune 500 Industrial companies are in the city of Chicago; another 18 are in the suburbs.[35] Large industrial corporations based in Chicago and its suburbs include Beatrice Foods, Borg-Warner, Consolidated Foods, Dart and Kraft, Inc., Esmark, IC Industries, Motorola, and Standard Oil of Indiana. The metropolitan area also serves as home for a number of large non-industrial corporations. Most notable in this group is the nation's largest retailer, Sears, Roebuck and Company. Sears' Loop headquarters —the tallest building in the world—also serves as a symbolic cornerstone of the corporate presence in the city's central business district. The activities of these large corporations make a major contribution to both the scope and the range of Chicago's regional economy.

One journalist characterized this economy in the following terms: "If the Chicago region were a country, its 'gross national product' of $112.1 billion would be the 11th biggest in the world."[36] *The Economist* identified the city as a

> sophisticated financial center. There is almost no financial need served in New York which is not also met in Chicago. Indeed, faced with Chicago's Board of Trade and Mercantile Exchange, New York has been forced to follow in its footsteps when it comes to dealing with commodities and futures. For international banking, LaSalle Street is second only to Wall Street in America.[37]

The importance of financial services in Chicago is likely to continue in the future despite problems experienced in 1984 by Continental Illinois Bank and Trust Company, Chicago's largest bank. In that year, Continental reported a $1.1 billion loss in the second quarter alone. This was largely due to defaults on over $5.1 billion in loans, loans to corporations such as International Harvester and Braniff Airlines as well as loans bought from an Oklahoma-based bank. It took an unprecedented $4.5 billion bail-out from the federal government and a shake-up of top bank executives to save the bank.[38] While Chicago's banking community received a black eye from Continental's near collapse, other parts of the financial services sector remain intact; its stock options and commodity futures exchanges as well as its insurance companies are thriving.[39]

Chicago's central geographical location has been a major attraction to corporations seeking a home. Not only is it attractive to the manufacturing firms that remain in the industrial Midwest; it is also ranked as the 26th most centrally located city in the United States (out of more than 900 cities), using markets and population as measures. To corporations seeking efficiency in their transportation and communications operations, this is an attractive feature.[40]

While Chicago's service economy has been replacing some lost manufacturing jobs, it has not replaced them all. One reason is that Chicago's service sector employment has not been expanding as rapidly as service economies in other U.S. cities. According to a study done by the Federal Reserve Bank for the Commercial Club of Chicago, between 1960 and 1982 Chicago employment changes in finance, services, wholesale and retail trade, and government lagged behind U.S. rates.[41] More importantly, the people who lose their factory jobs are rarely the ones who find employment in comparably paid service sector positions.

Nevertheless, all evidence suggests that it is the service sector and the concentration of service industries within the CBD, DuPage County, Lake County, and northwest Cook County that will be the thriving areas in the Chicago metropolitan area. The Chicago Department of Economic Development points to this traditional importance of the CBD:

> Almost 20.0 percent of the city's entire job base and over one-fourth of Chicago's non-manufacturing employment is concentrated within the central business district, an area of less than one percent of the city's total land base. If the surrounding business ring were added to the central business district, this larger central area would account for almost one-half of the city's non-manufacturing employment, 72.7 percent of its [finance, insurance and real estate] employment and 46.6 percent of all service and miscellaneous jobs.[42]

Metropolitan Area Income

Historically, employed workers in the Chicago region have maintained wage and salary levels at or above the national average. However, the changing fortune of the manufacturing sector, the weakening of labor unions, and the national trend of shifting investment to the South have been eroding the Chicago workers' wage advantage. Per capita personal income in Chicago has dropped to 119 percent of the national average in 1981, down from 130 percent in 1965.[43] While unskilled workers in Chicago still enjoy a relatively high pay scale—122 percent of the national average for unskilled workers in 1981 (of the large cities only Detroit was higher)—such workers represent a declining proportion of this region's work force. In the growing office and clerical occupations, 1981 Chicago pay scales were much closer to the national scale: 104 percent of the national figure.[44] While Chicago's per capita real income increased between 1970 and 1980 by 17.2 percent, this increase is below changes experienced in many other older industrial cities, including Detroit, Milwaukee, Cleveland, and St. Louis, all of which had increases of more than 23 percent.[45]

Chicago's past wage advantage was largely attributable to the strong influence of organized labor in heavy industries. A heavily unionized basic industry helped to maintain relatively high minority wages as well. However, the relatively high wages and salaries of Chicago labor have diminished in the wake of the recession of the late 1970s and early 1980s. Wage erosion has been an outcome of the severe employment decline in basic industries, extensive concessions made by labor unions in all sectors of the work force, and a restructuring of the work force to include a larger proportion of lower-paying service sector jobs.

Chicagoans have long enjoyed higher than average personal incomes. For example, in 1965, the Chicago SMSA's $4,847 per capita personal income (1972 dollars) represented 130 percent of the U.S. income figure.[46] Given such comparative figures, the Chicago area has the reputation for high wages and salaries. In 1981 a senior vice-president at First National Bank of Boston said about Chicago: "Your wage structure runs 50 to 75 percent above ours. That's because wages are set by the dominant industry and, in your area, that is autos and steel. Those industries may be dying, but their wage levels affect the entire area."[47]

Looking at income changes in specific industry categories, one can see slowed growth in most sectors. According to the 1984 Commercial Club study, "growth in Chicago's income lagged behind U.S. growth in every major industry category."[48] Even compared to other Midwestern cities, most notably Detroit and Milwaukee, Chicago fared poorly in personal income increases in both manufacturing and service sectors. Only in Chicago's finance industry did workers fare the same as or better than workers in other regional cities.[49]

Within the city, earnings inequities have also been more apparent. Because blacks have been segregated into certain areas of the city (and into a few suburbs with large black populations, such as Chicago Heights and Harvey), a localized oversupply of semi-skilled and unskilled production and service workers has developed. This, in turn, has lowered the black wage for these already low-paid occupations. John McDonald reports that "racial segregation in housing concentrates the supply of black workers in space relative to the demand for such workers, causing their wages to be

Chicago's Economy   41

Table 2.4   Changes in real income,
Chicago and its suburbs, 1969–1979

Area	1969 income (1979 dollars)	1979 income (actual dollars)	Percent change in real income
Chicago	$20,894	$18,776	−10.1
Suburban Cook County[a]	28,142	32,013	13.8
DuPage	29,494	30,430	3.7
Kane	23,372	25,046	7.2
Lake	26,538	28,045	5.7
McHenry	24,409	25,655	5.1
Will	24,054	25,740	7.0

Source: U.S. Bureau of the Census, *Census of the Population*, 1970 and 1980 (Washington, D.C.: U.S. Government Printing Office, 1973 and 1983).
a. Estimate based on published Census data.

relatively low."[50] Again these black neighborhoods in the city have been disproportionately affected by plant shutdowns.

A further income shift has occurred between city and suburbs. In 1959, city families earned 91.8 percent of the total wages and salaries paid in the SMSA; by 1979 that share had slipped to 76.5 percent.[51] Between 1969 and 1979, real income of families in Chicago —income adjusted for infla- tion—dropped by 10.1 percent. In the same decade, it rose in the suburbs (see Table 2.4). DuPage, Kane, Lake, McHenry, Will, and suburban Cook counties all showed increases. Suburban Cook County not only showed the highest rate of real income increase in the 1970s, but it also had the highest median income of all the suburban counties. In addition, while real income growth in Kane, Lake, and McHenry exceeded that of DuPage during the 1970s, DuPage still had the second highest median income of all suburban Chicago counties. In fact, in comparison with all counties nationwide, DuPage County is ranked as having the tenth highest house- hold median income.[52] Clearly suburban Cook County would also receive a high ranking if it were a separate entity from the city of Chicago. This income differential is a product of the middle-class exodus from the city along with the movement of businesses to the suburbs.

The middle-class exodus is particularly apparent when one compares city and suburban income distribution data. As shown in Table 2.5, be- tween 1960 and 1980, Chicago witnessed a more than 30 percent decline in the number of middle- and upper-income families. Middle-income families are defined here as those families falling in the middle third of family

Table 2.5 Distribution and change in number of families in low-, middle-, and upper-income groups, Chicago SMSA, 1959–1979 [a]

Area	1959 Families	1959 Percent	1979 Families	1979 Percent	Percent change
Chicago					
Low	164,566	18.1	230,711	32.4	40.2 [b]
Middle	578,254	63.6	376,686	52.9	−34.9
Upper	166,384	18.3	104,674	14.7	−37.1
Total	909,204	100.0	712,071	100.0	−21.7
Suburban Cook Co.					
Low	29,991	7.4	71,273	11.9	137.6
Middle	250,868	61.9	350,375	58.5	39.7
Upper	124,421	30.7	177,284	29.6	42.5
Total	405,280	100.0	598,932	100.0	47.8
SMSA less Cook Co.					
Low	33,329	12.4	54,759	11.4	64.3
Middle	172,628	64.4	287,596	59.7	66.6
Upper	62,102	23.2	139,322	28.9	124.3
Total	268,059	100.0	481,677	100.0	79.7

Source: Unpublished data from the U.S. Bureau of the Census compiled by Art Lyons, Institute on Taxation and Economic Policy, Chicago.

a. Low-income families are families with incomes less than 50 percent of the SMSA median income; middle-income families are those with incomes from 50 percent to 150 percent of the SMSA median income; upper-income families are those with incomes above 150 percent of the SMSA median. Median incomes for the SMSA were $7,342 in 1959 and $24,536 in 1979.

b. This percentage refers to the change in the number of low-income families living in Chicago between 1959 and 1979.

income distribution for the entire Chicago SMSA; upper-income families are defined as those families falling in the upper third. At the same time, suburban Cook County has seen an increase of more than 30 percent in families among the same income categories. However, the most startling growth of the middle class has taken place in suburbs outside Cook County, In the five SMSA counties other than Cook, the number of middle-income families has grown by 67 percent while the number of upper-income families has grown by 124 percent.

Aside from a few high-income neighborhoods in Chicago—such as the Gold Coast, Forest Glen, Edison Park, Norwood Park, Ashburn, and Beverly—the highest-income communities are concentrated in northwestern Cook County and the North Shore, which extends along Lake Michigan through northeastern Cook and eastern Lake counties.[53] The

Table 2.6 Unemployment rates in city and suburbs compared to U.S. (percent unemployed)

Year	U.S.	Chicago SMSA	Chicago (city)
1970	4.9	4.0	3.9
1972	5.6	5.1	6.3
1974	5.6	4.5	5.5
1976	7.7	6.7	9.0
1978	6.0	6.0	9.1
1980	7.1	8.3	11.3
1982	9.7	11.8	17.2
1983	9.6	11.2	16.8

Source: Mayor's Council of Manpower and Economic Advisors, *1980 Annual Update: Overall Economic Development Plan (OEDP) of Chicago* (Chicago: The Council, 1982), ADD (PN) Commercial Club of Chicago, "Economic Plan: Jobs for Metropolitan Chicago, Economic Scan." data prepared by Federal Reserve Bank of Chicago for a subsequent report: Commercial Club of Chicago, *Make No Little Plans: Jobs for Metropolitan Chicago* (Chicago: The Club, 1984), p. E 32.O; and data provided by the Chicago office of the U.S. Bureau of Labor Statistics

affluent communities of the North Shore include Kenilworth, Glencoe, Winnetka, Wilmette, Highland Park, and Lake Forest. These suburbs experienced among the highest income growth rates of all Chicago suburbs between 1979 and 1983.[54] Some of the newer affluent suburbs, most notably Barrington Hills, North Barrington, and South Barrington, in northwest Cook County and southwest Lake County also experienced increases. The concentration of wealth in the newer suburbs has been the product of zoning for large minimum lot size and effective opposition to commercial development that might adversely affect the exclusive image of the community.[55] This is similar to the history of earlier growth in the North Shore suburbs. Such suburban communities provide a sharp contrast to Chicago, which not only has experienced an exodus of moderate-and upper-income residents but is now seeing its better-paid, blue-collar residents put out of jobs due to a decline in manufacturing.

A disparity between city and suburbs has also been manifested in the area of unemployment. Although Chicago SMSA unemployment rates have only recently risen above U.S. averages, unemployment in the city accounts for much of this jump (see Table 2.6). While unemployment rates in both the city and the metropolitan area were below the U.S. average of

4.9 percent in 1970, this trend reversed itself in 1978, the beginning of a recession that hit older manufacturing centers quite hard. Since then both the suburban and the city rates have been above the national average. Even though 1983 unemployment is down slightly from 1982, the long-term impact of plant shutdowns and trimmed industrial work forces is apparent. For example, if one looks at the area in which Chicago's heavy industry is most concentrated—industrial Northwest Indiana—high unemployment rates have been quite apparent. In March 1984, when U.S. unemployment had slipped down to 8.1 percent, Northwest Indiana—the Gary-Hammond-East Chicago SMSA—still reported a 17.8 percent unemployment rate.[56]

Consistent with trends across the nation, regional black unemployment rates have been more than double those of whites. In 1982 black unemployment in the city and SMSA were 26.8 and 26.1 percent respectively, while white unemployment rates were 11.9 percent and 8.9 percent respectively.[57]

The Role of Organized Labor

Another community that has been dramatically affected by unemployment and the related economic decline of heavy industry is organized labor. Since the industrial union-organizing drives in the 1930s, Chicago and Northwest Indiana have been relatively strong union areas. In the mid-1970s, 28 percent of all private sector Chicago workers and 48 percent of all production workers were union members. The comparable figures for the Gary-Hammond-East Chicago SMSA were 55 percent and 69 percent, making the Indiana tri-city area the most heavily unionized in the country.[58] Both unionization rates exceeded the 1970s national average of 25 percent,[59] although the Chicago rate is not dramatically different from that of other large Northeastern and Midwestern cities.

Unions have been a prominent part of the region's economic and political landscape. The Amalgamated Clothing and Textile Workers Union, the American Federation of State, County, and Municipal Employees, the Chicago Federation of Teachers, the Electrical Workers, the International Association of Machinists, the Service Employees International Union, the Teamsters, the United Automobile Workers, and the United Steelworkers of America are among the larger unions in Chicago. The construction trades unions have been successful in maintaining a prevailing wage formula for city employees. This means that city workers in various trades are paid wages equivalent to those in private industry, even though city employees work 12 months and private tradespersons often work fewer months because of seasonal work schedules. Union leaders have been able to place their best friends or supporters in these city jobs, therefore becoming partners in the city's patronage system.[60]

However, there have been major shifts in the character of unions in the metropolitan area and in their role in the local economy, shifts reflecting national trends. Industrial unions have been weakened while service sector unions are gaining strength. Since 1979 industrial unions have experienced a precipitous drop in membership. The steelworkers union, which once had a regional membership of 130,000, now has fewer than 80,000 members in Northeast Illinois and Northwest Indiana. In addition to membership loss experienced by all the unions, recent rounds of concessionary contracts in most industrial unions have cut members' wage levels.

On the other hand, the growth of the service sector, combined with new Illinois state legislation giving government workers the right to organize, has given a boost to service sector unions, particularly those representing government employees in Chicago and Cook County. Illinois was the last industrial state to pass legislation allowing government workers—state, county, and city employees—the right to organize and strike in nonessential service areas.[61] The law went into effect in July 1984, and by the end of that summer service sector unions such as the American Federation of State, County, and Municipal Employees (AFSCME) and the Service Employees International Union (SEIU) had been able to swell their ranks by more than 10,000 members in Chicago and Cook County.

These new unions are likely to become more powerful in Chicago, while older industrial and craft unions become weaker. As already mentioned, plant shutdowns and disinvestment have hurt many of the older industrial unions. Suburban manufacturing employment has tended to be nonunion.[62] Shifts in the city's political climate have also changed the distribution of power among unions. Not only does state law now allow unions to represent public employees, but cooperative relationships between some "old guard" unions and the city's patronage system are disappearing. Because Mayor Harold Washington strongly supported unions and government workers' right to organize, he worked to dismantle the patronage system of which many construction and skilled trades unions have been a part.

As has been the case throughout the country, much of the established local union leadership has been unable to cope with the complex of economic and political changes. With the exception of the SEIU, AFSCME, and a handful of other unions, it has been business as usual for the veteran union leaders. The 40-year tenure of former Chicago Federation of Labor president Bill Lee, ending in 1984, was symbolic of this lack of new blood and new direction in union officialdom. When asked what input labor has had in working with the pro-labor reform government of the Washington administration, Rob Mier, head of the Chicago Department of Economic Development, replied, "Organized labor is in a shambles."[63]

The disarray has been apparent at a number of levels. Hit by substantial membership losses, union leaders have had a difficult time figuring out how to recoup losses within their unions, let alone figure out what role to play in Chicago's recent volatile political scene. Paul Booth, a staff member for the American Federation of State, County, and Municipal Employees in Chicago — a union that has made significant gains here in recent years — observes that these recent changes have "bewildered a large number of older leaders" in the Chicago labor movement.[64] These leaders want to maintain their positions of influence within their unions, within Chicago politics, and at the bargaining table; however, they find their power bases eroding and their traditional strategies ineffective.

Perhaps the most bewildering changes have been in the unions' relationship with city government. Booth notes that "labor unions were the bulwark of the Daley machine," the political organization that built up the post-World War II web of city patronage.[65] Court decisions, such as the Shakman decree outlawing patronage, and the general weakening of the Democratic machine eroded this traditional labor-government relationship.[66] Ironically, the state legislation that gives city employees the right to unionize has been important in weakening the power of those labor organizations — particularly the skilled trades unions — that have been part of the patronage system. At the same time that the skilled trades unions have experienced a loss of power in the city, service sector unions representing local government's clerical and administrative staff have made gains.

The unions that have organized city and Cook County employees do not have the strong tradition of elitism and behind-closed-doors deal-making that was characteristic of the skilled trades unions and allowed their involvement in the patronage system. For example, one union that gained over 3,000 new members in the state-mandated elections of 1984 was the Service Employees International Union. Much of this new membership was picked up by SEIU's District 925, a progressive arm of the parent union that has organized large numbers of women workers nationwide. Unlike many unions, the SEIU, not as dominated by male leadership, has challenged the second-class status of female office workers. In addition, it is not very likely to become a willing partner in the city patronage system. Explains SEIU District 925 staff member Bonnie Ladin:

People feel beholden to the patronage system for their job. They may even pay money to keep their jobs or do extra work for certain individuals to keep their jobs. With collective bargaining agreements and the union behind them, workers see that they don't need the patronage system to protect their jobs. Working as a union, you don't need to rely on patronage figures to move up the ladder.[67]

In addition to challenging skilled trades prerogatives and the overall patronage system, AFSCME and, to a lesser degree, SEIU openly supported Harold Washington's electoral bid in 1983 and his subsequent reform efforts.

Some of the older traditional labor leaders have not only lost their connections to city hall but are experiencing challenges from within their own unions as well. In recent years, political differences within unions have pitted older, more conservative, usually male labor leaders against younger, more militant, male and female grassroots activists. The successful 1970s rank-and-file insurgency in the steelworkers union—still one of the largest unions in the Chicago area—was a product of membership dissatisfaction with an unresponsive union leadership.[68] The ranks of militant young union insurgents have been thinned out by recent layoffs and plant shutdowns in the 1980s. As will be discussed below, despite their declining numbers, it is this younger, more militant group of trade unionists that has increasingly been working with local government agencies and community-based organizations to develop innovative solutions to deindustrialization. Nevertheless, while there may be some dramatic changes in organized labor's future here, the fact remains that organized labor, particularly those union members in the traditionally strong industrial unions, must be included in the losers' column when one looks at the results of the Chicago growth game.

The Direction of Chicago's Economy

Although there is some question about how substantial the growth of Chicago's service sector really is, corporate growth in the central business district is important to the city's economic well-being. Chicago's position as a regional center is an asset; it does pump private money and jobs into the Loop and North Michigan Avenue offices and retail developments. At the same time, the large corporations along with other CBD business interests have built a growth machine that reflects their private interests. Like all cities, Chicago has its prominent corporations, business associations, elite social clubs, and powerful business leaders. In the past these business leaders have won the cooperation of city officials in fueling their growth machine, often to the detriment of areas of the city outside the central business district.

The private economic institutions and the private-public cooperation in downtown economic development are part of broader economic processes that shape Chicago, just as they shape all urban economies. In essence, Chicago's growth machine is part of a national growth machine that directs revenue and investment to profit centers. At national and local levels economic development has been defined as the creation of a "good business climate."

The Good Business Climate

Much is written and said about the importance of the so-called business climate. Although this is a vague notion as used by the business community and economic development officials, Alexander Grant and Company "measures" this climate every year, state by state. States are then ranked from the perspective of business; for example, which states have lower wage rates or strike activity. In many ways a good business climate rating means that there is a poor labor climate—that is, workers and unions in such areas have been relatively weak when it comes to influencing wages and working conditions. Thus, given the traditional strength of Illinois labor unions, it is not surprising that, in 1984, Illinois ranked 48th in the U.S.; this was down from 42nd in 1983.[69]

This ranking suggests among other things that, in the eyes of business, Illinois wage rates and unionization levels are too high relative to other locations. Further, factors such as cost of living and levels of local government incentives produce a more positive business climate elsewhere. The presumed upshot is that, in the battle to attract new businesses or keep area businesses from expanding or relocating elsewhere, Illinois and Chicago do not have great drawing power in the eyes of the business community.[70] Yet the deteriorating business climate in Illinois and Chicago is part of a broader economic process affecting other regions as well.

In their book *The Deindustrialization of America*, Barry Bluestone and Bennett Harrison have documented this propensity of business to move to regions with a "procorporate environment." This has generally meant that firms have moved away from the Northeast and Midwest because of the strong influence of both organized labor and liberal state and local political

institutions. In the past such influences functioned to protect workers, con-
sumers, and residents from corporate excesses. This may no longer be the
case. Relocating firms and some new or expanding companies are likely to
gravitate toward the more pro-corporate environment of the South or of
Third World nations desperate to attract foreign capital.

In response to such regional shifts, metropolitan areas like Chicago believe they can compete only by offering bigger and better corporate incentives. In so doing they undermine what is termed the "social wage"—"that
amalgam of benefits, worker protections, and legal rights that acts to
generally increase the social security of the working class."[71] This move
toward a better business climate may not be entirely the outcome of a
conscious and calculated action on the part of identifiable individuals or
institutions. For example, the erosion of Chicago-area industrial union
membership—the result of plant shutdowns and layoffs in declining older
industries—combined with the persistence of relatively ineffective traditional trade union strategies has certainly weakened labor and consequently
helped to produce a positive business environment.

The growing low-skilled, unemployed minority population, created by
factors ranging from suburbanization to the CBD growth machine, makes
the city more desperate for jobs and ironically may be improving the business climate. A columnist for *Crain's Chicago Business* contended that the
city's high unemployment rate and increased labor pool size should be
encouraging developments for the business community.[72] Bluestone and
Harrison indicate that this trend in Chicago is part of a trend in older
industrial cities, in general, where one can now find a "proliferation of tax
breaks and other business subsidies, together with the weakening of pro-
labor, proconsumer regulations on industry." They go on to say that there
has been a "veritable orgy of 'incentive granting'" where state and local
governments are trying to compete with their neighbors for business'
hand.[73] However, at the same time as Chicago and other cities are trying to
muster limited resources to woo new businesses and keep remaining employers from leaving, other economic processes undermine this effort.

Economic Handicaps: Loss of
Taxes and Community Revenues

At a time when Chicago could use more federal tax dollars to help bolster
its sagging economy and redevelopment efforts, the city and the state are
experiencing a net loss in federal tax dollars. According to researchers for
the Federal Reserve Bank in Chicago, although the five states in its region

(Illinois, Indiana, Michigan, Iowa, and Wisconsin) produce approximately 15 percent of the federal government's revenues, these states receive only 10.7 percent of *all* federal support, ranging from welfare to defense industry expenditures. Illinois ranks 46th in per capita federal outlays of all kinds.[74] In federal grants to state and local governments in the 1984 budget, Illinois received $417 per capita, below the national average of $436. Interestingly, the six northeastern states are among the top 15 recipients of such government support.[75] This seems to indicate that aging cities of the Northeast are faring better, at least in this form of government aid, when compared to sister cities in the Midwest. Perhaps the most dramatic figure is the Chicago SMSA's loss in "defense taxes." In comparing that portion of Chicago taxpayers' money that goes for defense to what actually comes back to the area in the form of salaries, wages, or purchases, Employment Research Associates found that, in 1983, the average Chicago-area family lost $3,400 to this "defense tax." This is the largest per family "defense tax" loss of the ten largest SMSAs in the country.[76]

Other economic handicaps imposed on the metropolitan area include escalating energy costs and high interest rates for small business expansion. This has shifted money away from local businesses (and employees) and put it in the coffers of large corporations and banks. While these are "handicaps" affecting all parts of the country, it is another burden that can be added to the overall decline in this city's economy.

In many ways the "energy crisis" of the 1970s also brought about a shift in corporate wealth and strength. Small business, government, and private family budgets that may have had reserves in them for expansion, improved services, or home improvements prior to the crisis are now eroded by high energy costs. Completing research for two Chicago community organizations, the Organization of the Northeast and the Center for Neighborhood Technology, urban analysts Stanley J. Hallett and G. Alfred Hess Jr. noted that some Chicago neighborhoods that might have been resuscitated by minimal private and public moneys are now struggling for survival because of escalating energy costs:

> The effect of rising energy costs in urban neighborhoods is devastating. A recent study of the energy costs in the Edgewater/Uptown area on Chicago's North Side found that the residential electric bill for that community increased from nearly $17 million in 1978 to $19.5 million in 1979. Each 10% real rise in the price of electricity drains almost $2 million more from the community. There is no increase in the neighborhood economy as a result of this cost increase—no new jobs are

created in the neighborhood and no new business is generated locally from the utility's expenditure. In short, utility rate increases drain economic resources from neighborhoods least capable of losing those resources.

They add that in Chicago overall "energy costs rose from 11.2% of gross building income in 1968 to 23% in 1975." By the early 1980s energy costs had risen to almost 33 percent of building revenue.[77] One cannot assume that all the money "lost" to utility companies and energy conglomerates would have been pumped into the neighborhood economy. Nevertheless, rising energy costs do represent a drain on local economies.

The economies of neighborhoods have also been hit by high interest rates to small business. While large corporations can get prime interest rate loans, small businesses ($5 million or less in annual sales)—companies that are more likely to be located in neighborhoods outside the CBD—are much more likely to pay one or two percentage points above prime on loans.[78] Such banking policies serve to produce and reinforce the growth machine, forcing neighborhood businesses to struggle while downtown growth continues.[79]

Even for those who are not as quick to support the growth machine ideology wholeheartedly—as in the case of the Washington administration—the fact that the CBD has become such a keystone in the city's economy makes development of alternative policies a complicated affair. The CBD contains more than 42 percent of the city's jobs[80] and produces 40 percent of the city's property taxes.[81] Given these facts, any future plans for economic development must ask the question: does the city direct public resources to support the central business district or does it tax that area as a means of supporting less prosperous city neighborhoods? This dilemma and the political responses to it will be discussed in more detail in Chapter 6. At this point suffice it to say that downtown investment has been the long-standing focus of economic development policy in Chicago. Loop business leaders remain the single most influential force shaping the ongoing discussion of Chicago's economic future.

Challenging the Growth Machine?

Along with the urban economic crises of the 1970s and 1980s have come a series of proposed solutions. Some of these proposals, like the attraction of high-tech businesses or the establishment of enterprise zones, are firmly rooted in the growth ideology. In contrast, other potential approaches, including community-based economic development agencies, worker ownership, and the organization of a variety of neighborhood and civic group coalitions, do challenge the growth ideology. The following pages examine these various policies, some of which have already been implemented and others of which are still on the drawing board.

After Harold Washington's election in 1983, his administration worked to produce a city economic development apparatus that was more fair and more accountable to the public. Although it is too early to tell what long-term effect his reform efforts have had on CBD development and the growth machine, there have been substantial shifts in the focus of local government policy. Washington opposed development for development's sake and stressed the need to use city government money and power to produce and retain jobs for Chicago city residents. In addition, he vowed to pump more money into outlying neighborhoods and to allow residents of the communities more say in policy-making than did previous administrations. He met with some success in these efforts during his first year in office.[82]

For example, on the Southwest Side, city officials provided loans and development funds that convinced Sears and Roebuck not to close a neighborhood store. The administration of Mayor Jane Byrne, Washington's predecessor, had been unsuccessful in accomplishing this same task.[83] In addition, the Department of Economic Development helped to fund an "early warning system" in the depressed West Side. Developed in cooperation with the Midwest Center for Labor Research and the Center for Urban Economic Development of the University of Illinois at Chicago, the system is intended to give the city information about possible plant closings *before* they occur. This would allow city officials to intervene and possibly save neighborhood jobs by preventing a factory shutdown.

The Washington administration also intensified efforts to redirect funds to housing rehabilitation projects and other community support programs. At the one-year mark of the new administration, 5,500 living units were being rehabilitated by the city.[84] As the result of lengthy efforts by community organizations, the city and People's Gas financed a $15 million low-interest energy conservation loan program administered by community organizations.[85] The Washington administration also supported a policy to link downtown development projects with neighborhood projects.

Washington's first development plan, released in May 1984, differed from plans of earlier years, which rarely questioned unlimited CBD growth. Washington's proposal, subtitled "Chicago Works Together," advocated "a clearly articulated set of development goals . . . for the City as a whole, not just for the Central Business District and large scale public projects." Its top four goals were to "increase job opportunities for Chicagoans," "promote balanced growth," "assist neighborhoods to develop through partnerships and coordinated investment," and "enhance public participation in decision making."[86]

The Washington administration differentiated itself from its predecessors in attempting to meet these goals. However, despite the scrutiny it gave to past economic development policies, some of the Washington administration policies themselves followed the path of the growth ideology. These concessions to the growth ideology demonstrate some of the barriers that obstruct the creation of an economically democratic city.

The High-Tech Solution

In the 1983 Chicago mayoral debates, all three Democratic candidates —Jane Byrne, Harold Washington, and Richard Daley—said that they would invest city money to attract high-tech industries as part of the solution to the city's employment problems.[87] In many ways this is the ultimate expression of the growth ideology. Not only were the candidates proposing to spend money on a growth area, but they were proposing expenditures on a growth area that did not yet even exist in the city.

High tech is a highly questionable solution to Chicago's economic woes.[88] While the high-tech sector nationally has seen and will continue to see rapid growth in output, productivity, and profits, this does not necessarily translate into a boom in hiring, particularly for recently unemployed blue-collar workers. *Business Week* estimates "that the number of high-tech jobs created over the next decade will represent less than half of the 2 million jobs lost in manufacturing in the past three years."[89] The trade, service, manufacturing, and construction sectors are expected to produce more new jobs than high tech in the next ten years.[90]

In addition to the uncertainty regarding high-tech job creation nationally, the potential for high tech as a source of employment for workers in Chicago is questionable. First, there is considerable doubt that Chicago can become a center for high-tech industry comparable to Boston's Route 128 and California's Silicon Valley. Chicago is at a disadvantage to those areas that have been developing a broad network of high-tech industries and suppliers for more than thirty years. Moreover, while Stanford and MIT have been providing the high-tech sector in their regions with consultants, a constant supply of new entrepeneurs, and a highly skilled young work force, Chicago's universities have not been serving these same functions.[91]

A second major question about the appropriateness of high-tech industry for Chicago's occupational future involves the types of jobs that may be produced. In the final analysis, most high-tech jobs are not all that glamorous and are quite insecure. Although the label "high tech" brings with it images of highly skilled and highly paid workers in positions offering significant opportunities for advancement, most high-tech jobs are not much different from the types of jobs already available in manufacturing and service sectors. Of the 689,000 jobs that the high-tech industries are expected to produce nationwide between 1980 and 1993, 226,000, or 33 percent, will be for low-skilled operatives; another 150,000, or 22 percent, will be for managers and clerical workers.[92]

While these jobs might provide low-paying opportunities for the growing low-skilled Chicago work force, they are also very insecure jobs. Recent events have demonstrated that this new job market is even more volatile than the basic manufacturing industry job market. Like other mobile industries, such as electronics and garments, which have relatively little invested in machines and factory buildings, high-tech industries can easily pick up and leave if cheaper wage rates or more desirable employee relations beckon elsewhere. A notable indication of the instability of high-tech employment was Atari Inc.'s 1983 announcement that it was firing 1,700 workers in the United States because it was moving assembly of video games and home computers to Hong Kong and Taiwan. Domestic producers of digital watches, calculators, semiconductors, and computers have all moved their operations abroad when competition increased.[93] The operative and clerical-level high-tech jobs that Chicago might attract could disappear as quickly as they appear.

Despite the indications that high tech may not be the solution to Chicago's employment problems, there are attempts being made to develop a high tech base here. To attract high-tech firms, local government agencies have underwritten an "incubator" research building that can serve as an anchor to a new research park at Chicago's West Side Medical Center. There are also plans to establish a privately funded Chicago Science Foundation to support local research.[94]

Chicago does have potential to take the lead in certain areas of biotechnology, basing its growth on strong medical research institutions, university-based agricultural research in the state, and its proximity to

America's agricultural heartland. This area may also be more attractive to some developing high-tech firms because the Midwest is not expected to experience the rising costs plaguing Massachusetts and California. While this is somewhat encouraging, Chicago and the Midwest will most likely remain secondary locations for new businesses in this new sector of the economy. According to projections by the Congressional Joint Economic Committee, by 1986 high-tech plants in the Midwest are expected to represent only 9.6 percent of all the nation's high-tech plants.[95] It is also likely that those high-tech industries that do move into the metropolitan area will locate in DuPage County, not in the city of Chicago.

Enterprise Zones

Perhaps one of the more obvious signs of Chicago's desperate efforts to revive its economy is the establishment of enterprise zones. Set up by state legislation and subsequent city ordinances in 1982, as of 1985 enterprise zones had been created in five "economically depressed" areas. The legislation provides for tax incentives, zoning variances, building code modifications, and licensing variances for businesses entering the zones. To these are added other government incentives available citywide, including industrial revenue bonds, low-interest loans, and Urban Development Action Grants. The zones cover the predominantly black South Side and much of the depressed steel-producing Southeast Side. The city's publicity states that creation of the zones "is based on the expectation that the revitalization of a business community will produce a growth in jobs and overall improvement of the quality of life."[96] Yet there is substantial debate over whether such tax incentives really work.

Although attention is being directed toward the revitalization of economically distressed areas, the philosophy of enterprise zones is: if business is to stay in problem areas or if the private sector is to pump money into distressed neighborhoods, then it had better be guaranteed a good return on its investment. The city guarantees the return by overlooking ordinances, codes, and tax regulations, many of which were passed in earlier years to ensure future balanced development.

Chicago's enterprise zones have produced some results. At least one company, Spiegel, Inc., which employs 1,500 men and women, 90 percent of whom are minority workers, has changed its mind about moving to the sunbelt. Because it is included in one of the enterprise zones, the company has been able to get around some building codes and remodel its existing buildings to suit current needs.[97] Nonetheless, critics question the long-term impact of zones and incentives. The overall loss of tax revenue to incentive-giving may hurt the city more than it helps.[98]

The record, nationwide, of local- and state-level tax breaks and related incentives is not encouraging. There have been a host of such programs in recent years and little economic growth to show for it. In 1975 alone—by one count—more than 400 incentive programs were offered by state and city governments.[99] But the recipients of this aid have not been generating new jobs. Research by Ralph Nader and the Massachusetts Institute of Technology's David Birch shows that, while over two-thirds of the tax-free financing in the past two decades has gone to corporations employing 5,000 or more people, more than two-thirds of all new jobs have been created by firms with fewer than 20 employees.[100]

It appears that the jobs that are generated by incentive policies—particularly by enterprise zones—are low-paying and low-skilled. According to economists Bluestone and Harrison, those who will benefit from the zones are "employers who offer low-wage, low productivity jobs and who follow authoritarian or arbitrary personnel practices."[101] William W. Goldsmith, a professor of city and regional planning at Cornell University, describes enterprise zones as a way of bringing Third World wages and working conditions to American cities.[102]

The enterprise zone concept shares the fundamental flaw of other programs based on the growth ideology: it relies precisely on those market forces and profit incentives that caused economic problems to be the solution to the current economic crisis. The basic assumption underlying enterprise zones and supply-side theory generally is that, with additional financial incentives (or cost reduction through tax breaks and regulation), business will increase job-producing, economically stimulating investment activity. Stripped of its economic jargon, this approach portends a massive shifting of costs from the private to the public sector and from those most able to pay to those least able to pay.

Despite this rather bleak perspective on enterprise zones and similar incentive programs, cities like Chicago are in a bind. While public officials may not want to go on the public record as strongly supporting the growth of low-wage and low-skilled jobs, as indicated earlier, an increasing proportion of the Chicago labor supply is low-skilled. Although there may be plans on the books to implement training programs for low-skilled Chicagoans, such projects take time and are likely to serve only a small portion of those who need training. A 1983 survey of Chicago job-training programs found that few programs existed and few low-skilled Chicagoans were being served.[103] Federal support for even these limited efforts is quickly drying up in the mid-1980s.

Despite the dilemma facing city officials, there are winners in the city's incentive roulette: the city's corporate executives and their political allies. These groups are also the winners in the city's efforts to keep plants from shutting down or moving elsewhere; moreover, these businesses are winners in the battles between states of the industrial Midwest, all of which are vying for private enterprise's favor. Workers getting jobs and communities saving part of their economic base may not feel like losers, but in the long run they must ask the questions, "What price has been paid? What effects will the erosion of the social wage and the emergence of a good business climate have?" In the 1980s, the "City That Works" became the "City That Will Work for Less."

The Washington administration's pursuit of high-tech industries and the establishment of enterprise zones illustrate the dilemma faced by reform politicians in the 1980s. While they may openly question the inequities related to pro-growth assumptions regarding economic development, they may also find themselves adopting some of the very policies they have questioned. Dominant economic and political institutions severely limit the choices available to elected officials seeking more equitable solutions to urban problems. First, there is the reality that substantial sums of Chicago's tax money are generated by the growth sectors. Concomitant to this is the growth sectors' influence over private and public economic decision-making in the city. Second, while political reform swept through part of Chicago in the early 1980s, there still is an ongoing battle between the traditional political leadership and some of the newly empowered politicians who want to change priorities, economic and others, in the city. However, despite these barricades to sweeping reform in Chicago, there are noticeable grassroots efforts to challenge the prevalent growth ideology.

Community-Based Alternatives to Decline

The growth ideology represents one framework for seeking solutions to Chicago's economic woes. But, one must ask, "A solution for whom?" Throwing money at growth areas, such as the central business district, may keep the downtown healthy, at least temporarily. Building middle-class residential developments in deteriorating sectors or at the edge of the Loop can tidy up some neighborhoods, but these improvements frequently accelerate growth in already improving areas, at the same time as the lack of attention to the rest of the city may accelerate *decline* in other areas. Chicago's growth ideology has produced one of the nicest urban front yards in the nation; Chicago's downtown lakefront parks and skyline are spectacular. But the backyard—the deteriorating neighborhoods, the boarded-up businesses, the rusting factories, and the unemployed workers—presents a different picture. There are some working-class neighborhoods that appear to be surviving. But, even there, residents look beyond their communities at bordering neighborhoods experiencing increasingly serious economic problems. These more secure neighborhoods may be asking if leaders of economic institutions will pass them by too if they need help in the future.

There are alternatives to the growth machine. An emerging community of political, labor, neighborhood, and consumer organizations and activists is exploring other approaches to the city's problems. They envision a different future than do the industrial leaders, developers, and machine politicians. They have recognized that the growth ideology—though they may not use that term—carries with it enormous inequities for individuals and communities in the entire metropolitan area.

In the 1980s labor union activists and workers in Chicago's declining industries have been involved in a number of innovative projects. For example, in the first two years of its existence, the Midwest Center for Labor Research (MCLR) completed studies and produced public policy reports pertaining to improvement of health care for unemployed blue-collar workers, establishment of an early warning system for plant shutdowns, development of new models for employee ownership in financially troubled industries, and expansion of community support for depressed industries. The early warning system that MCLR set up with the assistance of the Chicago Department of Economic Development and the University of Illinois Center for Urban Economic Development will seek to retain businesses and jobs in Chicago's poor, predominantly black West Side. The labor activist group already has worked with a coalition of public and private health care agencies both in identifying health care needs of the newly unemployed and in implementing new policies and practices designed to meet those needs. Its work has reached into the suburbs and the Northwest Indiana industrial areas.

MCLR has distinguished itself from traditional labor union approaches to these problems. It has completed community-based research and made policy recommendations on problems transcending traditional collective-bargaining issues. In so doing, the Center has worked with academics, community activists, religious leaders, and public officials in seeking solutions to social problems of the 1980s. Dan Swinney, director of MCLR, explains that "we are not willing to write off industrial workers, industrial plants, and industrial communities as a lost cause." There is potential productive power in the Chicago region's industrial communities, in its factories, and in its labor force. Swinney adds that "we need to exhaust this potential before we throw it away."[104]

Building on its strong base among labor union activists, MCLR sees itself as a consultant organization and coalition builder, working with labor, government, community, and business organizations. It is currently involved in feasibility studies to decide whether there is productive capacity left in closed or soon to be closed industrial plants and whether worker or community buyouts may succeed. They are working with government officials to determine whether or not shutdown sections of USX's South Works are still viable. MCLR is also assisting employees and managers at Blaw Knox—an East Chicago, Indiana company that lost its Defense Department contract to build armored tank shells—to determine the feasibility of converting to non-defense production.[105] In 1985 MCLR organized a nationwide boycott of Playskool Toys after the parent company, Hasbro Bradley, decided to move production outside of the Chicago area, leaving more than 700 jobless. What has made this case particularly noteworthy is the fact that, in 1980, Playskool received a low-interest loan via an industrial revenue bond from the city and had promised to stay in the area and increase the size of its work force.[106] While the boycott and the threat of a city suit against the company did not stop Playskool from moving, it did delay the shutdown by one year and helped force the company to provide $300,000 to support a job-placement program for the dislocated workers.[107]

Other organizations, such as the Chicago Jobs Council and the Wisconsin Steel employees' Save Our Jobs (SOJ) Committee, have also looked beyond traditional approaches to saving jobs in older industrial areas. Although unsuccessful in reopening the Wisconsin Steel facility on Chicago's Southeast Side and regaining jobs for its 3,500 workers, the SOJ Committee promoted the idea of employee ownership as a means of saving jobs and preventing the devastating ripple effect of job loss in the community. Although the naysayers in Chicago shouted "I told you so" as some of the furnaces and mill buildings were dismantled in 1984, the concept of employee and community ownership gained credibility.

In January 1984, 60 former managers and union workers purchased Scully-Jones Corporation on Chicago's South Side. After paying $2 million to Scully's parent company, Allied Corporation, workers now elect their own board, which in turn hires management. According to the new president of this company, which manufactures electrical switches, productivity has risen well over earlier levels.[108] The United Food and Commercial Workers Union is currently working with the Midwest Center for Labor Research and a community economic development corporation on a feasibility study for buying out a small leather tannery on Chicago's near Northwest Side.[109] While these are small examples of the viability of worker or community ownership as an alternative to plant shutdowns, recent cases of worker buyouts of larger industrial and service operations in other parts of the country have encouraged Chicago planners.[110] However, despite the fact that employee ownership has proven to be a viable alternative to plant shutdowns, efforts have not received much support from private or public agencies. In the absense of government support and cooperation from the business community, it is unlikely that such alternatives to conventional enterprise will become commonplace.

Challenges to the growth ideology have also been generated outside the workplace. A number of community-based organizations are using innovative ways of helping small businesses and building owners survive. For example, the Center for Neighborhood Technology (CNT) has provided technical assistance to over 100 community organizations, particularly in the area of energy conservation and lower-cost alternative energy sources. In the past three years it has helped to distribute grants and low-interest loans to community organizations investing in new energy systems. Many of these organizations are based in Chicago's low-income communities. CNT executive director Scott Bernstein reports that not one organization has defaulted on its loans. He notes that "you wouldn't expect community organizations in poor neighborhoods to be good lending risks, but they were not risks."[111] Communities still have viable neighborhood economies; Bernstein adds, "If they weren't good [investment] risks, how could the South Shore Bank and the Northside Community Federal Credit Union [both banks that invest in local communities seen by some as economically unstable] be as profitable and as successful as they are?"[112]

Such efforts—and others to be discussed in later chapters—currently operate at the fringe of Chicago's economy. However, the evolution of Chicago's economy, along with the changing dynamics of race and ethnic relations, of community organization involvement, and of politics generally, suggest that such efforts may play a far more significant role in the future.

3

From Machine Politics to ?

It has been said that in Chicago
the term "clout" was invented.
Nicholas von Hoffman[1]

In 1955, when Paddy Bauler reportedly observed that "Chicago ain't ready for reform," big city political machines were in general decline, although the Cook County Democratic organization was considerably more operational than most. At present, three decades later, some of Bauler's successors continue to make this claim.

In order to understand political developments in Chicago since World War II, one must come to terms not only with shifts in voter sentiment and the electoral calculus of politicians but also with the virtually mythic dimensions of "The Machine" and its longstanding leader, Mayor Daley. A decade after Daley's death, mayors continue to be measured by the standards of toughness, attention to management and fiscal detail, and love for his city that Daley's memory, if not his performance, evoke.[2] Moreover, mayors are held to these standards by media commentators, the business community, and working politicians, even if neither their personalities nor their programs are congruent with "Hizzoner's." Efforts to carry on electoral politics and coordinate governmental operations in ways contrary to the practices of the Cook County Democratic party run up against far more than a party hierarchy and some holdover payrollers in city government; reformers find themselves adversaries of a broadly internalized political subculture.

The character of metropolitan politics and city-suburban relations in the Chicago region also reveals the mark of the Democratic party. As one might expect, the several dozen relatively small suburban towns arrayed to Chicago's north, west, and south view the giant central city with considerable trepidation. In the Chicago area this commonplace suburban apprehension is aggravated by party cleavages. Unlike in Chicago, Republicans are an important force in most suburbs. Furthermore, political style divides Chicago from its suburbs, most of which have been ruled by fairly low-key non-partisan governments. The result is that the metropolitan area has not been very successful in developing cooperative solutions to its collective problems. Instead, informal and often temporary accommodation is the primary vehicle for resolving intergovernmental conflict and addressing metropolitan problems.

Within the city the salience of this inflation of party and mayor to local cultural symbols was highlighted by Harold Washington's successful mayoral candidacy in 1983. There were a number of reasons for supposing that the passing of the mayoralty from white to black hands might have been reasonably uncontentious. Quite early in the twentieth century, Chicago elected blacks to significant political office as alderpersons and state legislators.[3] Throughout much of the 1950s and 1960s the mainly black wards overseen by Congressman William Dawson turned out huge majorities in support of Democratic party candidates, white and black. Furthermore, Harold Washington himself served an apprenticeship in the regular Democratic organization. Though he broke with his political mentors in the 1970s, so had any number of disaffected organization politicians, most notably a string of Polish Democrats including Benjamin Adamowski and Roman Pucinski.

In fact, the mayoral election of 1983 was highly divisive, because the record of black Democratic loyalty and Harold Washington's roots within the Democratic organization did not diminish the threat that black political leadership poses for the regular Democratic organization. The Democratic party had come to signify a style of governance and interpersonal relations among political figures that could not bend to the demands of a mobilized black electorate. This was in large part because a significant component of the party's style of governance and politicking required the subordination of blacks and their political interest to the psychological and material needs of the party's white ethnic factions. These attitudes and the interests they promote did not relent even though the ideological orientation and policy implications of the Washington candidacy were hardly at odds with the neighborhood maintenance and service delivery concerns of many white ethnic Chicagoans. Thus, the Harold Washington ascendancy must be viewed as a political watershed in Chicago. To understand it one must recall the political circumstances that produced the Democratic machine in Chicago as well as the requisites for its stewardship by Richard J. Daley from 1955 to 1976.

Chicago Politics, before Daley

Politics in Chicago from the late nineteenth century to the Great Depression is the exemplar of Raymond Wolfinger's distinction between machine politics and political machines. The former he identifies as

the manipulation of certain incentives to partisan political participation: favoritism based on political criteria in personnel decisions, contracting, and administration of the laws. . . . Now there is no necessary relation between incentives and centralization: machine politics (patronage incentives) need not produce centralized organization at the city level or higher.[4]

During this period both the Democratic and Republican parties were formidable electoral organizations, each winning the mayoralty with frequency and electing sizeable delegations to the city council. This is mainly attributable to the relative numerical balance of their voting coalitions. The Republicans drew support from Protestant natives of the United States, from older immigrant groups such as the Germans and Scandinavians, and increasingly toward the end of this period from blacks. Democratic support derived from newly arriving Central and Southern European immigrants and older Catholic immigrants such as the Irish.[5]

Nor were the Republicans and Democrats readily distinguishable with reference to ideology or their relative proclivity for "favoritism based on political criteria." The leading local Republican during the two decades preceding the Great Depression was three-time Mayor William Hale ("Big Bill") Thompson, whose cultivation of black political leaders and electorate was unusual for the day. Nonetheless, historian Allan H. Spear characterizes their alliance in this fashion:

The Negro community paid a price for political recognition. Its leaders allied themselves with the least progressive, most corrupt element in Chicago politics. Under Thompson, prostitution and gambling flourished openly on the South Side, and underworld figures enjoyed not only protection but political power in their own right. At the same time, housing conditions grew worse, alleys and streets accumulated filth, zoning and health regulations were ignored.[6]

In short, Thompson steered a particular voting faction into his coalition by awarding its leaders just the sort of patronage and other favors that were the currency of Chicago city politics. The business of politics was being carried on as usual. The Democrats for their part occasionally nodded in the direction of political propriety by nominating for office reformers such as William Dever, the latter even serving as mayor from 1923 to 1927. But far more impressive in the long run was the willingness of local party chieftains such as "Hinky Dink" Kenna and "Bathhouse John" Coughlin of the First Ward to coexist with and profit from the activities of organized crime. Thus, well in advance of the electorally indestructible Cook County Democratic machine was a pattern of politicking in Chicago that featured individual self-aggrandizement, coalition-building on a base of mobilized ethnic factions, and the use of government to reward friends and punish political foes.

The main architects of the modern Democratic machine were Anton J. Cermak and Herbert Hoover, the latter of course inadvertently. A Czech immigrant, West Side political power, and anti-Prohibitionist, Cermak during the 1920s took control of the Democratic organization and in 1931 defeated the Republican incumbent, Thompson, in the race for mayor. Cermak's victory was assisted by popular hostility to the Hoover administration, which in Chicago as in other parts of the country was blamed for the spreading ravages of the Great Depression. By the mid-1930s a substantial reorientation of the Chicago electorate had occurred. The result was that many traditionally Republican voters, most notably the city's rapidly growing black population, had shifted permanently into the Democratic column.[7]

The series of electoral setbacks experienced by the Republican party in the 1930s eliminated its access to government patronage, thereby eradicating the ranks of its activists.[8] Within the city the party never recovered from this body blow. However, since the Second World War and with the expansion of the metropolitan area, it has become a powerful force in some Cook County municipalities outside Chicago—and the dominant party in "collar" counties such as affluent DuPage, directly west of Cook County. Republicans typically hold the majority of suburban seats on Cook County's legislature, the Board of Commissioners.

In 1933 Anton Cermak was murdered by a would-be assassin of President-elect Roosevelt. Cook County Democratic party chairman Patrick Nash, a Cermak associate, tapped Edward Kelly as his successor. Kelly served as mayor until his ouster was engineered by another party chairman, Jacob Arvey, in 1946, and under the joint tutelage of Kelly and Nash the modern Democratic machine took shape. This occurred along two dimensions. First, the characteristic style of ward organizations was formalized during this period. For instance, the peculiar statutory measures that have tended to perpetuate the power of local ward bosses, technically known as committeepersons, were legislated.[9] More important —and following Cermak's lead—the Democratic organization learned that, by careful slating of candidates for city and countywide office, geographically and ethnically based party cadres could sustain control of city and county government even as they separately fostered the ambitions of individual politicians and oversaw the distribution of favors among family and friends. Second, a generation of leading local politicians came of age during the 1930s: later County Board president Dan Ryan, future party chairman Jake Arvey, mayoral advisor and city council leader Thomas Keane, and, not least, Richard Daley.

The structure of Democratic party ward organizations is a constant from this era to the present. Heading each of the city's 50 wards is a committeeperson, who is elected in a party primary every four years. The committeeperson appoints precinct captains, who are responsible for bringing in the vote in the ward's individual precincts. Precinct captains in turn may select assistant precinct captains to assist them in serving their constituents, this practice being especially common among captains serving an area whose ethnic composition is diverse or does not match their own.

With the exception of many assistant captains, who are just entering on the road to making a living from political activity, most of these ward officials parlay politics into an occupation. It is commonplace for Democratic committeepersons in Chicago also to hold public office, some as elected alderpersons on the city council, others as municipal administrators in departments such as Streets and Sanitation, and a few as legislators in Springfield or Washington, D.C. Longtime South Side boss William Dawson represented Illinois' First Congressional District. Northwest Side committeeman Dan Rostenkowski is chairperson of the House Ways and Means Committee. The occupational status of precinct captains is more modest, most holding fairly inconspicuous posts with the city or county governments or one of the local special jurisdictions such as the Chicago Park District.

For ward politicians disinclined to seek public office, there are a variety of other available professions. Many are attorneys and handle work for local governments. Those maintaining a predominantly private practice often find a surfeit of local clients attracted by their reputation for what is termed "clout" within city government. Other ward politicians trade in real estate or sell insurance, again seemingly advantaged by their proximity to political power in the city and county.

Although the structure and occupational proclivities of Democratic ward organizations have been extremely consistent for several decades, just what the local organizations do has always been more variable. Even at specific points in time, the variety of neighborhoods and constituencies ensures this. Formally speaking, the committeeperson manages local electoral activities and by law is responsible for nominating election judges to officiate at polling places on election day. As a member of the Cook County Democratic Committee, the committeeperson participates in the slating of candidates for office, as well as other party decisions. In general, protecting the local ward organization's interests is the committeeperson's touchstone in these deliberations.

Yet just how the local organization presents itself to its community and just what tactics it employs to mobilize its electoral constituency are not so amenable to generalization. In Harold F. Gosnell's classic study of the machine in the 1930s, he describes the activities of three precinct captains: "Grady," "Czech," and "Murphy." The first was in connivance with illegal gambling operations; the second sought direct aid for his mainly impoverished constituents; the third talked issues in his precinct. At any one time the combination of local constituent characteristics and the politicians' personal inclinations makes for a wide array of constituent mobilization-electoral strategies.[10] Again, to engage in risky generalization, although polling place fraud and the use of strong arm tactics are by no means absent (especially in the dilapidated black and Hispanic areas of the Near West and South Sides), contemporary ward organizations depend more on homeowner-oriented service delivery (dispersing garbage can lids, alley shoveling following winter blizzards, writing letters of recommendation for college-bound children, and so on) and put a more professional face on their operations than in the 1930s.[11]

A sketch of ward-level politics in Chicago would be incomplete without noting another consistent motif: the peculiarly narrow vision of these politicians. In 1984, at the close of a discussion with a Southwest Side alderperson the interviewer asked: "What do you see happening to Chicago in the next twenty years?" The reply: "I'm scared between now and '87. People are wondering about moving to the suburbs, what with busing, the utilities, and taxes. The mayor is talking about increasing city taxes. I don't know if I'll run in '87. The money doesn't look good right now, either."[12] A question regarding the future of the city was thus met with a statement concerning the immediate circumstances of the alderperson and his ward.

Sometimes this overriding concentration on things local seems to run counter to conventional notions of personal ambition, as one might infer from Alderman Roman Pucinski's decision in the mid-1970s to leave the House of Representatives and run for the city council. In general though, politics in Chicago is taken by both participants and observers to be a game in which the achievement of power and fortune is not merely a legitimate but virtually the sole end. Indeed, a remarkable irony of Richard Daley's regime was the popular perception of his personal integrity, which turned on the inference of his not having financially profited from the wielding of political power. This assessment seems to have been little undermined by the extremely circumscribed parameters of the mayor's commitment to propriety, which, judging from the record of indictments and criminal convictions racked up by his political confidants and allies, did not extend to include the behavior of those immediately surrounding him.[13]

To return our attention specifically to the machine of the 1930s and 1940s, it should be evident that the very term represents a mischaracterization. During this period the Democrats very effectively dominated local elections and turned out large majorities for candidates for statewide and national office, but as an occupational vehicle for individual politicians and a local service delivery device, this was a highly decentralized mechanism. Nor were Mayor Kelly or party chairman Nash personally inclined to enforce an undue amount of discipline on local ward chieftains. As a result, the siphoning off of municipal resources by way of direct city council action was considerable, and within the bureaucracy it is safe to say that the first loyalty of most patronage workers was to their ward boss.[14] Kelly was finally driven from power, in fact, when criticism of the school system's operations reached deafening levels in the mid-1940s. Similarly, the alliances between ward politicians and organized crime in the Loop and adjoining South Side and West Side wards also received much attention by the 1940s, again inviting criticism from newspapers and reform groups. Thus, the loose-reined leadership of Kelly and Nash (then Kelly alone, following Nash's death) encouraged the free-wheeling character of the early Democratic machine, but in turn generated such shenanigans that public disaffection, newspaper harassment, and party insider misgivings finally brought down the curtain on this phase of Democratic party domination in Chicago. In 1946, apparently led by party chairman Jake Arvey, the Democrats refused to reslate Ed Kelly for mayor. Another eight years passed before Richard Daley's seizure of the mayoralty, but from this point the countdown began.

Life with Daley

In 1947 the Democrats turned to Martin Kennelly as their mayoral candidate. Kennelly was a businessperson and civic leader who had not previously been active in the Democratic party. Nonetheless, he won the 1947 and 1951 mayoral elections, and during his two terms in office oversaw a mildly reformist administration.[15]

Although support for him was by no means unanimous, Richard J. Daley was elected Democratic party chairperson in 1953. A year and a half later the central committee snubbed Kennelly and slated Daley as its 1955 mayoral candidate. In a three-way Democratic primary, Daley handily defeated Kennelly and Benjamin Adamowski but with only a plurality of the vote. In the general election Daley defeated South Side liberal Robert Merriam, the Republican candidate—but previously a Democratic alderperson—by 127,000 votes.[16]

With the advantage of hindsight, one can observe that this election marked the transition from the old to the new Democratic machine. At the time, few in Chicago would have supposed so. Daley, who celebrated his fifty-third birthday after moving into the fifth floor of City Hall, had not rocketed to the mayoralty. In his past was a career of loyal service to the Democratic organization, marked usually but not exclusively with personal successes. As a state legislator in the late 1930s and 1940s, Daley had been Mayor Kelly's mouthpiece in Springfield, introducing legislation and directing the Chicago delegation. In the late 1940s he became the committeeperson of his 11th Ward. During the same years Daley participated in another Illinois political tradition—double-dipping—by holding an appointive post in the Cook County Comptroller's Office in addition to his legislative seat. Later Daley served as state revenue director under Governor Adlai Stevenson and then as Cook County clerk. It was probably while holding these latter, fiscally related, positions that Daley developed his acumen for controlling expenditures as a political tool. In short, Chicago's ward bosses had promoted to first among them a colleague whose loyalty was unquestioned, whose ambitions seemed controllable, and whose public record had been unsullied during the decline of the Kelly regime.[17]

In the following years they learned that their new mayor was much more than this, but it is also clear that Daley's maintenance of congenial ties with the bulk of the city's Democratic ward organizations formed one important buttress for the new machine. Unlike his predecessors Cermak and Kelly—the former widely identified as an advocate of liquor interests, the latter touched by personal improprieties even before becoming mayor — Richard Daley, until the late 1960s, scrupulously avoided identification with political controversy and maintained an inconspicuous lifestyle. By assuming far greater oversight of the budget-making process than his predecessors, and by devoting unending attention to the mundanities of personnel appointments, Daley certainly narrowed the field available for some sorts of political graft. However, he did not direct police power into the spheres of influence of local organizations, nor by his own choice of associates or powers of persuasion attempt to steer party insiders in new directions. Moreover, as his personal popularity mushroomed, his heading the local party ticket provided long coattails for many unimpressive candidates for city council and other elective offices. In this fashion Daley achieved a tremendous degree of loyalty among ward-level politicians throughout the city.

During most of Daley's tenure as mayor and party boss, the mechanics of electioneering in Chicago were highly labor intensive. Through most of the 1960s the techniques of media candidacies had yet to be worked out, and by that time in this particular city no opponent of Daley could raise sufficient cash to vie with the mayor through the airwaves. Daley, on the other hand, as chief executive of a municipality with above 40,000 employees — and one who authorized the filling of even the most trivial positions — had at his disposal a huge army of patronage workers.[18] Most of these were not just willing to work precincts but had been favored in the first place due to skills of this sort. Moreover, it was widely recognized that patronage jobs in city government had to be approved by the mayor. Though an individual might be a resident of Rogers Park on the North Side, and sponsored by the 49th Ward committeeperson, that same individual viewed Daley as his/her ultimate benefactor. In this sense as well, Daley centralized party allegiance without coming into direct confrontation with ward bosses.

The Daley administration was also most forthcoming with organized labor, especially by its practice of paying workers on city-contracted projects at private scale. Union organization was not encouraged among municipal employees such as the police; however, in compensation, Daley's wage offers were among the most generous by big city mayors.[19] Thus, Daley provided employment to a large cadre of party workers and cultivated the voting loyalty of a far larger number of city workers and unionists mainly dependent on city-initiated projects.

From a political standpoint, Daley's most impressive achievement was his courtship of Chicago's business elite. Culturally, Daley's youth in what was then one of the more impoverished Irish neighborhoods in Chicago did not prepare him for this task. Nor were Chicago business leaders especially well disposed to the Democrats at this time—in part as a result of the misadventures of the Kelly administration, in part due to the party's unceremonious disposal of Martin Kennelly, who had been drawn from the business ranks. Nonetheless, by Daley's second term in office he appears to have overcome both barriers. Biographer Len O'Connor suggests that Daley's decorous behavior during his frequent social forays to business-persons' clubs broke the interpersonal ice.[20] More significantly, Daley pursued several courses of action favorable to the business community.

Paramount among these initiatives, and coincidental with Daley's arrival on the scene, was the city's decision to move forward with urban renewal and its sponsorship of several additional massive public works projects. These included the construction of the city's expressway network, the expansion of the mass transit system, and the development of O'Hare International Airport.[21] As we shall detail in Chapter 6, this physical reordering of Chicago was carried out in close consultation with leading business groups. Moreover, it signified the municipal government's acceptance of and contribution to the growth ideology that dictated post-World War II urban redevelopment in Chicago and cities nationwide.

In addition, Daley regularly consulted with business leaders on more routine planning matters, municipal finance, and related topics. He also made a point of sprinkling his nominations for the school board and other municipal commissions with business and civic notables as well as politicos.[22] Finally, Daley was willing to bring in administrative managers of national reputation to head up city departments. For instance, one of his most savvy political moves was to mop up an early 1960s police scandal by hiring a respected academic criminologist, Orlando Wilson, to serve as superintendent of police.[23] Ironically, atop city agencies whose staffs were mainly filled by patronage workers were administrators whose professional credentials most impressed the local business elite.

The Daley machine, although an extension of the Democratic organization built by Cermak and unbridled by Edward Kelly, was a new model. A cadre of relatively autonomous party chieftains remained. Indeed, the likes of Thomas Keane on the West Side and Paddy Bauler on the near North Side remained in power through most of Daley's tenure. And in the city's rough neighborhoods on the near West and South Sides, the style of politics remained much the same as a generation earlier. However, by centralizing patronage as had never been done before, Daley brought the electoral organization much more under his command than had his predecessors. Further, by building new ties with the business community and by professionalizing the upper echelons of city administration, Daley managed to limit editorial page criticism of his mayoralty and, maybe more importantly, close off the financial spigots essential for mounting serious opposition political campaigns in the city.

The Metropolitan Context of Politics in Chicago

Until the Second World War, metropolitan politics was effectively Chicago politics. Eighty percent of Cook County's population resided within the city of Chicago, and the surrounding "collar" counties of the contemporary metropolitan region were considerably less populous than Cook County outside Chicago. In the succeeding four decades the city of Chicago's population increased to 3.6 million and then declined to its present figure of 3 million. There are now 2 million residents in suburban Cook County and another 2 million in the Illinois collar counties of Lake, McHenry, DuPage, Kane, and Will. In addition to Chicago and the surrounding six counties, this metropolitan population of 7 million is served by 260 municipalities, 315 school districts, and 519 special districts stretching over 50 miles north, west, and south of Chicago's Loop.[24]

The governmental apparatus seeking to manage this region is much expanded from 40 years ago, yet the fundamental ingredient of postwar metropolitan politics has been the Chicago Democrats' intention to ride out regional population and economic shifts in order to hold control of city government. In the mid-1970s political scientist and local Democratic insider Milton Rakove characterized the party's attitude toward the suburbs in this fashion:

> In the past, the interests of the suburban population in the Democratic machine's internal dynamics were of little relevance to the machine's programs and planning. The machine's leaders went about the business of choosing candidates, electing them to office, and distributing the rewards and perquisites of office, with little regard for the interests of the people of the suburbs, either Democrats or Republicans.[25]

For much of the postwar period the Chicago Democrats could avoid consulting suburban interests by dominating several governmental units whose activities extend beyond the corporate limits of the city. The Cook

County Board of Commissioners oversees law enforcement in the unincorporated portions of the county, appropriates funds for the Cook County jail and County Hospital, and approves property tax assessments. Its members are elected at large. Chicago Democrats have used party discipline and the city's population advantage to hold the board's majority. Chicago and its suburbs also rely on several special districts, such as the Metropolitan Sanitary District and the Regional Transportation Authority (RTA), to coordinate particular government services. Although the governing boards of these units have not been so thoroughly dominated by the city, they have frequently selected executive staff with experience in Chicago government. Charles Orlebeke of the University of Illinois-Chicago, in a review of the activities of these special purpose governments, observes: "Chicago-area governments have not been under any sort of monolithic control, even under Daley, but an intricate network of personal and political relationships does crisscross the nominal legal boundaries of these governments."[26] In short, one reaction of the Chicago Democrats to metropolitan suburbanization has been to extend their influence to the governmental jurisdictions that serve the population outside the city.

Chicago Democrats have also sought to circumscribe the power of suburban politicians—and without much regard for party affiliation. Although suburban Cook County now accounts for a sizeable share of the Democratic vote in countywide elections (that is, for state's attorney, county sheriff, county assessor, and so on), the party's endorsement is normally reserved for a city resident. After the 1980 census, Chicago Democrat Michael Madigan oversaw the Illinois House of Representatives' redistricting plan. Madigan himself acknowledged that several angular districts reaching out from the city to include smaller suburban constituencies were designed to reduce Republican representation of Chicago's suburbs.[27]

In the two decades immediately following World War II the character of suburban politics seemed to invert politics Chicago-style. Many of the suburban communities elect officials via a non-partisan ballot, and most of the larger suburban towns employ a city manager to oversee their day-to-day operations. During this period reform-style suburban government also seemed to be associated with quiet, non-confrontational politics. The Republican party was a much stronger force in suburban politics as well, both in municipal government and in state legislative and congressional races.

City-suburban relations were uneasy, and in spite of occasional calls for increased intermunicipal cooperation or even metropolitan government, only limited metropolitan cooperation developed.[28] Chicago Democrats were able to exercise a considerable voice in suburban affairs through the Cook County Board. Moreover, their ability to hold most of the elected countywide offices offered a growing supply of patronage jobs and government contracts. Suburban politicians, Democrats and Republicans alike, resented the high-handedness of the Chicago Democrats. Suburban Republicans in the state legislature frequently vented their hostility by endorsing or rejecting legislation based on their perception of what would cause Chicago the most discomfort.[29] The suburban towns, if at all possible, simply avoided dealing with Chicago. This environment was not conducive to the effective development of crosscutting metropolitan units such as the Cook County Council of Governments and the Northeastern Illinois Planning Commission (NIPC). Given their access to Cook County government, Chicago Democrats had little reason to participate in the Council of Governments or support NIPC's initiatives. Conversely, the suburbanites feared that if these units assumed real power they would soon enough fall under the sway of the city.

Since the 1960s the tenor of suburban politics and city-suburban relations has undergone substantial change. Outside the city of Chicago, reform-style government no longer seems to guarantee placid politics. The economic accessibility of many suburbs to relocating Chicagoans of moderate means has greatly increased the suburban Democratic vote. Moreover, suburban politics frequently assumes an ideological, confrontational tone that was largely absent a generation ago. Interestingly, neither the ideological right nor left wing seems predominant. On the one hand, west suburban congressman Henry Hyde became a nationally known anti-abortion spokesperson, and in the late 1970s the "tax revolt" mustered considerable support in several suburban towns.[30] Yet at the other end of the spectrum, Oak Park, which adjoins Chicago's West Side, implemented a policy of managed residential integration.[31] In 1981, northwest suburban Morton Grove was but the first of several suburban communities to pass an ordinance restricting the possession of handguns.[32]

Chicago-suburban relations have also passed beyond the point where the city can consider its neighbors superfluous and its neighbors can remain aloof from the squalor of city affairs. Mass transit has been a headache for Chicagoans and suburbanites alike since the early 1970s. Several northern and northwestern suburbs purchase their water supplies from Chicago, and the city's pricing of this essential resource has often been disputed by these clients. The city's expansion of O'Hare Airport on its far northwestern corner has been opposed by several nearby towns, whose residents complain of the airport's noisy air traffic.[33] The metropolitan area's aging infrastructure, in contrast, is an emerging issue that unites Chicago and many suburbs, especially the older towns such as Evanston, Oak Park, and Cicero that directly adjoin it.[34]

Given the intermunicipal hostilities that divide Chicago and its suburbs, the main avenue for metropolitan cooperation has run from Chicago to Springfield, specifically from the mayor's office through the governor's mansion. Mayor Daley for the most part maintained good relations with Illinois governors and, with Republican Governor Richard Ogilvie, resolved the early 1970s transit crisis by the creation of the RTA.[35] A few years later Mayor Byrne and Republican Governor James Thompson agreed to reallocate to mass transit funds initially designated for highway construction and to restructure the RTA's financing.[36] More recently, Mayor Washington worked with Thompson to reorganize the RTA's governance and achieve state legislative enactment of infrastructure appropriations beneficial to Chicago and its suburbs.[37] Yet, as the repeated tinkering with the RTA demonstrates, the ability of Chicago's mayors to negotiate settlements with governors resulting in state legislation amenable to the suburbs does not prevent stresses at the point of implementation. Chicago and its suburbs do not trust one another, and thus far the mounting circumstances that require metropolitan cooperation have not resulted in either formal or informal mechanisms that routinely deal with metropolitan and intermunicipal problems.

Three Counterforces

Richard Daley's revival of the Democratic organization, whether grounded in intuition or in a rational calculation of shifting political forces, successfully extended its life as a vote-getting apparatus. Given the widespread esteem for his personal leadership, it was possible for a time to suppose the Daley machine held a hammerlock on the local body politic. In fact, even as Daley reshaped the machine, three factors were working at crosspurposes with its continued political hegemony. Each was rooted in factors transcending the local social and political system, although the role they have played in altering politics in Chicago has been much affected by local circumstances. These factors were the emergence of block and neighborhood organizations as a political force, the growing electoral success of "Independent" politicians, and disaffection of blacks from the Democratic machine.

Neighborhood Organizations

The formation of neighborhood groups is a long-standing practice in Chicago, reaching back at least to the settlement house movement at the turn of the century. In succeeding decades, Saul Alinsky's approach to the militant mobilization of city neighborhoods was in part forged in Chicago, notably by the Back of the Yards Neighborhood Council (BYNC) in the 1930s and The Woodlawn Organization (TWO) a generation later.[38] By the 1950s, however, the most numerically significant variety of neighborhood group was the indigenous block, neighborhood, homeowners, taxpayers, or civic organization.

The latter also represent the most ambiguous political institution in Chicago. As in most parts of the country, the postwar erection of single-family home tract developments and the accompanying rise in homeownership were pervasive spurs to the appearance of neighborhood groups. As such, these groups mainly shunned partisan politics while giving attention to the quality of public services, the promotion of self-help activities, and simple boosterism. In Chicago, however, many of these organizations have had a more explicit agenda: the preservation of neighborhoods in the face of rapid racial turnover. Sometimes, as in the case of the Hyde Park-Kenwood Community Conference, the mainly white membership sought to slow the flight of white residents and create a stable, integrated community. Public discussion of redevelopment initiatives, monitoring of landlord maintenance practices, and resident placement services were among its activities. In contrast, organizations in working-class and lower middle-class neighborhoods often resorted to harassment and outright violence in order to prevent blacks from renting apartments or purchasing homes.[39] Of course, the potency of the dual issue of race and residency is not limited to city neighborhoods, as evidenced by the varying responses of Chicago suburbs, many populated in large part by former Chicagoans, to the prospect of racial transition.

The relationship between the more virulently racist neighborhood organizations and party politicians has been quite complex. During the 1950s mainly white neighborhoods on the far South and Southwest Sides (as well as the Northwest Side, which, however, was not in the line of racial transition) were not reliably Democratic. For example, they turned out heavily in support of liberal Robert Merriam, the Republican candidate in the 1955 general election for mayor. Yet white Democratic committeepersons and alderpersons must have recognized that racial transition would end their careers. Blacks moving beyond the near South Side tended to be

Democrats, but the Dawson organization—although subservient to the regular party structure—was a thoroughly black organization. This continued to be the case as its geographical reach increased.

Thus, the substantive interest of neighborhood groups and ward organizations was the same, but the outspokenness of the former was uncharacteristic of machine politicians. In the short run, more visibly racist local policies took shape in the early Daley years, notably the concentration of public housing on the near South and West Sides by way of the aldermanic veto privilege over Chicago Housing Authority siting.[40] More subtly, the rhetoric of neighborhood stability and maintenance of the racial status quo entered the lexicon of South Side Democratic politicians.

Neighborhood organizations in Chicago, however, have sprung up all over the city and with highly variable agendas. In black neighborhoods they have often focused on shortcomings in city service delivery, and since the 1960s have themselves engaged in the provision of family services, local housing construction and rehabilitation, the management of community centers, and other related activities. However, such groups have not been immune to penetration by representatives of the Democratic party. This circumstance is described by one political organizer from the West Side (where for years white ward bosses continued to dominate increasingly black and Hispanic wards): "A lot of block club leaders are coopted. Some organizations are actually initiated by the machine. As we started getting to the ones already in existence, the machine got involved too. Assistant precinct captains . . . out of civic duty . . . will organize them and they're controlled."[41]

Nor are the hazards of organizational atrophy and attachment to the status quo unique to orthodox neighborhood groups. For instance, the Alinsky-organized Back of the Yards Neighborhood Council has become sufficiently static in its agenda to have elicited the creation of a new local group, the United Neighborhood Organization (UNO), whose members claim that the BYNC is resistant to Hispanic participation in its affairs.[42]

Thus far, the primary successes of the new wave of neighborhood coalitions have been oppositionist in nature, successfully blocking initiatives of downtown business interests, particular firms, or city hall. Furthermore, they have often had to ally themselves with less progressive individuals and groups in order to achieve their ends. In 1981, community organizations allied with dissident Democratic politicians and downtown hotel owners to block a Byrne administration plan to provide Hilton Hotels with an estimated $70 million investment subsidy.[43] Nor are these groups' militant rhetoric and confrontational tactics thoroughly assimilated by the prevailing Chicago political culture. The Southwest Side alderperson quoted earlier had this to say about the Southwest Parish and Neighborhood Federation: "I don't like them. They've been involved in a couple of precincts at the south end of the ward. . . . They just get involved in the same things politicians do . . . who are elected by the people. I think they're mainly liberals from Hyde Park."[44] In spite of this characterization, the number and vigor of such organizations suggest that for many Chicagoans they have become an important way to participate in public affairs and influence local public policy. Furthermore, their explicit interest in government programs and their participatory ideology represent a sharp break with the long-standing style of politics in Chicago.

Independent Politicians

As was the case in other cities in the late 1940s, the 1950s, and the early 1960s, Chicago witnessed the emergence of "amateur Democrats" as a significant local political force. Also in common with cities such as New York and Los Angeles, these reformers in the main were young professional persons, who, galvanized by the national candidacies of Adlai Stevenson and John Kennedy, were also disaffected from the personalities and operations of their local Democratic organizations.[45]

In Chicago, the presence of the Daley machine was central to both the successes and failures of this movement. On the one hand, the dominance of city government by a handful of political insiders in tandem with recurrent political scandals has provided local reform Democrats—or, as they typically call themselves, Independents—with whole magazines of ammunition for their campaigns. This has been especially useful in that the structuralist agenda typical of amateur Democrats—expansion of civil service, tighter election procedures and policing, and open government in general—could be convincingly posed as an antidote to both the practices and the perceived policy failings of the machine. On the other hand, the electoral sinews of the regular Democrats kept Independents out of government far longer than in other cities. With the exception of the South Side Fifth Ward, which includes the University of Chicago community, Independents made no electoral headway at all until the late 1960s.

Although Independent politics in Chicago has been chiefly identified with the crusades of individual reformers—initially Fifth Ward alderpersons such as Robert Merriam and Leon Despres, more recently North Siders William Singer, Dick Simpson, Martin Oberman, and David Orr—a succession of reformist organizations has struggled against the machine.

Initially there were the Independent Voters of Illinois (IVI). and the Democratic Federation of Illinois (DFI).[46] In 1968 the Independent Precinct Organization (IPO) appeared, which has since merged with the IVI.[47] The consolidated IVI-IPO endorses candidates, raises funds via a dues-paying membership, and actively electioneers in some parts of the city. However, none of these groups has been active throughout the city, and unable to raise large campaign war chests, they have never blitzed the media in behalf of their endorsed candidates. Finally, dependent as they are on volunteers to canvass precincts and patrol polling places, their electoral impact has varied dramatically from campaign to campaign. With attractive candidates and hot issues, the contemporary IVI-IPO's effect in some portions of the city may be formidable; when these conditions are not present, the IVI-IPO wanes as well. If anything, the most consistent electoral function the organization now performs is by way of its endorsement, which, when two or more non-machine candidates vie to oppose an organization designate, often throws the bulk of campaign volunteers and contributions behind a single individual.

In the 1970s, in conjunction with the collapse of the Republican party as an electoral force in Chicago, Independents became *the* political opposition in the city. Two or three usually managed to attain city council seats, and a handful found places in the state legislative delegation from Chicago. Hopelessly outnumbered on the city council (which until the Washington administration was wholly subservient to the executive branch, its committees seldom meeting, its budget review a rubber-stamping process), Independents took solace in at least throwing some light on the iniquities of their colleagues. Often this has meant futile oppositionism. For example, in his two four-year terms as an opposition alderperson, Independent Martin Oberman never voted in support of a municipal budget ordinance. Independents often ruefully noted that legislative initiatives that were their brainchildren but had become lost somewhere in committee, when examined and dusted off by the machine, would then sail through the council under the sponsorship of regular alderpersons.

In the mid-1970s 44th Ward Independent alderman Dick Simpson sought to short-circuit these constraints in an intriguing fashion. While campaigning for office he pledged to, if elected, create a Ward Assembly. This assembly, partially filled by individuals elected to represent blocks in the ward, the remainder of its members neighborhood organization delegates, met regularly and advised Simpson on locally relevant issues and its reaction to city council business. Indeed, when an extraordinary majority of the assembly voted in support of or opposition to a particular measure,

Simpson in the council voted in consonance with the majority's wish. Later, Simpson and the Ward Assembly established a Community Zoning Board to review zoning variance requests by developers. Although the statutory responsibility for such decisions rests with a city council committee, this ad hoc mechanism, by its informal, preliminary hearing process, seems to have exercised some influence on the committee's deliberations.[48]

It was Simpson's intention to leave in place the 44th Ward Assembly and Community Zoning Board once he vacated office. However, following his retirement from the council in 1979, both atrophied. Nonetheless, his initiatives as well as those of other Independents left a legacy. In the 1979 aldermanic elections a West Side black Independent candidate, Danny Davis, ran a campaign in the 29th Ward in which he promised, among other things, a Ward Assembly. Davis, who defeated his machine-affiliated opponent in that contest, was not the first anti-machine alderperson elected from a black ward. However, by successfully grafting to his campaign Independent-style programs in the last part of Chicago where white politicians still dominated black constituencies, Davis' victory was a significant indicator of the growing reach of this form of anti-machine sentiment. Furthermore, by explicitly recognizing the concerns of neighborhood organizations and their members, Simpson (again, along with some of his Independent colleagues) was beginning to forge an important new form of anti-machine alliance.

Disaffection of Blacks

The most deceptive truism of Chicago politics is that the bulwark of the Democratic organization is the white ethnic enclaves of the city's Northwest, Southwest, and far South Sides. At present, if one goes searching for paeans to the administration of Richard J. Daley, these are the places to visit. Nevertheless, such was not always the case and even in recent years voters from the Northwest Side, for example, have more than once bolted from the machine camp.

In Richard Daley's first mayoral campaign, 11 wards extending from the near South Side through the Loop and across the West Side—all of them predominantly black or then undergoing substantial racial turnover —provided him with a plurality over Robert Merriam that almost precisely corresponded to his citywide margin of victory. Indeed, if one adds to these wards Daley's home 11th Ward, in the remainder of the city Merriam carried a slight majority.[49] Up until the mid-1960s, the loyalty of the city's growing black population to the Daley machine was central to the latter's success. From that time onward the diminished allegiance of Chicago blacks to the machine, in conjunction with their expanding portion of the electorate, foreshadowed problems for the regular Democrats.

However, before examining the sources and implications of this shift in loyalties, we will look at the later Daley years and the political wake of "Hizzoner." Shifts in the black electorate's commitments will then be examined in some detail by way of interpreting the success of the Harold Washington insurgency.

The Later, Lesser Daley Machine

After a fairly tight run for re-election in 1963, Richard J. Daley piled up huge majorities in his three remaining mayoral campaigns, and to judge from this evidence alone, one would suppose that his organization was in fine condition. Even the three trends discussed in the preceding section were sufficiently distanced from the mainstream of local electoral considerations to generate little attention until the last half-decade of Daley's rule. Thereafter, their impacts snowballed. Yet it is commonly asserted that the machine unraveled only after Daley's passing in late 1976. In fact, there were clear signs of its diminished capacity even while he was still on the scene.

Significant indications of the Daley machine's declining vote-getting power can be inferred from Daley's last mayoral campaign in 1975, particularly the Democratic primary. Uncharacteristically, Daley had three challengers: William Singer, the first Independent to win a North Side aldermanic election; Robert Newhouse, a black state legislator and machine defector; and Edward Hanrahan, the Cook County state's attorney whose agents in 1969 had carried out the infamous shootings of Black Panthers Fred Hampton and Mark Clark. Daley was the clear victor, carrying a majority of the turnout, but the geographic distribution of his support is revealing. Along the North Side lakefront wards where Independents were beginning to make inroads, Daley just barely outpolled Singer. Even more remarkably, in the 11 central wards that had provided Daley his entire margin of victory over Robert Merriam in 1955, Daley's vote exceeded the Singer and Newhouse total by only 16,000. In general, Daley's command of the city's black wards had been lost, not just to opponents but also to apathy. Political scientist Paul Kleppner notes, in a detailed examination of this campaign: "In Daley's last primary battle, only 16.5% of the voting age population in the fifteen black wards supported him."[50]

In Daley's later years, maintaining organization discipline also became more arduous. At the beginning of his last full term, from 1971 to 1975, a group of young, white, regular Democrats demanded and won concessions from city council floor leader Thomas Keane, their main objective being more say-so in council affairs.[51] In 1972, Daley refused to support Edward Hanrahan's reslating as state's attorney, but Hanrahan entered the Democratic primary anyway and defeated the organization's designate.[52] Shortly thereafter, South Side congressman Ralph Metcalfe bolted from the organization and subsequently withstood an organization-sponsored challenge to his re-election.[53]

In the early 1970s the Daley machine was vulnerable to attack from beyond the boundaries of its immediate influence, those boundaries themselves seeming to shrink. After 1972, Bernard Carey, a Republican who had received considerable support from Chicago blacks and white Independents, held the Cook County state's attorney post. Carey's election demonstrated that, without sufficient discipline among Chicago Democrats, countywide election victories were well within the reach of the Republican party. Another Republican, U.S. attorney and later governor James Thompson, built his reputation during this period by successfully prosecuting corruption charges against machine insiders.

Finally, this same period in Daley's governance revealed chinks in his central programmatic claim as mayor, that his was "The City That Works." A series of teachers strikes periodically closed the Chicago schools from the late 1960s until 1971, with Daley initially intervening as a bankroller of the school board's salary concessions. The uncharacteristic boldness of the teachers' actions was in keeping with national developments at that time, and Daley—as friend of labor—took a fairly congenial stance toward the teachers' union. However, his final intercession in 1971 was to offer a salary package that the school board had to finance and that in fact put it in serious financial straits.[54] In 1974, Daley sought state legislation to slide the Chicago Transit Authority under the aegis of the Regional Transit Authority, a move that not only acknowledged the fiscal failure of the former but also ceded important institutional resources to a governing board drawn from throughout the metropolitan area, representing constituencies in many cases quite hostile to the city's transit needs, and not much subject to the mayor's influence.[55]

Richard J. Daley died in December 1976, immediately setting in motion a sequence of backroom conferences among party leaders and producing days of uncertainty regarding the city's future.[56] At the time of Daley's passing, Wilson Frost, a South Side black and eminently regular Democratic alderperson was serving as president pro tempore of the city council. The municipal charter seemed to indicate that he succeed Daley as acting mayor. The white inner circle of the Democratic party would have none of this, of course, and it maneuvered to have Michael Bilandic, alderperson from Daley's 11th Ward, installed as acting mayor. Bilandic also announced that he would not enter the mandated special election to elect a successor for the remainder of Daley's four-year term of office. Wilson Frost was named chairman of the City Council Finance Committee, a post that could be used to considerable political effect.

Not surprisingly, Bilandic found himself drafted to enter the Democratic primary preceding the special election for mayor. He had two opponents, Northwest Side regular alderman Roman Pucinski and South Side black state legislator Harold Washington. With most of the Democratic organization well in hand, Bilandic overpowered his opponents and then triumphed in the general election. Nonetheless, this primary sustained the trend of formerly loyal black politicians' breaking with the organization to challenge it. Just as significantly, Pucinski's support on the Northwest Side was indicative of factionalism among even the white regular ward organizations. The domination of the party by the Daley faction of South and Southwest Side politicians was so long-standing that resentment of the management of the succession was probably unavoidable. When pushed forward to succeed Daley, Michael Bilandic was insufficiently powerful in his own right to generate much overt opposition. Yet, by the same token, ward leaders cut off from real organizational power certainly viewed Bilandic as a captive of the 11th Ward circle. As a leading figure among the large Chicago Polish community, Pucinski sought to capitalize on the sentiment of this group that their loyalty to the organization had not been satisfactorily rewarded. Unfortunately for Pucinski, he was unable to extend this appeal beyond his geographic base; even South Side Polish precincts tended to remain in the column of party-designate Bilandic.[57]

Between 1977 and 1983 the deficiencies of the Democratic machine were increasingly visible, notably by virtue of Jane Byrne's upset of Michael Bilandic in the 1979 Democratic mayoral primary and the increasing number of Independents winning aldermanic elections. By considering what was happening to the ward organizations during this period we can find some of the roots of the party's decreasing effectiveness as an electoral device. The centralization of patronage that Richard J. Daley had accomplished by sheer willpower and by joining the power of mayor and party chairman was lost. Both Bilandic and Byrne controlled the flow of city jobs, but they also had to cooperate with a separate party chairperson, first

George Dunne and later Edward Vrdolyak, and undoubtedly gave up some patronage control in doing so. Further, heads of autonomous jurisdictions such as Dunne, president of the Cook County Board of Commissioners, and Edmund Kelly, commissioner of the Chicago Park District, had more leeway to use as they saw fit the political resources at their disposal.

Secular trends have tended to diminish the value of patronage as well. As an increasing portion of the city population has assumed middle-class occupational aspirations, even if they are not yet in the middle class, the attractiveness of jobs in patronage-rich departments such as Streets and Sanitation is reduced. Furthermore, judicial decisions in the wake of the famous Shakman decree of 1970, which by and large have limited the injection of political considerations into the hiring, disciplining, and firing of public employees, have diminished the control that politically connected administrators or ward committeepersons can exercise over government workers. In particular, once an individual is in a local government post in the Chicago area, removal is now rather difficult, even if this individual was politically sponsored in the first place. Practically speaking, there have been two consequences of these developments: first, jobs available to patronage appointees have diminished, and, second, once appointed, patronage workers are not so controllable by their sponsoring ward organizations.[58]

In an illuminating case study of machine politics in a ward that is not headed by one of the party kingpins such as Richard M. Daley, Edward Vrdolyak, or Edmund Kelly, Thomas Guterbock terms the electoral strategy of the local organization "defended venality":

> The need to preserve a legitimate image increases the complexity of the ward club's internal structure for two reasons. First, it is essential to the party's effectiveness that its members portray the party to outsiders in positive terms — as an organization seeking community goods through democratic means. . . . Second, the members themselves are recruited from an environment which is opposed to the use of material incentives in politics. . . . To the extent that the members share the value that venality in politics is wrong and have low personal stakes in the club's success, it is not possible for the party to secure their genuine commitment through the use of patronage alone.[59]

In effect, local constituents would not necessarily follow the lead of a party that only sought support by patronage, personal favors, and the like. Moreover, party activists themselves are not so motivated; thus in Guterbock's ward the organization espoused neighborhood preservation while marginally sweetening the lives of party loyalists by employing traditional machine-style incentives.

In the Chicago of the late 1970s and 1980s this sort of machine presence is commonplace. Aided by a totally inept Republican opposition, the Democratic organization sustains itself via consistent electoral success. However, it is also evident that in portions of the city where the machine, per se, generates considerable antagonism, this sort of party style and tactical approach does not guarantee much success. Since the late 1960s Independents in the belt of affluent wards running north from the Loop along the lakefront, and as well in the anomalous South Side Fifth Ward, have converted popular antipathy for any style of machine politics into electoral successes. An analogous trend that also dates from the 1960s, but ballooned in the late 1970s, has been the electoral support garnered by opponents of the machine on the black West and South Sides.

The Harold Washington Insurgency

The roots of Harold Washington's mayoral triumph in the spring of 1983 can be traced back in time at least a generation. In *Negro Politics*, a study of South Side black politics in the late 1950s, political scientist James Q. Wilson already identified a wide chasm separating regular Democratic politicians from civic and civil rights leaders.[60] In the years that followed, as national civil rights activism expanded, it is none too surprising that black disaffection from Congressman Dawson, whose consistent practice was to subordinate civil rights concerns to considerations of party realpolitik, would emerge. Then from 1966 through 1969 a succession of events virtually ensured the permanent alienation of large parts of Chicago's black electorate from the machine. First, in 1966 Martin Luther King Jr. chose Chicago as his site for turning the focus of the civil rights movement to issues such as open housing that were especially pertinent to blacks in Northern metropolitan areas. The reaction to King-led marches in white Chicago neighborhoods, as well as suburban Cicero, was violent, and Mayor Daley's dealings with Reverend King were hardly cordial.[61] Following King's assassination in the spring of 1968, rioting, burning, and looting broke out on Chicago's West Side. Daley's generally unimplemented "shoot to kill" order to the police was nevertheless widely publicized, and the subsequent expressions of loathing from local black leaders were a further indication of less visible popular shifts in party loyalty.[62] At the end of 1969 the Democratic state's attorney's officers, in highly suspicious circumstances, shot and killed Black Panthers Hampton and Clark. If this were not enough to enrage Chicago blacks, two years later Edward Hanrahan, who had authorized the Hampton-Clark raid, overcame rejection by the Democratic party slating committee and won renomination in the party primary.[63]

Despite this storm of events, and even with the growing proclivity of machine-bred black politicians such as Ralph Metcalfe to exit the organization, until the very late 1970s machine insiders seem not to have seriously countenanced mass renunciation by the black electorate. One reason may have been a perceptible sense of apathy that marked many black voters' initial disaffection from the machine. Thus, in the early and mid-1970s the proportion of voting blacks supporting Democratic candidates held up; however, the proportion of eligible blacks registering to vote and, in particular elections, the proportion of the registered voters actually attending the polls both declined. Further, had the regular Democrats sifted through the electoral data for the 1970s, political scientist Michael Preston notes, they would have discovered a most ominous development. Black middle-class voters, while supporting national Democratic candidates such as Jimmy Carter in 1976, were significantly less inclined to cast votes for or against local Democrats. Writing after the 1979 mayoral election, Preston concluded:

> The data indicate that increasing numbers of qualified black voters are avoiding the system in mayoral elections. Considering the difference in Democratic support at the polls in national and local elections, the increased or steady machine support in local general elections, and the decreased black turnout, it would seem that many of the black voters who are staying away from the polls are potential anti-machine votes.[64]

In fact, evidence to support this contention had already been provided in the 1979 mayoral primary. Michael Bilandic, seeking re-election, had been challenged by Jane Byrne, a Daley protegé and former city commissioner of consumer affairs. Until the very close of what had been a pleasingly uneventful administration, Bilandic was considered a shoo-in. However, when two huge snowstorms struck the city in January 1979, the response of city agencies was slow and quite erratic. At one point, the Chicago Transit Authority sought to maintain schedules on the Dan Ryan "el" line by skipping stations on the black near South Side, thus expediting the ride home for white commuters to peripheral neighborhoods. Though Byrne's anti-machine credentials were always suspect, on primary day in February, she carried 15 of 19 black majority wards. The plurality provided Byrne in these wards more than doubled her citywide margin of 16,000.[65]

Jane Byrne worked a sufficient rapprochement with Democratic regulars between the primary and the general election to overwhelm her Republican opponent. Then, in the next three and a half years she carved a record marked by extreme fluctuations of policy and personal style. This was commonly attributed to her temperament, but it is just as reasonable to contend that she was striving to build an autonomous administration and enlist a personal political constituency, when in fact neither was available. As a candidate in the Democratic primary she posed as a political opponent of the machine, yet when it came time to fill administrative positions in her government, she had two groups to choose from: political novices who previously had not been involved in municipal affairs or Democratic organization veterans. In running through a succession of police superintendents and budget directors she demonstrated the uncertainty of her own agenda as well as the constraints confronting any political outsider assuming the mayoralty in contemporary Chicago.

In regard to the police superintendency, by passing over a particularly eligible black candidate, Byrne did not serve well her black voting constituency. Later she appointed to the school board two white women who were ardent opponents of busing, and criticism from black politicians and civic leaders escalated. In short, by 1982, when Byrne's intention to run for re-election became clear, she must have been aware that her support in the black community was soft.

A sure sign of black disaffection was the 1982 boycott of "Chicagofest," a late summer food and entertainment festival sponsored by the city and a hallmark of the Byrne years. The Reverend Jesse Jackson, who called for the boycott, claimed that black vendors were excluded from participating in this lucrative event, and the substantial decrease in black attendance that he engineered cut into its revenues. Far more ominously for the Byrne administration, Jackson also sponsored a massive voter registration drive in preparation for the fall general election. Led by Operation Push and other community organizations on the black South and West Sides, the drive was joined by groups serving Hispanics and Appalachian whites in other parts of the city. In the November campaign, longshot Democratic challenger Adlai Stevenson III came within a few thousand votes of upsetting incumbent governor James Thompson, in no small part due to huge turnouts in several Chicago wards. Indeed, by the time of the mayoral primary in February 1983 nearly 171,000 names had been added to the voter registration rolls in Chicago. In nine largely black wards alone the increase in registration was above 96,000.[66] Following the fall election there were commentaries in the Chicago press suggesting a new lease on life for the regular Democratic party. This proved to be a serious misreading of events.

In effect, two of the long-standing subcurrents in modern Chicago politics were joining in late 1982. First, black alienation from the politics of the machine was becoming focused, and given the increasing minority proportion of the city's population and the sudden jump in their voter registration—one might say a return to the electoral fold—a major political eruption was in the offing. Second, the growth of community groups, so many of which had serious interest in the policies and service activities of government even as they eschewed politics Chicago-style, served as the fulcrum for the 1982 registration drive. They passed the word, staffed the registration tables, and seem to have taken seriously the prospect of using the upcoming mayoral election to upset the machine's apple cart. The seeds of the regular Democrats' indifference to blacks' and most neighborhood organizations' interests were at last bearing fruit.

Like so many black politicians in Chicago, Congressman Harold Washington was a product of the Dawson machine, although again, like many apprentices in that group, he had long since severed his ties with the regular Democrats. In 1977 he was one of Michael Bilandic's challengers in the Democratic primary for mayor but was decisively defeated. Following the November 1982 general election and mindful of its import for a black mayoral candidacy, Washington announced for the February primary. It became a three-way race when Richard M. Daley, the late mayor's son, 11th Ward committeeperson, and Cook County state's attorney also entered.

Paul Kleppner in his analysis of this race contends that the two white candidates, in spite of the voter registration drive that had preceded the November election, disregarded the chances of a black mayoral candidate. Furthermore, Byrne and Daley were both firmly in the machine camp at this point, and their candidacies promised to split the vote among white party loyalists. We have already noted the geographic strains within the Democratic party, Northwest Siders in particular tending to view the practices of the party as favoring the interest of South and Southwest Siders. Daley was, of course, the heir to the old party style of politics. Byrne hailed from the Northwest Side Sauganash neighborhood and during her term often seemed to depend more on regular alderpersons from this portion of the city. Once Washington's place in the primary was solidified in January 1983, notably by competent performances in a series of televised debates spotlighting the three candidates, this split opened the way for Washington to win the primary though carrying only a plurality of the vote.[67]

The implications of this electoral calculus forced the white candidates to exchange claims that the other was the spoiler who threatened to allow Washington's victory. Until the very end of the campaign this was mainly implicit. The weekend before the election Byrne supporter Edward Vrdolyak finally broke the silence in a talk to Byrne precinct workers, when he implored:

> A vote for Daley is a vote for Washington. . . . It's a two person race. It would be the worst day in the history of Chicago if our candidate, the only viable candidate, was not elected. . . . It's a racial thing. I'm calling on you to save your city, to save your precinct. We're fighting to keep the city the way it is.[68]

Washington was left to promote his "80-80" campaign among blacks (an 80 percent turnout, with Washington drawing 80 percent of their vote) and still appeal for votes among white machine opponents. Furthermore, the certain effect of Vrdolyak's eleventh hour appeal for white unity behind Byrne was to close off any chance of either Byrne's or Daley's pulling substantial black votes.

The vote tally was exceedingly close, Washington carrying 36 percent to 34 percent and 30 percent for Byrne and Daley respectively. The ward-by-ward vote is especially revealing of the ethnic-geographic bases of the three candidacies. In a number of South Side wards Washington outpolled his opponents' combined vote by a factor of eight to one. Daley's main strength was in wards on the Southwest Side, including his home 11th Ward. Byrne's strength was more evenly distributed, she being the only candidate to carry at least 1,000 votes in each ward. In contrast, and evidence of the fear his candidacy generated in some wards, Washington received fewer than 300 votes in the Southwest Side 13th and 23rd Wards.[69]

The seven-week general election campaign following the primary was the most interesting in a generation, if only because of the strong run made by the Republican challenger, Bernard Epton. To his evident surprise, Epton, who had previously followed a fairly liberal course as a state legislator, found himself embraced by a growing array of white Democratic

alderpersons and committeepersons from the racially defensive neighborhoods of the Southwest and Northwest Sides. Their retrospective claim to
have followed the will of their constituents has the ring of truth, as well as
ingenuousness. Having whipped their wards into near frenzy in the effort
to turn out the anti-Washington primary vote, they were in no position less
than two months later to subordinate race to party loyalty.

The degree to which Democratic party chairman Edward Vrdolyak encouraged surreptitious campaign work for Epton is unclear. In any case,
powered by intensive attacks on Harold Washington's personal affairs—he
had failed to submit federal income tax returns for several years and had
also in the past failed to complete some contracted legal work—Epton's
campaign lumbered to some momentum. Epton was not an impressive
orator, and as the campaign wore on time and time again he exhibited a
penchant for testiness. Nonetheless, many Chicagoans were determined to
prevent a Washington victory. Jane Byrne even re-entered the race as a
write-in candidate, but apparently sobered by the logistical problems, she
gave up hope of a second term and withdrew in just a few days.

The campaign ground to a fairly predictable close. The flinging of accu-
sations was unrelenting; on the streets arguments and even fisticuffs among
pedestrians were commonplace. Washington carried the city by just under
45,000 votes, out of 1,300,000 cast. In some black wards his proportion of
the vote was above 99 percent, and he ran strongly enough in the lakefront
wards and among Hispanics to carry the city. Ironically, while Washington
this time polled at least 1,300 votes in every ward, Epton received under
300 votes in eight wards.[70] The vote was highly polarized along racial lines,
but as Paul Kleppner notes, the racial distribution of votes was not incon-
sistent with figures from Philadelphia in 1983, where Wilson Goode was
also the first black elected mayor, in a reputedly harmonious campaign.[71]

In the aldermanic races coinciding with the 1983 mayoral election,
Washington swept in a number of insurgents to join the Independent faction on the city council. These victories were especially significant because
of the council's considerable statutory voice in municipal affairs. Speaking
precipitately in advance of the first session of the new council, the mayor
predicted that he would fashion a working majority of alderpersons, by
combining the block of black alderpersons with the white Independents.
In fact, party chairman and 10th Ward alderman Vrdolyak lined up a
majority block of 29 (out of 50) alderpersons, none of whom was black. In
the initial weeks of the new administration a heated debate over committee
assignments ensued, with the Vrdolyak faction eliciting cries of "foul" from
the Washington loyalists when the latter were excluded from important

committee assignments. In the long run, the configuration of the factions was given to stalemate, as the Vrdolyak faction without reinforcements was 5 votes short of the 34 necessary to override mayoral vetoes.

The early years of the Washington administration witnessed a politics of violent accommodation in which the symbolism of power and its use further clouded events. When the city council was in session, Edward Vrdolyak strode about the chamber buttonholing colleagues and offering only token attention as the mayor presided. The point of this calculated nonchalance seemed to be its stark contrast with Mayor Daley's authoritarian direction of the council.[72] One day in the gallery overlooking the council chambers, a youngish fellow in a dark raincoat—probably a city worker killing lunchtime—sat as close as possible to the front rail. After a remark by Vrdolyak, the smiling observer muttered as if at a prize fight: "Attaboy, Eddie. Stick-it-to'em." Washington for his part, when addressing black audiences, characterized Vrdolyak as evil incarnate.

Substantively speaking, the acrimonious talk was the prelude sometimes to compromise and sometimes to stalemate between the mayor and the Vrdolyak faction. For the first time in a generation the city council reviewed in some detail the mayor's budget proposal for 1984, much of its attention focused on appropriations for personnel. Vrdolyak ally and Finance Committee chairman Edward Burke negotiated some changes in the mayor's document only to have members of his own side express misgivings. In the end the two sides agreed to a comparatively frugal appropriations ordinance for the new year.[73] However, by summer 1984 the Vrdolyak faction's insistence upon oversight of all city contract awards in excess of $50,000 led Washington initially to veto a series of major public works authorizations, among them funds for the expansion of O'Hare Airport.[74]

Having campaigned as an advocate of neighborhood interests, regardless of their particular demography, Mayor Washington sought to open his administration to communication with neighborhood, civic, and local planning groups. In terms of the provision of access to city data and personnel, community groups were quite satisfied with the Washington administration.[75] Nonetheless, the momentum of projects carried over from previous administrations inhibited the charting of a wholly new policy of downtown and overall economic development. For instance, the Washington administration went forward with the controversial North Loop redevelopment project, a complicated public-private arrangement whose implementation stymied both the Bilandic and Byrne administrations. Washington, although taking a fairly skeptical stance toward the private group sponsoring the 1992 World's Fair—especially in reference to its estimates of municipal costs engendered by the event and the identification of fiscal sources to underwrite such expenditures—also distanced himself from the opposition that ultimately blocked Fair plans. The administration also continued negotiations with the Rouse Corporation to redevelop the Navy Pier area just east of near North Side Streeterville. It in fact succeeded in eliciting the developer's commitment to couple Navy Pier improvements with a series of neighborhood projects around the city. The Navy Pier proposal, a carryover from the Byrne administration, ironically enough came under fire from the formerly supportive city council.[76]

The Washington administration in many respects confronted the same political and economic constraints in evidence when other reformist black mayors have taken over in major cities. The business community, rendered somewhat anxious by the nasty election campaign, needed to be assured of the acumen and reasonableness of the new regime. Tight municipal finances further limited the policy alternatives available, and, as a result, efforts were made to improve the quality of ongoing projects and to modify, not dramatically reorient, future action. Washington's economic development commissioner, Robert Mier, suggested that significant gains could be made by the city's merely taking a "hard bargaining approach" with developers, that is, insisting on auxiliary joint ventures in neighborhoods and specifying employment targets to derive from particular projects.[77] In evident conformity with the commissioner's comments was the "1984 Chicago Development Plan," released in May 1984, which specified the reallocation of municipal resources toward neighborhood housing and economic development investments, but not without asserting the administration's commitment to also improving the Loop and its environs.

The Transformation of a Political Subculture

The recent period of transition in Chicago politics reflects not just the substitution of one local political faction for another or a redirection of local public policy. An indigenous political subculture has been severely undermined by events since the late 1970s. Edward Vrdolyak's swaggering defiance of Harold Washington was not so much a result of personal antipathy, as is often suggested, but instead a need on the alderman's part to demonstrate that the machine and its way of doing things were not dead. Further, by portraying the mayor as the opponent of all that the machine has aspired to accomplish, Vrdolyak skirted a central paradox within the myth of the machine. For Chicago is a city in which downtown rebuilding has taken precedence over neighborhood maintenance, and its Democratic party politicians bear much of the responsibility. During the Daley, Bilandic, and Byrne administrations they accepted without question a Loop-centered planning and redevelopment policy. Nor have they shown much sympathy for indigenous neighborhood action, which from their standpoint has offered the prospect of threatening political competition. In contrast, though he pitched his 1983 campaign to black voters and committed himself to increasing minority participation in city affairs, Harold Washington's vision of Chicago was not at odds with the aspirations and needs of Chicago's white working-class and middle-class neighborhoods. Thus, rather paradoxically, Chicago's first reform administration in a half-century sought to emphasize some of the same values given routine lip service by leading regular Democrats.

The city's painful political transition has had another important by-product, which is to reduce the salience of metropolitan issues. Both the Washington administration and the regular Democratic opposition pursued a single, compelling objective: control of city government. Outside Chicago no municipal or county official possesses the stature to lead the fight for metropolitan cooperation. Furthermore, federal aid cutbacks have reduced the ongoing work of units such as the Northeastern Illinois Planning Commission. The Washington administration took advantage of the mayor's background in the state legislature and worked with Governor Thompson to push through legislation with metropolitan impacts. Nevertheless, this represents an extension of the long-standing practice of metropolitan cooperation by way of Springfield. Until the battle for Chicago is settled this is likely to remain the principal means of resolving metropolitan problems in the Chicago area.

The myth of the machine, in addition to magnifying the accomplishments of the Cook County Democratic party, has also provided an implicit explanation of Chicago's turbulent race relations and neighborhood affairs. This explanation has been built on notions of ethnic solidarity, interethnic hostility, and the sanctity of neighborhood. Thus, to comprehend the nature of Chicago's political transition fully, one must also consider in some detail its social, demographic, and neighborhood conditions, which are the focus of Chapters 4 and 5.

4

Race, Class, and Residence

The Committee recognizes that a great immigration of negroes
have arrived and are arriving in Chicago, and that some feasible,
practicable and humane method must be devised to house and
school them. . . . The Committee is dealing with a financial business proposition and not with racial prejudice, and asks the
cooperation of the influential colored citizens. Inasmuch as more
territory must be provided, it is desired in the interest of all, that
each block shall be filled solidly and that further expansion shall
be confined to continuous blocks, and that the present method of
obtaining a single building in scattered blocks, be discontinued.
Chicago Real Estate Board[1]

The growth and decline of the city as a manufacturing center as well as the
struggle between the traditional political machine and the movements for
reform have shaped the spatial distributions and life chances of Chicago-
area residents. Market and political considerations are both major forces
in determining where, how, and whether different groups of people find
shelter and create community.

The spatial structure of the Chicago metropolitan region is not a spontaneous expression of natural forces, contrary to the theories of some
ecologists. And residence is not just coincidentally related to race, ethnicity, and class distribution of populations in the metropolitan area. This
spatial structure is the result of decisions made by key institutional actors
about where various kinds of housing will be constructed. Banks and
savings and loan institutions determine where mortgage money will be
made available and which neighborhoods will be denied credit; municipal
zoning regulations determine the kind of housing that can be constructed
in segments of the metropolitan area; government agencies make decisions
about what kind of public housing will be built and where it will be located;
real estate companies decide which racial groups will be "steered" to which
neighborhoods; the federal government enforces or relaxes its guidelines
about what housing projects will be funded under urban renewal or com-

munity development block grant programs; the Chicago Housing Authority decides on locations for public housing; and the courts determine which housing policies are constitutionally acceptable.

There are, of course, individual decision-makers in the housing market, people who determine for themselves where they will locate. The cumulative result of these individual decisions does influence the ways in which populations distribute themselves: a middle-class white family will move to the suburbs because the schools are better; a pioneering black family will move into a predominantly white suburb for the same reason; a poor black family will remain in the neighborhood where there are social support networks rather than move to another neighborhood where the affordable housing may be better. But the collective impact of these individual decisions pales in comparison to the impact of the large-scale institutions whose single decisions about construction or investment can have sweeping and permanent consequences for thousands of people. The decision made 30 years ago to house Chicago's poor in high-rise buildings is certainly one of the most dramatic examples of how whole generations can be affected.

The most salient characteristic of the spatial structure of this city is the rigid separation of blacks from whites that has earned Chicago the title of America's most segregated city. This chapter examines the institutional forces that have created and perpetuated that segregation throughout Chicago's metropolitan area.

A City of Contrasts

Three of the nation's 12 most affluent communities are located in Chicago.[2] The country's second wealthiest neighborhood, the lakefront area just north of Chicago's Loop, boasts a per capita income of $27,000 at a time when the national per capita income is $7,200 and the Chicago per capita income is $6,933.[3]

At the same time, Chicago houses the nation's very poorest neighborhoods. Public housing projects in Chicago contain 10 of the country's 16 most concentrated areas of poverty. The poorest community in the country is a four-block segment of Robert Taylor Homes, with a population of 5,681 and a per capita income of only $1,339.[4] The situation is not improving: during the 1970s, the proportion of city residents with incomes below the poverty line increased from 14.5 percent to 19.9 percent.[5]

Race and class, to no one's surprise, overlap in Chicago. Chicago's long-standing practice of segregating its populations has persisted into the

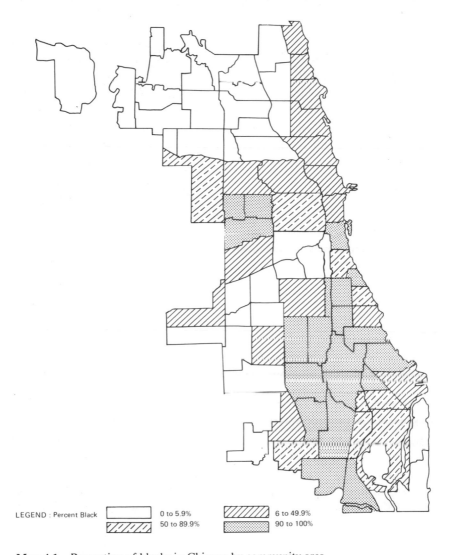

LEGEND : Percent Black   0 to 5.9%   6 to 49.9%
50 to 89.9%   90 to 100%

Map 4.1   Proportion of blacks in Chicago by community area
Source: Chicago Fact Book Consortium, Department of Sociology, University of Illinois at Chicago (eds.), *Local Community Fact Book: Chicago Metropolitan Area, 1980* (Chicago: The Consortium, 1980).

1980s; today more than two-thirds of the black families in the metropolitan arca live in census tracts that are more than 95 percent black.[6] The distribution of the black population by community area (aggregates of census tracts) is given in Map 4.1. The 1980 census brought new evidence as well of the economic disparities between blacks and whites in Chicago. From

1970 to 1980 this city grew both blacker and poorer. The city's black population in the decade of the 1970s grew from 33 to 40 percent of the total. Fifty-six percent of black census tracts in the city experienced a significant increase in poverty during that decade, compared to 14 percent of white census tracts. The Chicago metropolitan area, in fact, shows greater disparities between blacks and whites on all socio-economic indicators than any other major metropolitan area in the United States.[7]

Yet this city, with its incredible racial segregation and black poverty, elected its first black mayor in 1983, fielded the first serious black presidential candidate in 1984, and has blacks as leaders of its police department, school system, and public housing authority. The political resources of this community appear to outstrip its financial resources.

Economic hard times have hit white communities too. A large percentage of the city's white population is experiencing economic decline; 58 percent of white census tracts showed some increase in poverty in the decade of the 1970s. Yet a sizeable minority of whites reap the benefits of the uneven economic development of the metropolitan area that was discussed in Chapter 2. Twenty-eight percent of white census tracts in the city actually experienced a *decrease* in poverty during the seventies. The white residents of Chicago's lakefront, near North Side, and northern suburban communities are affluent, powerful, and mobile, while the thousands of residents in the white ethnic neighborhoods on the Northwest, Southwest, and Southeast Sides of the city struggle with unemployment, declining public services, and the fear of racial change in their neighborhoods. In the face of both economic stress and a black mayor in city hall, they feel beleaguered.

That Chicago is a city of contrasts does not make it unique among American cities. But Chicago has always carried its contrasts to extremes. In 1929, Harvey Zorbaugh wrote of the Gold Coast and its adjoining slum, "in which the physical distance and social distance do not coincide."[8] In 1987, it is this same community area that contains both the extremely wealthy Gold Coast neighborhood mentioned above and the extremely poor Cabrini-Green public housing project.

To understand the contrasts that characterize Chicago in the 1980s, one must understand both Chicago's history and recent economic and political developments at the national and local levels. Contemporary Chicago must deal with the legacy of decisions made in the past by major institutional actors. Decisions about housing development and land use have combined with an industrial infrastructure, strong ethnic neighborhoods, and a political machine, all of which are now in a state of decline. Each of these phenomena in and of themselves, their interactions with each other, and their connections with related national developments have given Chicago the class and racial patterns it exhibits today, as well as its potential for adaptation and change in the future.

The pattern of uneven distribution of resources was set early in Chicago, just as ethnic and racial dividing lines were early established. The social divisions and geographical dispersion of Chicago's population along both class and ethnic lines has been a persistent feature of the city. Chicago, of course, shares such a history with other cities that developed during the time America's industrial infrastructure was being built. Immigrants from European countries were welcomed as workers, if not always as neighbors. Ethnic colonies were formed early in Chicago. Irish, German, and Scandinavian immigrants built their communities before the Great Fire of 1871. A decade later, the geographic sources of immigration had shifted to Southern and Eastern Europe; Russians, Poles, Italians, Hungarians, Lithuanians, Greeks, Serbians—all came in great numbers until the immigration quotas of 1927 went into effect.

Chicago's periods of economic growth and decline have given shape to the city's ethnic make-up and have, along with national legislation, determined periods of heavy in-migration of Europeans, blacks, and Latinos. Around the turn of the century, railroad construction companies, slaughter houses, and other industries aggressively recruited workers in Mexico and in large European cities in order to create a cheap and "cosmopolitan" work force, not dominated by one ethnic or racial group.[9] Their efforts paid off. Thousands of laborers came to Chicago each year between 1880 and 1930 to provide manpower for the growing industries, but ethnic and racial divisions discouraged unionization efforts.[10]

Initially settling near their workplaces, by the time of World War I and the expansion of streetcar lines, these white ethnic groups had begun to establish communities further away from the downtown area. Many of these communities, such as the Polish, Lithuanian, and Greek, persist today with second- and third-generation residents. Although these neighborhoods no longer have the concentrations of people sharing a single national background that they once had, the identity of a culture with a place continues to be important and celebrated.

Chicago's population peaked at 3.6 million in 1950, about the same time that Chicago's businesses began moving to the suburbs and the city's share of manufacturing jobs began to decline. Much of the white middle-class and working-class populations began to move along with the jobs. But many other workers—blacks, Latinos, and lower-income whites—or potential workers—young people coming of age and older women attempting to enter or re-enter the labor force—frequently could not follow those jobs. Transportation was expensive by car and frequently impossible by bus or train, either because there were no mass transit routes to the new locations or because the time and cost involved were prohibitive.[11] In many cases, workers could not follow jobs to the suburbs because housing there was beyond their financial means or not available to them because of their race. In other cases, the jobs no longer existed as automated equipment replaced line workers.

So the descendants of those same Chicago industries that had welcomed European immigrants during their period of growth and had invited black and Latino workers into the job market when labor was scarce and it was necessary to discipline white workers now abandoned a work force of no further use to them. Indeed, they abandoned a city for which they had no further use.

As Chicago's white population declined after 1950, its minority population grew in absolute numbers as well as in relative proportions. The black population increase was most dramatic: from 493,000 blacks in 1950 (13.6 percent of the city's total population) to 1,197,000 in 1980 (39.8 percent of the city's population). But the increase in Latinos has been most significant in recent years. It is estimated that the Latino population increased between 1960 and 1983 from 3 percent to 17 percent of the city's total population.[12]

Members of all ethnic groups can now be found in Chicago's suburbs. Some groups dispersed in outward directions fairly quickly, moving from the inner city to the city's fringes to the suburbs in just a generation or two. While white ethnic settlements have not altogether disappeared in the city, two factors have substantially changed their nature. First, the largest white ethnic groups now have a majority of their populations living in the suburbs rather than in the city. Second, in the city race has come to be a far more significant characteristic for defining group membership and neighborhood residence than ethnicity.

The fear of losing "their" neighborhoods to "the blacks" is deeply rooted in Chicago's white communities. During the 1960s and 1970s many white neighborhoods went through a total racial transition and became completely black. In the 1970s economic conditions made it difficult for working-class and middle-class families to finance home purchases, the political pressures of the 1960s subsided, and the expansion of the black population slowed. Thus the process of neighborhood residential change slowed too. Indeed, in 1981 the Chicago Urban League concluded that, "although black demands for improved housing and white flight from the city may continue to create the demand imbalance which is the precondition for transition in selected areas of the city, the era of massive resegregation is probably over as far as Chicago itself is concerned."[13]

Nonetheless, the election of a black mayor in 1983 and the political power of the black community that this portends, along with the intransigence of many white elected officials with respect to cooperation across racial lines, set racial conflicts and tensions off on a new course. According to both the Leadership Council for Metropolitan Open Communities and the Chicago Police Department, incidents of racial violence in the Chicago area markedly increased in 1984.[14] The real struggle in the next few years may be between the white community, losing its political clout and cultural hegemony, and the newly empowered black community, growing in numbers, in voting strength, and in institutionalized political power.[15] "It's our city, too!"—while it may sound like the cry of Chicago's blacks in the 1960s—was actually the theme of the city's first White Ethnic Conference held in April of 1984.[16]

Housing: White and Black

Blacks have lived in Chicago since the birth of the city in 1833. But as late as 1900 they numbered only about 30,000 of a total population of 1.7 million.[17] World War I altered the racial composition of Chicago, as migration from Europe virtually ceased and the black population of the city more than doubled. Chicago early showed its inability to house blacks and whites together peacefully. The riot of 1919, the worst in the city's history, lasted five days, cost 38 lives, injured hundreds, and left thousands homeless.[18] The riot began on a hot July day and was triggered by a white mob's stoning of a black youth who swam across an imaginary line dividing the beach for whites from the beach for blacks. However, a major aspect of the tension and hostility between white and black Chicagoans before that riot had centered around housing. From that time into the 1980s, housing has been a major area of contention between the races in Chicago.

The housing that was available to low-income people in Chicago in the 1920s was in deplorable condition. After the fire of 1871 had destroyed one-third of the city's buildings, the city council passed an ordinance allowing "temporary" wooden structures for emergency housing.[19] Many of these "temporary" houses still stand today, a testimony to the city's enduring capacity to enforce selectively its own ordinances. Overcrowded tenements thrived in early twentieth-century Chicago despite the efforts of reformers like Jane Addams. Into these substandard, unhealthy buildings crowded thousands of black and white newcomers to the city. Blacks, however, were concentrated into a small, rigidly defined geographical area on the South Side. Between the end of the First World War and the beginning of the Second, this Black Belt became the Black Metropolis, in Drake and Cayton's words.[20] It rapidly established its own churches, commercial areas, civic associations, and newspaper, and in 1928 the district elected its first black representative to Congress.

World War I generated a need for labor that brought blacks to Chicago in growing numbers. Steel mills and other industrial establishments that had long been closed to minorities now had large military contracts, were desperate for labor, and welcomed the newcomers as cheap workers. Tensions between white workers trying to organize unions and black workers eager to step into jobs previously closed to them were exacerbated by the practices of employers skilled at playing one group off against the other.[21]

Chicago's black population grew by 114 percent during the decade of the 1920s, but that growth dropped to only 19 percent in the following decade. The Depression meant no jobs and a virtual halt to residential building in Chicago. From 1930 to 1938, a period when the city had an increase of over 60,000 families, it suffered a net loss of over 10,000 housing units.[22] Despite the slowdown in population growth, the housing crisis was worsening.

In 1937, Congress passed the National Housing Act to assist local governments in the job of slum clearance. While the federal government was prepared to assist with the costs of providing new low-income housing, local municipalities were encouraged to establish independent authorities to build and manage the housing. That year, in response to the federal mandate, the Chicago Housing Authority (CHA) was incorporated with two specified purposes: "to provide decent, safe and sanitary housing to poor families and individuals who live in substandard dwellings and cannot get adequate housing in the private housing market and to remove slums and blighted areas."[23]

The CHA assumed control of four public housing projects that had been built in Chicago by the Public Works Administration. These projects were located in different parts of the city, but all adhered to the "Neighborhood Composition Rule," which was federal policy in the 1930s. According to this guideline, a public housing project was not to alter the racial make-up of the neighborhood in which it was built. Thus, units in Lathrop Homes and Trumbull Park Homes were rented exclusively to white families; Jane Addams Homes reserved a few units for blacks; and Ida B. Wells was rented exclusively to black families.

The Ida B. Wells project opened in 1941, with more than 10 applicants for each of its 1,662 units. Construction of the project did little to relieve overcrowding in the ghetto because the units destroyed for the project almost equaled the number of new ones built. The growing black demand for housing increased the pressure on the white neighborhoods to the south, where a flurry of restrictive racial covenants were added to property deeds in the early 1940s.[24]

When World War II began, blacks, along with many whites, were part of a vast labor surplus. Although whites received the war-generated jobs first, President Roosevelt's 1941 Executive Order calling for an end to discrimination in hiring by government agencies and manufacturers holding defense contracts, along with stepped-up war production, brought blacks into industrial life in Chicago at an unprecedented rate.[25] The black population expanded dramatically during the war and the years immediately after, increasing from 8 to 14 percent of Chicago's population during the 1940s. Many of the blacks who migrated to Chicago during the war years were successful at finding employment, but were literally unable to find shelter in the ghetto. As a result, many black families doubled up. Others began to move into formerly all-white neighborhoods, either through the private housing market or through the public housing system.

A 1948 Supreme Court decision (*Shelley v. Kraemer*) rendered racially restrictive covenants unenforceable. After the war, white families moving to the suburbs made housing available for some black families who were now financially able to make the purchase. But violence routinely met the newcomers. In the public sector, the Chicago Housing Authority, under the leadership of Elizabeth Wood, vowed to place returning veterans regardless of race into the temporary housing quarters that were established in white areas of the city. In doing so, CHA, its residents, and Wood were met with a hostile community response.

In December of 1946, 400 policemen were assigned to the neighborhood around Airport Homes on the city's far West Side to keep order after several black families moved in. Following two weeks of harassment, the black families left; no others replaced them. The next summer, when black veterans were placed in Fernwood Park Homes, thousands of residents of the nearby community rioted for three successive nights. This community had earlier been angered by Elizabeth Wood's clear statement with respect to CHA's housing policy: "We must invite them all in the exact order of their priority and on the basis of their need."[26]

White resistance to black movement across the imaginary racial barriers resulted in what historian Arnold Hirsch has called "an era of hidden violence and guerilla warfare."[27] Most of the riots of the 1940s that arose around housing desegregation were spontaneous, unplanned, "communal" riots.[28] White residents—often including women, older men, and teen-agers—reacted to the attempted integration of their neighborhoods with name calling, rock throwing, arson, and assault. The guerilla warfare of the 1940s continued into the 1980s. In the spring of 1984, a black family renting a house in a white neighborhood on the Southeast Side was forced to move after its garage was burned and windows were repeatedly broken. Later that same year in another white neighborhood, a black couple and their small son escaped unharmed from their newly rented apartment where they had been under seige for six hours, as neighborhood residents hurled rocks at their home.[29]

Public Housing and Urban Renewal

From its inception, public housing has received mixed reactions in Chicago. On the one hand, both social reformers and downtown businessmen in the 1930s wanted to eliminate the worst of the slum housing. On the other hand, many building, banking, and real estate interests in the city, as well as nationally, opposed government's moving into the business of providing housing. Initially, public housing was viewed as temporary assistance for families hurt by the Depression. But by the 1950s the functions of public housing in Chicago, as well as the population served, had changed dramatically.[30]

When Martin Kennelly succeeded Edward Kelly as mayor in 1947, Elizabeth Wood lost her chief supporter. Mayor Kelly had given her free rein to run the Housing Authority as she wished and had insulated her from the politics of the city council. With Kennelly's election, Wood was no longer protected from the citizens and alderpersons outraged at her integrationist policies. In 1948, the state of Illinois at the behest of powerful Chicago politicians had granted the city council veto power over CHA site selections and, finally, in 1954, Wood was fired. "The firing of Elizabeth Wood not only signaled the change in power of CHA from liberals to conservatives, but the end of an almost twenty-year period where public housing was viewed as a vehicle for social change."[31] It also brought public housing squarely into the politics of the city council.

One legacy Wood left behind was, in hindsight, most unfortunate; this was her commitment to high-rise buildings for the poor. Wood believed that bold, decisive steps were necessary in planning low-income housing: blighted areas should be totally rebuilt into complete residential neighborhoods, provided with all the necessary community services and facilities.[32] Wood's thinking was in line with that of most progressive urban planners of the period, but the long-range consequences proved to be a disaster.

The construction of high-rise buildings for family housing proceeded at a rapid pace in Chicago during the 1950s. Seventy-five percent of the apartments constructed in that period had three, four, or five bedrooms, thus assuring that large numbers of children would be concentrated in a few buildings. When Robert Taylor Homes opened in 1962, with 4,312 units, it was the largest public housing project in the world; the families that originally moved in averaged 5.8 persons. There were more units than families on the CHA waiting list that year, so a number of unscreened tenants were allowed to move in.[33] This was the beginning of a shift in policy that continues to plague public housing residents. As the screening process broke down, apartments were rented to families with active gang members, drug dealers, and criminals of other stripes. Concerned about safety, families that could do so began leaving the projects. By the 1970s, Robert Taylor Homes and other high-rise projects had hundreds of empty, unrented units that had been taken over by gang members.

Decisions about site locations for public housing added to the architectural decisions to isolate Chicago's poor completely. Martin Meyerson and Edward C. Banfield, in their 1955 study of how public housing locations were selected in Chicago, demonstrate clearly that the intention of the city council members from the moment they wrested control of sites from the CHA was to do whatever was necessary to keep public housing out of white neighborhoods. Consequently, the CHA staff was defeated in its 1949 plan to build on vacant sites in outlying areas. The council insisted that blighted housing in the ghetto be torn down and new housing rebuilt on the same location. The problem of residential displacement and the fact that the severe housing shortage would be little alleviated by such a strategy were of minor significance to the council members. The really important task was achieved: Chicago's poor black residents remained segregated.

In looking at the consequences of urban renewal for Chicago's inner city, it is important to be aware of what was happening in the broader metropolitan area. After the war, large amounts of federal money went into the interstate highway program and mortgage subsidy programs for veterans, stimulating the growth of housing in Chicago's suburban rings. The suburban population in the Chicago area had been growing before the Depression, but after World War II it took off with a new vigor. The city of Chicago grew by 6.6 percent between 1940 and 1950 while the suburbs grew by 32.7 percent. During the 1950s, with the federal programs in full operation, the pattern became even more pronounced: Chicago declined in population by 1.9 percent and the suburbs increased by 71.5 percent.[34] In the 15 years following the end of World War II, over 688,000 new houses were built in the Chicago area. Seventy-six percent of these were single-family homes, and 77 percent were located in the suburbs.[35] The housing shortage for whites had effectively been resolved.

The Housing Acts of 1949 and 1954 provided federal funds for local governments to acquire and clear land in blighted areas and then sell the cleared land to private developers or local authorities for public housing. The legislation was passed in a spirit of granting to the cities the tools necessary "to combat urban blight." Thus, the legislation not only made $1 billion available in federal loans and $500 million available in federal capital grants but also gave local governments the necessary powers to acquire land for redevelopment. Chicago was a major beneficiary of this federal money; by 1970 the city had received over $150 million in urban renewal funds.[36]

The urban redevelopment program, or urban renewal as it came to be called after the 1954 legislation, was always intended to limit projects to those that were for "predominantly residential uses."[37] Yet in 1954 Congress responded to pressure for assistance to non-residential projects by raising from 10 percent to 20 percent the limitation on federal capital grant funds that could be used for non-residential projects.[38] In later years, the "predominantly residential" requirement was waived altogether for projects that would benefit universities or hospitals or aid industrially depressed areas.

The requirement that funds be used primarily for residential purposes had been opposed from the beginning by those who felt the intent of the legislation should be the overall rehabilitation of the downtown areas of older cities. On this side were local government officials who wanted more discretion in planning projects. An additional voice was that of organized business, which veered from its normal opposition to federal expenditures to speak in favor of federal assistance in reconstructing blighted business and industrial properties.[39]

From the time the program began there were competing interpretations of what urban renewal should really be doing in and for cities, what aspects of redevelopment should be emphasized, and which populations should be targeted for assistance. It was clear to politicians and civic and business leaders that the central cities were in a state of serious economic decline, as middle-class populations, retail establishments, and industries all relocated to the suburbs in growing numbers. A central contention of the growth ideology many of them espoused was that focusing resources on the economic rehabilitation of downtown commercial areas would be the most beneficial for all urban residents in the long run, as both jobs and housing would eventually trickle down to the poor.

The growth ideology prevailed in Chicago though few resources trickled down. Urban renewal projects ultimately worked more to the advantage of the middle class than of the poor and working class. One observer characterized the program in Chicago as "urban renewal for M.D.'s and Ph.D.'s" since so many of the funds were used for the revitalization of major nonprofit institutions such as the University of Chicago, Illinois Institute of Technology, and Michael Reese Hospital.[40]

It is certainly arguable that middle-class revitalization was necessary to assure the economic viability of Chicago. The problem is that the poor and minority populations continued to be the losers, even under programs that were designed with them in mind. Indeed, urban renewal projects frequently did the poor substantial harm, forcing them out of inexpensive though substandard housing but seldom providing alternative, affordable housing. For example, one Chicago Housing Authority report, which looked at those displaced from cleared sites in 1957 and 1958, concluded there was an increase in the median rent/income ratio following relocation from 16.6 percent to 26.3 percent.[41]

Urban growth, renewal, and planning in Chicago have always entailed close collaboration between the private and public sectors, as will be demonstrated in Chapter 6. The focus of these efforts has been on economic growth and development, not revitalization of existing structures. The notion of using renewal funds primarily for low-income residential purposes was never seriously considered by Chicago decision-makers. When poor people were displaced by development projects intended to benefit other populations, relocating them was at best a secondary concern to the principal objective of land clearance for development.

The Chicago Housing Authority was left to handle the housing problems of the city's displaced families. Between 1950 and 1954, more than half of all public housing units constructed were allocated directly to families displaced by building programs. In Hirsch's words, "Public housing had become the cornerstone of private redevelopment and, in turn, was dominated by it."[42]

Chicago's Dual Housing Market

Public and private housing developers share credit for perpetuating the dual housing market in the Chicago area. While most large American cities offer somewhat distinct housing markets for whites and for blacks, the segregation in Chicago has been particularly severe.

Since 1950, Chicago has had the greatest degree of racial segregation among major metropolitan areas.[43] One study done in the 1960s showed that blacks would range from a minimum of 10 percent to a maximum of 27 percent of each census tract in the city if the black population were distributed in a color-blind, income-determined housing market.[44] In fact, in 1960 two-thirds of Chicago's blacks lived in census tracts that were over 90 percent black. There was no improvement in later years: the segregation index in Chicago was 88.8 in 1970 and 91.9 in 1980.[45] These statistics show clearly the persistence of segregated populations and a dual housing market based on race, not income.

Both whites and non-whites suffer in a dual housing market since neither group has access to the entire housing of the city or the wider metropolitan area. However, the additional consequences for minority populations are particularly harsh. When there is less housing available to non-whites, they tend to pay more than whites for comparable units.[46] In the single-family home market blacks generally pay about one-third more for housing at any given income level.[47] Rents frequently increase after a community experiences a racial transition from white to black. Both Carole Goodwin in her study of Austin and Harvey Molotch in his study of the South Shore document the existence of a "color tax" on rentals and purchases as those Chicago neighborhoods changed.[48]

Minorities are restricted to purchasing or renting within a much smaller geographical area when a dual housing market is operative. It was precisely this restriction of a swelling black population to a narrowly defined ghetto that produced much of the racial tension, anger, and conflict of the postwar decades in Chicago. Chicago newspapers did not end their practice of running separate housing ads "For Colored" until 1951. By the late 1960s, however, the legal and commonly recognized replacement for such headings had become the geographical listings: an ad under "South" or "West" invariably meant the house was in a black community.[49] Large areas of the northern and western suburbs, historically unavailable for minority home purchasers or renters, still had minority populations under one percent in 1980.

The existence of a dual housing market is strengthened by the perspective of many urban planners, as well as real estate brokers, that the ideal community is the homogeneous community. As noted in the Introduction, until 1950 the code of ethics of the National Association of Real Estate Boards stated that realtors were not to play a role in bringing into a neighborhood members of particular races or nationalities whose presence might hurt local property values.[50] Rose Helper, in her study of Chicago real estate practices, documents that realtors, themselves often residents of the communities they served, believed they should not be the first to sell a home to a non-white family. Of course, realtors have had pragmatic as well as ethical concerns. As Robert Lake concludes after his study of real estate agents, "To introduce blacks into one's territory is to risk alienation of potential white clients [and] to replace whites with blacks in whose social networks one does not participate."[51] Indeed the question with which realtors in Helper's study wrestled was: at what point in the entry of blacks into a market will the community not hold it against me if I sell property to a black family?[52]

During the period of Helper's study, the mid-1950s, the black population of Chicago was increasing in great numbers, but little of the new housing being built was available to them. In addition much of the old housing in white communities was off limits to the black population. Consequently, the housing density rate within the ghetto continued to increase. Inevitably, the boundaries of the black community were pushed—further west and further south into adjacent neighborhoods of lower density. The pattern that followed has now come to be seen as that of classic resegregation: block by block an area undergoes racial transition. If the Census Bureau takes its picture of the population at the right moment, it might even appear that some blocks are integrated; in reality the transition has just not completed its full cycle. A situation described as integrated is often simply an ephemeral moment between the time when the first black moves in and the time when the last white moves out.

But in the 1970s a different situation developed in Chicago as the growth of the city's black population slowed down. During the 1950s, Chicago's black population grew by 65 percent; in the 1960s, the increase was 36 percent; but between 1970 and 1980, the increase was only 9 percent. The expansion of black residential areas has been occurring much more rapidly than the numbers alone would warrant. While much of the media focus continues to be on those areas where whites refuse to accommodate blacks as neighbors, there are other areas of the city where middle-class blacks are increasingly able to compete in the single-family housing market with whites, and other neighborhoods of rental housing that are racially and ethnically quite diverse. One recent study, acknowledging the persistence of residential segregation for most families, notes that about 10 percent of the metropolitan area's white population has lived for more than a decade with significant numbers of blacks or Hispanics in census tracts that are not experiencing rapid racial transition.[53] Whether these changes reflect a softening of the dual housing market in the area, or simply the fact that white housing demand in some areas is declining, remains an open question.

A critical component of the dual housing market has historically been a dual finance market in which conventional loans for home purchases are available to white families while blacks are compelled to buy with cash, on contract, or through government-guaranteed loan programs such as FHA (Federal Housing Authority).[54] For example, between December of 1974 and August of 1976, 275 houses were sold in the Southwest Side community of Chicago Lawn. The neighborhood was experiencing racial transition and virtually all the new home-buyers were black. FHA or VA (Veterans Administration) mortgage programs financed 82 percent of home purchases; only 15 percent were secured through conventional mortgages. Many black families purchasing these homes could comfortably have afforded conventional mortgages, but the banks had designated that area as one "in transition" and were not lending.[55] The concentrated use of FHA mortgages in Chicago became a signal during the late 1960s and 1970s that a neighborhood was in decline and had essentially been written off by the city's lending institutions that had chosen instead to invest their money in lakefront or suburban "up-scale" areas. Conventional mortgage or home-repair loans were sweepingly denied on the basis of address alone.

This practice of "redlining," systematically denying mortgages or home improvement loans to certain communities, was the target of massive organized community action in Chicago throughout the 1970s, as the next chapter will show. At this point, it is worth noting that the federal Home Mortgage Disclosure Act of 1975, coupled with the Community Reinvestment Act of 1977, provided important leverage for community groups, requiring lending institutions to disclose by census tract the number and amount of loans and be responsive to the credit needs of the community. There was a significant increase in the volume of conventional lending in Chicago minority neighborhoods after this legislation took effect.[56]

The Chicago Reinvestment Alliance (CRA), a coalition of community, housing, and local development organizations, has played an important role in convincing Chicago's large banks to follow the intent of the Community Reinvestment Act and reinvest in the city's neighborhoods. This coalition presents a sophisticated analysis of the current lending situation, its causes, and its likely consequences. The Alliance then offers suggestions for change and has the mass-based membership necessary to exert considerable pressure on non-cooperating lending institutions.

The Chicago Reinvestment Alliance recognizes that the nature of the financial industry has changed in recent years as smaller banks have been bought up by larger banks and financial institutions have lost interest in making traditional mortgage loans in urban neighborhoods. Many banks are moving away from local lending and are seeking out higher-risk loans nationally and abroad. One bank vice-president in Chicago admitted that his bank knew more about investing in South Africa than it did about investing in the neighborhoods of the South Side of Chicago.[57] Savings and loan institutions prefer to make their home loans to rich or soon-to-be-rich borrowers. In researching lending patterns in Chicago, CRA found the city was receiving a decreasing share of the metropolitan loan pie. In 1980, 34 percent of the total housing lending in the SMSA went to Chicago, but in 1982 this had decreased to 22.7 percent. In other words, the suburban share increased from 66 percent to 77.3 percent of the metropolitan total over those two years.[58]

But even these figures tell only a part of the story. Within the city, three lakefront communities (out of a total of 77 Chicago communities) received 29 percent of the total number of Chicago housing loans. Further analysis showed that 56 of the city's 868 census tracts (about 6 percent) received almost 40 percent of the city's housing loans in 1982. The home lending patterns in the area, not surprisingly, are closely associated with race: predominantly white census tracts in the metropolitan area (those with a minority population of 39 percent or less) combined to account for 91.6 percent of the total SMSA housing lending. The racial impact of lending patterns persists even when income level is controlled.

Latinos, the Emerging Minority

While Chicago's total population is declining, Chicago's Hispanic population is increasing at a rapid pace. Between 1970 and 1980, the number of Latinos increased by 71 percent.[59] Nationally, the Chicago area ranks fourth among urban areas in Latino population, trailing only Los Angeles, New York, and Miami. Chicago's population is unique, however, since it combines large numbers of Mexicans, Puerto Ricans, and Cubans as well as many immigrants from other Central and South American countries. While Chicago's patterns of black-white segregation have been intensively studied for decades, only recently has light been shed on Latino housing patterns. For these minority groups, the housing market has operated in substantially different ways than it has for blacks.

Several historical factors appear to account for some of these differences. Latinos early on tended to establish distinct and dispersed areas of settlement in Chicago rather than concentrating in one large area as did the black population. Mexican migration to the Chicago area began in earnest around the time of World War I. By the 1950s, three distinct areas of settlement had already been established. The first was around the steel mills and other heavy industry on the far Southeast Side of Chicago and in Northwest Indiana. This area is now 30 percent Latino, predominantly Mexican. (See Map 4.2) The second area, Pilsen-Little Village, located west of the Loop, is home to over one-third of the city's Mexican population. The third area, a little further north and west of the Loop, incorporates parts of West Town, Humboldt Park, and Logan Square and also has almost one-third of the city's Latino population, with large numbers of both Puerto Ricans and Mexicans. By 1980 two other areas of Chicago had large concentrations of Latinos as well: Back of the yards on Chicago's near Southwest Side was 31 percent Latino, predominantly Mexican, and the northern lakefront communities of Lakeview, Uptown, and Edgewater had increasing numbers of Mexicans, Puerto Ricans, and Cubans.[60]

These housing patterns reflect in part the fact that Latinos tended to settle near jobs in such industries as steel and meat packing; they also tended to settle near transportation lines and where housing was cheap. Very few Latino families have lived in public housing, although, even today, approximately one-quarter of the population is poor. In 1981, only 2 percent of the population in CHA projects were Latino; 3 percent were white; the remaining 95 percent were black.[61] One geographer has suggested that Latinos are reluctant to give up a living space where they have control over who enters and leaves and are further reluctant to be a minority within the large, spatially restrictive housing developments.[62] Despite these realities, it is also the case, as we have seen, that the largest public housing projects in Chicago were constructed in all-black neighborhoods and Latinos, like whites, tended to distance themselves from areas of black settlement. In Chicago, public housing for families was constructed, in effect, as black housing. The policies for selecting housing sites virtually assured there would be no integrated subsidized housing in the city.

In recent years, however, black and Latino populations have tended to live, if not together, then in greater proximity to one another. Indeed,

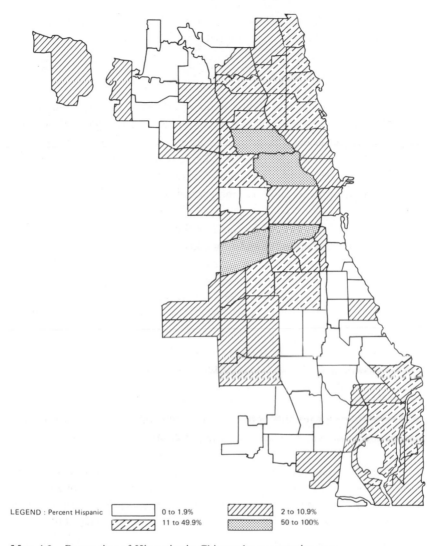

Map 4.2 Proportion of Hispanics in Chicago by community area
Source: Chicago Fact Book Consortium, Department of Sociology, University of Illinois at Chicago (eds.), *Local Community Fact Book: Chicago Metropolitan Area, 1980* (Chicago: The Consortium, 1980).

Hispanic settlements increasingly have tended to function as "buffer zones" between black and white neighborhoods. At the same time, Latinos have tended to move into outlying areas more rapidly than blacks. This is particularly true for Mexicans, whose numbers in the suburbs increased from 25,555 in 1970 to 113,179 in 1980.[63] They tend to be concentrated in several cities, particularly those like Aurora, Waukegan, Joliet, and East Chicago, Indiana that have substantial amounts of industry.

Housing Classes in Chicago

Homeowners, renters, and public housing tenants have had different experiences in Chicago's housing market. The major struggle over housing in recent years has been largely between blacks and whites of moderate income who are competing for the same scarce single-family housing. Blacks who are the first to penetrate an all-white community in their quest for good housing generally have incomes above the median for that community.

Almost two-thirds of the Chicago population, however, are renters with a different relationship to the housing market. In the city, black renters are less likely than whites to move outside their own community. Minority renters are even less likely than home-buyers to have access to the suburbs. Many suburbs, especially the more affluent ones, have zoning ordinances that prohibit multi-family housing units. Others limit rental developments to one and two bedroom units, effectively excluding all but single individuals, childless couples, or those with only one child.[64]

Thirty-eight percent of Chicago renters pay more than 30 percent of their income for housing; 21 percent of renters spend more than 50 percent of household income on rent.[65] Until recently, there has been no citywide organized voice for tenants. The lack of a single powerful voice for tenants became painfully clear to middle-income renters during the condominium craze of the late 1970s, when residents were regularly forced out of their apartments by landlords or developers eager to convert rental units into purchase property. The absence of such a voice had long been felt by lower-income tenants, who rarely have legal recourse with landlords who do not provide necessary repairs, heat, or maintenance. David Orr, as city council representative from a far north lakefront community where 84 percent of housing units are renter-occupied, for years led the fight for legislation to strengthen the rights of tenants. He worked with the Coalition for the Tenants Bill of Rights, which represents over 40 groups and, by 1986, they had successfully pressured the city council to pass an ordinance that adds significantly stronger protections for tenants. The most controversial section of the bill, "repair and deduct," allows tenants to make repairs that are necessary for health or safety reasons and deduct the costs from the rent. Other components of the bill limit security deposits and provide a mechanism for resolving conflicts outside the strained housing court system.

In Evanston, the suburb just to the north of the city, both a tenants' rights ordinance and a tenants' organization have been functioning successfully since the mid-1970s. Chicago's Orr modeled his legislation along the lines of Evanston's ordinance and claims the purpose is to "slow the deterioration of Chicago's rental housing stock, which lost about 84,000 units in the past decade."[66] As William Tabb notes, social control of the rental market "opens a Pandora's box of potential democratic decision making into the market."[67] Thus, not surprisingly, the ordinance has met with stiff opposition from the real estate industry, which argues the ordinance will raise building operating costs and discourage new apartment construction and renovation.

The third housing class in Chicago, those who are unable either to purchase or to pay full rent, are obvious losers in the city's housing market.[68] These are the residents of public housing. Chicago's 142,000 public housing tenants, overwhelmingly black, are also overwhelmingly women and children. They constitute almost 5 percent of the city's population and have been treated with particular harshness in this city.

The 20,000 people who live in the huge housing complexes of Robert Taylor Homes are there mostly because they have no other option. Robert Taylor Homes, in the admission of most housing experts, is a disaster. The 28 16-story buildings are unsafe for children and offer the antithesis of community to their residents. The Newman Report, commissioned by HUD in 1982, found the CHA "to be operating in a state of profound confusion and disarray."[69] Charles Swibel, a confidant of Mayors Daley, Bilandic, and Byrne, chaired the CHA board from 1963 to 1982, a period of huge CHA deficits and federal bail-outs as well as continuous scandal regarding patronage in CHA hiring and purchasing and inflated maintenance costs.[70]

Far more overwhelming have been the human costs. In 1980, one report on Robert Taylor Homes concluded:

Minors made up 72 percent of the population and the mother alone was present in 90 percent of the families with children. The unemployment rate was estimated at 47 percent in 1980; some 70 percent of the project's 200 official households received AFDC. Although less than one-half of one percent of Chicago's population lived in Robert Taylor Homes, 11 percent of all the city's murders, nine percent of its rapes, and ten percent of its aggravated assaults were committed in the project in 1980.[71]

Chicago has not followed the example of St. Louis and demolished tall public housing structures, although this is regularly suggested. These high-rises continue to provide shelter in a city where far more housing has been lost than built in the past two decades. Despite the fact that Chicago's population is declining, the housing shortage of the past persists for low-income families. Throughout the 1970s, approximately 6,000 housing units per year were lost due to arson and abandonment. In some areas of the city, gentrification has replaced renewal as a cause of displacement of poor people.[72]

Because high-rise public housing, with its concentration and isolation of thousands of poor people, was judged by experts and novices alike to be a massive social failure, no new high-rise public housing has been built in Chicago (or the nation) since the 1960s. The U.S. Housing Act of 1968 mandated that no new family public housing be constructed above the third floor. Public housing units built in Chicago over the past two decades have been in low-rise buildings. Yet, as a result of the city's unwillingness to comply with a court order on where public housing should be constructed, only 114 new subsidized family units were built in the entire city of Chicago between 1969 and 1980.[73]

In 1966 a class action suit was filed against the Chicago Housing Authority on behalf of Dorothy Gautreaux and other tenants of public housing. The lawyers for the plaintiffs claimed that CHA had fostered segregation by systematically constructing public housing in black neighborhoods. In 1969, federal district court judge Richard Austin agreed, finding CHA in violation of the equal protection clause of the Fourteenth Amendment. At that time, 99 percent of the residents of CHA family housing were black and 99.5 percent of its units were in black or racially changing neighborhoods. CHA was ordered to build its next 700 units of housing in predominantly white areas; after that a majority of future CHA housing units were to be built in white neighborhoods.[74]

Chicago resisted the court order. Mayor Daley publicly expressed his opposition to court interference in the CHA site selection process. From 1966, when the suit was initially introduced, until 1981 there was continuous litigation. In 1981, Judge John Crowley approved an agreement to modify the initial court decision. Under the earlier Austin decision the city had been divided into two segments, white and black. Crowley added a third designation, "revitalizing," a reference to racially mixed areas undergoing gentrification, and indicated court approval for construction in those areas.[75]

It was during the years that the case was in court that so few housing units were built. Austin's court order, of course, had not changed the social and political conditions that led to the initial housing concentration policies. The city council, for example, maintained effective veto power over site selection until 1974, and this continued to assure white communities with strong alderpersons that no housing would be built in their wards.

To add to the already complicated nature of the court proceedings, when the case reached the Supreme Court in 1976, the focus had shifted from building public housing in the city to opening up the suburbs. The suburbs, however, were under no mandate to accept projects that conflicted with their local zoning ordinances. Six years after that 1976 decision, the Leadership Council for Metropolitan Open Communities, the agency charged with placing families, had placed only 970 city families in suburban locations.[76] Neither Chicago nor the suburbs accepted responsibility for changing the racially segregated public housing practices defined by the courts.

The city, unable to avoid the court order since federal funds were involved, chose not to build new housing units at a time when thousands of homes were being lost and the poverty population was increasing. By the 1980s, blacks were questioning the value of moving into all-white neighborhoods and demanding that decent housing be built in their own communities.[77] Some critics argued that the entire legal procedure had been counterproductive since it had produced neither integration nor new housing for the poor.[78]

After the 1981 decision and under threat of further legal action, CHA finally began to move ahead with plans for constructing low-income scattered site units. Such housing was eventually built under Mayor Byrne, but the units tended to be few in number and concentrated either in black neighborhoods or the few "revitalizing" communities that were open to racially mixed populations. The reactions of some communities, both black and white, believing that they have received more than their "fair share" of subsidized units has been intense.

With Harold Washington's election in 1983, Chicago for the first time had a mayor with a commitment to building new housing for poor people and building it in the communities mandated by the courts. Many residents of white communities feared that Washington would encourage (or at least not discourage) the building of subsidized units in their neighborhoods. Washington, for his part, attempted, as much as possible, to distance himself personally from the issue. He consistently maintained, both in his campaign and his first months in office, that his administration would simply carry out its obligations as defined by the courts. While this was little comfort to some white citizens who wished to have their neighborhoods remain exempt from scattered site housing, others hoped that at last the housing sites would be truly scattered throughout the city.

But Washington, like his predecessors, was unable to resolve either the low-income housing problem or the CHA community relations problem. He encountered a series of roadblocks, both legal and political, with the administration of CHA in general and the scattered site program in particular. His administration continued to purchase sites in communities that already had substantial amounts of subsidized housing. A court-appointed Citizens Advisory Committee to CHA met with then interim CHA director, Erwin France, who acknowledged that in trying to move ahead quickly with land purchases, he did not address the issue of fair distribution of sites across communities. "I . . . took what I could get," he admitted.[79]

What he could get were more units in neighborhoods which already had a disproportionate amount of subsidized housing, either through the scattered site program or through other subsidized housing programs such as Section 8.[80] And what he found was considerable anger and resistance from community groups in those areas. Their concerns over such issues as management of existing CHA units and tenant selection were not being addressed and their major concern—that certain neighborhoods, their neighborhoods, not be saturated with a disproportionate amount of the city's public housing—was being rejected in practice by the acquisition of additional sites.

The Washington administration in its first years also made little progress in improving management of the public housing high-rise projects. In 1983, Washington appointed Renault Robinson, CHA board member, former police officer, and founder of the Afro-American Patrolman's League, to direct the CHA. Because Robinson had been a frequent and outspoken critic of the agency and an advocate for the tenants, many had hopes that the cycle of crises and mismanagement would come to an end. Unfortunately, Robinson's term in office served only to perpetuate the problems: he hired friends and relatives but was unable to keep the elevators operating or the apartments heated in winter. These basic maintenance problems persist despite the fact that Chicago's housing authority has monthly maintenance costs that average more than twice those of other Midwestern public housing authorities.[81]

As long as Chicago's more affluent neighborhoods are not willing to share the burdens of having some subsidized housing in their communities, residents in other parts of the city will feel justified in complaining about the absence of "fair share" policies. The issue of equitable distribution of social costs, however, cannot be adequately addressed as long as the solution is presumed to reside solely within the city's political boundaries.

Housing Chicago's Suburbanites

Kale Williams, director of the Leadership Council for Metropolitan Open Communities, concluded, after a review of the 1980 census data, that the Chicago metropolitan area remains heavily segregated with most black home-seekers housed within the black segment of the dual housing market. Nonetheless, after acknowledging this, he went on to say there had been modest progress over the decade in opening previously closed areas to blacks. Chicago's black population grew by 94,000 during the 1970s, increasing from 32.8 to 39.5 percent of the city's total; the black population of the suburbs increased by 102,000, from 3.5 to 5.6 percent of the metropolitan ring's population.[82] This increase in black suburbanites, as we will show, has generally *not* meant integration since most black families are concentrated in a few municipalities. The approximately 4 million residents of suburban Cook, Lake, DuPage, McHenry, Kane, and Will counties are virtually all white, with higher average incomes and better education than Chicago residents. Nonetheless, within those counties lies a good deal of variability.

Along the lakefront north of Chicago are some of the most affluent communities in the United States. In both median household income and per capita income, Northbrook, Highland Park, and Wilmette are among the nation's ten wealthiest communities with a population of 25,000 or more.[83] There are other salient characteristics of these three communities: they are virtually all white and they have virtually no subsidized housing. In 1980, Northbrook had three subsidized housing units out of a total of almost 10,000. Highland Park and Wilmette were slightly less exclusive; each had approximately one percent of its housing subsidized.[84]

The suburban areas to the northwest of the city tend to be newer, having experienced most of their growth after World War II. The fastest-growing suburbs in the last two decades have been those surrounding O'Hare Airport, which opened in 1955. This World War II test airfield had become the world's busiest airport by 1962, spurring economic development for miles around. Transportation problems, however, kept many city residents from taking advantage of the job opportunities in and around the airport. As of 1983, 41 percent of Chicago-area black households and 27 percent of Hispanic households lacked cars.[85] Rapid transit to the airport was unavailable until 1984, the same year the city announced a privately funded $1.4 billion redevelopment program at O'Hare Airport, projected to create an estimated 9,000 construction jobs and create or retain over 35,000 direct and indirect permanent jobs.[86] Firms involved in this expansion agreed to a 25 percent minority hiring goal. Further, with completion of the new Chicago Transit Authority spur to O'Hare, mass transit will finally be able to take workers back and forth within reasonable time and cost limits.

Because of Chicago's narrow east-west dimension, suburbs to the west of the city are the ones closest to the Loop; some are only eight to ten miles from Chicago's downtown. Those adjacent to the city are also some of the oldest suburbs, often home to families that have lived there for several generations. They contrast sharply with the newer suburbs further west. Yet the histories of these old, close-in suburbs, their relationships to Chicago's varied populations, and their responses to the possibility of racial change are as diverse as can be imagined. Three suburbs—Oak Park, Cicero, and Maywood—demonstrate the diversity.

Oak Park is an attractive, middle-class residential suburb, noted for its homes designed by Frank Lloyd Wright. It is adjacent to Austin, the community marking Chicago's western boundary. Austin experienced almost complete racial resegregation over a period of 20 years. In 1960, there were no blacks in Austin; in 1970, the community was about one-third black; in 1980, Austin was 75 percent black. By 1986, with the exception of a small section in the north end, the community was all black. Oak Park has managed to avoid the block by block resegregation that Austin experienced, but not without concerted community efforts. In 1986, blacks were about 16 percent of Oak Park's population. Although there is some concentration of blacks in the eastern sections, black families have been rather successfully dispersed throughout the village. Thus far the Chicago experience of racial change has been avoided.[87]

Oak Park first created a housing authority in 1946 to provide housing for returning veterans. Once that task was completed, the agency was dormant until the late 1960s, when it joined with the Oak Park Residents Corporation to upgrade the quality of local housing stock. More recently, both of these groups have worked closely with the Oak Park Housing

Center, which was founded in 1972 to "'manage' integration in Oak Park by influencing the locational choices of its newcomers."[88] The Housing Center refers tenants to available apartments in a way that encourages racial deconcentration. All these housing organizations, along with the community's leaders, are publicly committed to both racial integration and a prevention of the complete racial transition that occurred in Austin.

In 1980, Oak Park had over 800 subsidized housing units and had carefully scattered these throughout the community in order to avoid either economic or racial concentration. This community has one of the country's most aggressive programs for promoting a single housing market for all racial and income groups. The village has been referred to as "a living laboratory for an experiment watched by the entire nation,"[89] and has become a national model for its series of efforts to manage integration. In 1978, the village initiated a home equity insurance plan that guaranteed to home owners the value of their property even if anxieties over racial change caused prices to fall. Since that time, property values have increased and no one has made a claim against the fund. For years the village has advertised the advantages of a racially mixed community. Most recently, the Oak Park Board of Trustees voted approval of a plan to give financial subsidies to building owners who agree to integrate their buildings.

These efforts to control integration have met with opposition. The president of a real estate company that manages 200 units in the village says Oak Park is "trying to manipulate socially who lives in town" and its recent ordinance will be found illegal by the courts.[90] Nancy Jefferson, a black West Side community leader, has also protested that "they are keeping the town for the elite."[91] Oak Park's programs are not universally affirmed nor is it clear that they will achieve their goals in the long run. Nonetheless, the efforts that have gone into peaceful integration make this village unique among Chicago's suburbs.

To its south, Oak Park is bordered by Cicero, a blue-collar community of about 61,000. Like other old industrial towns, Cicero is in a state of economic decline. The town's largest employer, Western Electric, has steadily reduced its work force since World War II, with its most extensive cuts in the 1970s. At its peak, Western Electric employed about 12,000; by 1984 it employed 4,000 and was scheduled to be closed altogether. Town leaders are hopeful that the abandoned industrial land will be developed by new companies, since Cicero was recently designated a state enterprise zone. Cicero is a fully developed community with no further room to grow. Its population is aging, with one in five residents over the age of 60.[92] And it is projected the town will suffer a 6 percent decline in population by the turn of the century.[93]

In 1980, over 20 percent of the population of Cicero identified itself as Polish. Irish, Italians, and Germans also settled here in large numbers.[94] Cicero too shares a border with an all-black Chicago community, Lawndale, yet there were only 74 blacks (one-tenth of one percent) living in the entire town in 1980. Sixty-seven of these black residents are employed at Hawthorne Park, a horse-racing track, as trainers and animal caretakers and live in cinder-block huts during the eight months the track is open.[95] The other seven blacks are nursing home residents. Blacks have been employed by some of the industries in Cicero, but have been welcomed only as commuters.

Also like Oak Park, Cicero has been the object of national attention, beginning in 1951 when a young black veteran and his family attempted to move into an apartment in the suburb. Members of the local police department allowed community residents to harass the black family with impunity. A Cook County grand jury, ignoring the rioters, indicted the three blacks and one white involved in the rental of the apartment. They were charged with conspiring to reduce property values; a white Communist who distributed leaflets at the scene of the riot was also indicted.[96] Later, in the 1960s when the Southern Christian Leadership Conference had headquarters in Chicago, Cicero received further notoriety when it was dubbed "the Selma of the North" by Martin Luther King Jr. Cicero's attempts to keep its neighborhoods all white over the years have been successful.

While Oak Park has striven to "manage" integration, Cicero has steadfastly refused to open its community to minority residents in any way. The village of Oak Park passed a fair housing ordinance in 1968. The Cicero Town Board is being sued by the Justice Department for systematically excluding blacks from housing and employment. The federal government is demanding that Cicero town officials promote integrated housing, adopt an open housing ordinance, and repeal the one-year residency requirement for municipal employment.[97]

A third model, the Chicago model, is evident in the suburb of Maywood, which has gone through the transition from being an all-white community, to a briefly integrated community, to an all-black community, over the past 20 years. Maywood is located just west of Oak Park and Cicero. During the 1960s, Maywood was considered an integrated suburb with a black population around 20 percent. In the 1970s Maywood gradually lost its integrated character and became increasingly black. By the time of the

1980 census the town was 75 percent black and growing poorer. Five percent of Maywood's 8,600 housing units are subsidized.[98]

These three suburbs—Oak Park, Cicero, and Maywood—are neighbors and all are in the path of possible westward expansion of the Chicago ghetto. Each has responded in a different way to the prospect of racial change. Each community had different populations and resources to begin with: in 1969, for example, Oak Park's per capita income was $5,021, compared to $3,819 for Cicero and $3,342 for Maywood.[99] Each community had different traditions and different political leadership. By 1986, each community had a very different profile.

Growth and Exclusion

Further west, away from the city and the suburbs of Cook County, lies DuPage County, where the median family income is over $30,000, the political mood is distinctly conservative, and there are so few blacks that they have formed their own organization, the Black Suburbanites Club.[100] Bigotry against blacks is a problem in this county of over 700,000 to be sure: as recently as 1980, a wealthy black businessman was forced to wage a court fight for the right to purchase and live in a $675,000 house in an all-white subdivision in Oak Brook. Two years later the U.S. Court of Appeals upheld a lower court decision that found the Hunter Trails Community Association in violation of the Civil Rights Act of 1964 and the Federal Fair Housing Act. The Community Association had attempted to block the sale after the fact by enforcing a covenant giving them the right of first refusal.[101]

In 1970, DuPage County had no subsidized housing at all. But during the decade of the 1970s, public officials began to take advantage of federally assisted housing programs and by 1980 there were 4,154 subsidized units in the county. There is no public housing, however; all low-income units are subsidized through Section 8 or Section 235 or 236 programs. Overall, 2 percent of the county's housing units are now subsidized; the overwhelming majority of residents of this housing are white. Although there are an estimated 20,000 people living in poverty in the midst of DuPage County's affluence, only 1.2 percent of the entire county's population is black.

The restricted nature of the housing market in DuPage County was challenged in court in 1971, when several fair housing groups filed a lawsuit against the county claiming housing discrimination on both racial and economic grounds. Plaintiffs charged that the overall zoning policies and practices deterred developers of subsidized housing from even trying to build in the county. In 1982, after years of delay, Judge Hubert Will of the U.S. District Court ruled that the county used housing and zoning regulations to discriminate against minority groups and low- and moderate-income families, and he ordered the county to cease. As part of that order, DuPage County was to provide housing assistance to 1,810 needy families over a 20-month period and start a ten-year plan to provide a "significant number" of low and moderately priced housing units. The judge further forbade the county from enforcing ordinances setting minimum acreages and lot sizes for housing development in unincorporated areas.[102]

As a result of this court's ruling, the federal Department of Housing and Urban Development froze $7.2 million in community development funds "because of doubts about the county's commitment to assisting the poor and minorities."[103] In the face of this economic threat, the DuPage County Board went on record in May of 1984 as being in favor of open housing and opposed to discrimination, block busting, and racial steering. The resolution was widely perceived as expedient, non-binding, and un-enforceable.

It also appears to have been unnecessary since the U.S. Court of Appeals in June of 1984 overturned the wide-ranging ruling by Judge Will on the grounds that the plaintiffs did not have standing in the case when they first filed suit—that is, none of them were victims of discrimination by the county. The DuPage County board chairman, Jack Knuepfer, was quoted as expressing the hope that this latest ruling would finally get the fair housing groups and the federal government "off our backs" and would change HUD's position on withholding funds.[104]

The plaintiffs briefly considered an appeal to the Supreme Court but dropped the idea, discouraged that the outcome of 13 years of litigation should be so unsatisfactory. "I don't think [the courts] want to deal with the issue of discrimination head on," said the director of one fair housing group. "The problems remain, low-income families are still here, minority families are still discriminated against."[105]

The west suburban high-tech growth corridor, where new office and research development centers are sprouting, runs through the heart of DuPage County. Naperville, a boom town with a population projected to increase 143 percent by the year 2005, is home now to national or regional headquarters for such firms as Bell Labs, Nabisco, Nalco Chemical Company, Standard Oil Research Labs, and the Wall Street Journal. Naperville's housing is 94 percent single family with a median value of $98,400. If the new industries there hire extensive numbers of workers unable to afford the kind of housing that DuPage County now offers, pressures for more moderate-income housing again may hit the county's government.

Managing Integration in the South Suburbs

The suburbs to the south of Chicago tend to be the ones with the greatest concentration of heavy industry and blue-collar workers, as well as the ones with the largest black populations. These suburbs have never been as affluent as those to the north and the west, but recently this area has suffered serious economic decline as a result of the closing of the steel mills and other industrial plants. A few southern suburbs have populations that are almost entirely black. Indeed, it is important to keep in mind that figures indicating greater numbers of blacks in Chicago's suburbs are more a reflection of the continuing concentration of blacks in a few of these communities than they are of any meaningful integration in the wider metropolitan area.

In 1974, Robbins, an all-black suburb, had a median family income of $10,200, the lowest in the metropolitan area.[106] A number of other southern suburbs with a greater range of working-class and middle-class residents also had sizeable black populations as of 1980. In some of these suburbs, the increase in black population between 1970 and 1980 was substantial. Park Forest South, for example, went from 3 percent black in 1970 to 44 percent in 1980. Calumet Park was 30 percent black in 1980, although no blacks had been counted in the 1970 census. Hazel Crest and Country Club Hills, both without black residents in 1970, were each 12 percent black in 1980.[107]

Some of these communities experiencing considerable racial change have, like Oak Park, publicized their commitment to open housing. They have enacted fair housing legislation and established or worked with housing groups to facilitate the process of peaceful integration. They have also taken measures to forestall total resegregation. These measures, which have come to be known by terms such as "managed integration" or "integration maintenance," encourage black home-seekers to rent or buy in white areas rather than congregate with other blacks and encourage white home-seekers to move into integrated rather than all-white areas.

At least 14 Chicago suburbs, most south of the city, have attempted such programs in recent years. Many work together through groups like the South Suburban Housing Center in Park Forest. The director of the Center says the essence of the integration process is "blacks and whites competing for housing in the same market."[108] These suburbs, for reasons of enlightened self-interest, are attempting to eliminate the dual housing market from their region. In the absence of such self-conscious attempts at citywide integration or "reverse steering," suburbs that are open to blacks believe they will experience total racial transition.

These attempts at racial balance, again like Oak Park's program, have met with resistance and controversy, and their legal status has been challenged. The major opponent of these efforts is the real estate industry. The National Association of Real Estate Boards "deplores the combinations of efforts like those of the South Suburban Housing Center with such municipal actions as bans on solicitation and 'for sale' signs. . . . The basic problem is, how can we comply with [federal laws] that require us not to steer and [local laws] that require us to steer."[109]

"Freedom of choice" has become the slogan of the real estate industry's campaign against efforts to maintain integrated housing through affirmative marketing techniques. "'Freedom of choice,'" says the assistant village manager of Park Forest, "has become the slogan for segregation and resegregation, ethnic purity, separate and unequal, business as usual, American apartheid. 'Freedom of choice' has become the code phrase that serves as once did 'States rights.'"[110]

The real estate industry has chosen to file suit against those communities that are struggling to maintain integration while business as usual prevails in those predominantly white communities that refuse access to black home-seekers. The federal government has taken no steps to support the efforts of those municipalities that are trying to break down the dual housing market. In addition, some civil rights organizations have objected to these efforts, arguing that the black community's need for good housing is more important than allaying the fears of whites. There is also resentment at the implication that "too many" blacks are by definition "a problem." History suggests, however, that if attempts at "managed integration" cannot be made to work, total resegregation is the likely outcome for some of Chicago's suburbs, just as it was for many of Chicago's neighborhoods.

Economic Integration in the Suburbs

Historical practices like restrictive covenants and realtors' steering in the suburban housing market, along with self-steering by both blacks and whites, and the absence of any plan for housing at the metropolitan level, have resulted in housing patterns whereby a few suburbs have many black residents but most have next to none. In a similar vein, while the total number of subsidized housing units in the suburbs increased substantially in the 1970s—from 5,235 units (.04 percent of all housing) to 29,463 units (2.2 percent of all housing)—they tended to be clustered in a few municipalities.[111] Only a handful of communities had 1,000 units or more. These were the industrial cities—Joliet, Elgin, Waukegan, Aurora, and Chicago Heights—all of which have ethnically diverse populations and long-established ghettos. In each of these cities between 5 and 9 percent of all housing is subsidized. Among the other suburban communities that bring up the metropolitan-wide count of subsidized units are the suburbs with almost exclusively black populations—for example, Robbins or East Chicago Heights (now Ford Heights)—or those suburbs with "open housing" for example, Evanston, Oak Park, Park Forest. Fifty-two of the area's 260 suburbs have 88.5 percent of all the suburban assisted housing.[112]

Successful efforts at opening up suburban housing to middle-class blacks would offer only a partial solution to resolving the regional patterns of inequality, as long as economic segregation remains. If the city is any barometer, efforts to integrate low-income housing into middle-class areas is likely to meet with resistance comparable to that directed toward racial integration. Urban renewal efforts in Hyde Park, Lincoln Park, and the near West Side were fairly successful in creating stable, partially integrated, middle-class communities, but often this was done at the expense of the displaced poor. Indeed, successfully opening up the entire suburban ring to black middle-class families while ignoring the poor would actually exacerbate one of the major dilemmas now facing Chicago: how to provide for an increasingly impoverished, unemployed, dependent population. Much of Chicago's vitality in recent years has been a result of the strength of its black middle class. This group may well choose to remain in the city even with broader housing options, but if they should follow their white counterparts to the suburbs in increasing numbers, the economic divisions between the inner city and the outer suburban rings will intensify.

Directions for Housing Reform

As long as housing remains a commodity to be produced and distributed according to the dictates of a market economy, the concept of housing classes expresses well the relative political and economic power of different groups in the metropolitan areas. But, while a privileged few profit from the operation of real estate and finance markets, those growing numbers of families and individuals excluded from the traditional single-family home are developing alternative strategies. As more people are permanently cast in the role of renters, a new tenant consciousness is developing and a sleeping giant is beginning to awaken in Chicago as in other cities.[113] City coalitions like the Chicago Reinvestment Alliance have played a leadership role in monitoring the reinvestment policies of lending institutions, as more people come to realize that the days when houses and neighborhoods were cast off like used cars must end. Neighborhood housing groups, like Voice of the People in Uptown, are purchasing and rehabilitating old buildings abandoned by their former owners. Concerned professionals like the Lawyers Committee for Better Housing have worked with community groups to assume receivership of abandoned buildings and ensure that vandals and arson do not destroy sound housing. Coalitions of community organizations and research and policy groups, like the Woodstock Institute, are working together on housing issues in Chicago. Permanent umbrella organizations like the Housing Agenda or temporary coalitions like the Housing Abandonment Task Force are beginning to hold both public agencies and the private sector accountable for housing conditions and opportunities in the city. Increasingly, those denied adequate and affordable shelter are viewing housing as a public good, not simply a marketable commodity, and they are demanding changes in the behavior of the institutional actors who have historically controlled access to housing throughout the nation.

Enforcement of fair housing laws, an end to displacement, an expansion of residents' rights, retention and improvement of housing stock, and an adequate supply of low-income housing are the essentials laid out by the National Low Income Housing Coalition.[114] The housing problem is a national one, rooted in housing policies set by the federal government and the behavior of major actors in the private housing industry. The most creative solutions for redressing the shortcomings of the past, however, may be those being put in place today at the neighborhood level.

5

Conflict and Cooperation
in the Neighborhoods

Cities are not about neighborhoods.
Bowden and Kreinberg[1]

Official business in Chicago has traditionally been handled by a few men:
the mayor and several key advisers, perhaps in further consultation with
selected business leaders. Although the gender of one major figure changed
when Jane Byrne was elected mayor in 1978, the dynamic of decision-
making remained the same. Until recently, the ward representatives in the
city council merely rubber-stamped administration proposals. Neither debate, discussion, nor review have historically been a part of the legislative
process. Many alderpersons served entire terms without ever introducing a
major piece of legislation. During Daley's years it was not unusual for the
mayor to turn off the microphone when the lone Independent alderperson
would attempt to raise an issue or object to procedures.[2]

If the elected representatives were little involved in formulating city
policy, citizen involvement in the workings of the government has been
even more limited. Perhaps only in Chicago in the 1980s could Mayor
Harold Washington's move to give citizens access to public records be seen
as revolutionary. In previous administrations, legislation, budgets, and development plans were seldom made available to the public for their scrutiny. As recently as Jane Byrne's administration, citizens were forced into
the courts to obtain the release of reports that were prepared with public
money. Indeed, over the years Chicago has wasted enormous amounts of
its taxpayers' money fighting in the courts what were inevitably losing
battles over citizen access.

During the years the machine was strong, Chicago's brand of ethnic
politics sustained white communities that were well provided for by local
politicians, at least in the short run. Indeed, the maintenance of local
streets and alleys and the delivery of jobs, favors, and contracts to con-

stituents—not the development of legislation to guide the governance of the city—were seen as the alderperson's job. The residents of favored neighborhoods had their streets cleaned in the summer and plowed in the winter and their garbage picked up on a regular basis. Correctly or incorrectly, they attributed these to the efforts of their representatives in city council. More important, the residents had jobs: city jobs with the Fire Department, the Police Department, or Streets and Sanitation and county jobs with the Sheriff's Office or the Tax Assessor's Office. The neighborhoods with the most clout—that is, those where the most influential politicians resided—had the most public payrollers, since those officials had the most patronage to dispense. Mayor Daley's neighborhood of Bridgeport, was, during his career as mayor, home to thousands of city employees. As recently as 1982, the 11th Ward (where the Daley family still lives) and three other white Southwest Side wards had 8,189 city workers, 20 percent of all city jobs, although they contained only 8 percent of the city's population. All four wards had Democratic committeepersons with long and close personal ties to the Daley family.[3]

Ed Kelly, the long-time Park District superintendent, always managed to "locate" numerous jobs for constituents in his 47th Ward. Clout-heavy politicians have delivered other special favors to their constituents as well. For example, Bridgeport has, through the years, retained the only family public housing project in the city with no black residents, and in 1978 the parks in white wards averaged 79 percent more indoor facilities and 23 percent more outdoor facilities than the parks in black wards.[4]

Over time, of course, the machine was weakened by fair employment regulations, civil service procedures, and the landmark Shakman court decision, which made it illegal to hire, fire, or promote city workers for purely political reasons. Nonetheless, patronage—a city job for friends and relatives or a special favor or contract for campaign contributors—has remained alive if not as robust as in the past. It may well have been Harold Washington's message of reform more than his race that sent the regular Democratic organization into a frenzy when they realized he might become the mayor of Chicago. Jane Byrne had demonstrated that the business as usual patronage game could be played just as well by members of groups previously excluded. But significantly changing the patronage system in Chicago, in effect stripping local politicians of their source of power, was a reform that would be fought to the bitter end.

In any case, many white ethnic communities in Chicago held their own with special services and secure jobs throughout the urban turmoil of the 1960s and the fiscal crises of the 1970s. Other communities, of course, were not so fortunate; these were the communities with black or Hispanic populations or those that had elected an Independent alderperson. While the liberal Independent wards tended to house white, middle-class voters not dependent on the city's political system for jobs and favors, the minority communities felt the impact of neglect.

It was these minority communities that expressed their anger and frustration in the 1960s and 1970s, not only through riots and demonstrations but also through organized political protest. Much of the community-based protest of this period revolved around schools and housing, two issues of paramount concern to a community that expanded as rapidly as did black Chicago in the 1950s.[5] Overcrowded schools and a shortage of decent housing, both resulting from institutional efforts to maintain blacks in their ghetto, brought them instead to the streets in the 1960s.

Prior to that decade, problems in the black community were largely responded to through individual rather than collective action. The leaders of Chicago's political machine early on learned the value of co-opting key figures from the black community for individual material and symbolic rewards. These rewarded individuals—politicians such as William Dawson and Ralph Metcalfe before his conversion—were able to maintain their own sub-machines and dispense their own patronage in the black wards of the city. While the number of blacks benefiting from these arrangements were few, the most vocal and potentially most troublesome could be rewarded for playing within the existing system.

Confrontation and Change

All this began to change in the 1960s. With a national civil rights movement capturing the support, participation, and imagination of thousands of Chicagoans, there was a clear context for pushing change at the local level. Institutional resistance to change and the racism of Chicago's leaders made it clear that rational negotiation among concerned parties was not a feasible route to timely solutions.

When the huge unmet demand for moderate-income housing forced black families into previously all-white areas of the city's South Side, they were met with violence. The Concerned Task Force, a watchdog group of citizens representing different religious groups, claimed, "The absence of firm and unequivocal statements by city officials, religious leaders, and representatives of the business and civic community have encouraged white Southwest Side residents of the righteousness of their beliefs."[6]

In 1975, when it was pointed out by an investigative team for the *Chicago Reporter* that Chicago had the highest fire death rate of the nation's largest cities and, furthermore, that this problem was most serious in poor black and Hispanic ghettos, city fire commissioner Robert Quinn responded, "The ghetto? I don't know of any ghettos in Chicago."[7] His response echoed that of Mayor Daley a few years earlier when he was informed of poor housing conditions in the same Chicago neighborhoods.[8]

The insensitivity of Chicago's white leadership to the black community and its intransigence to change was nowhere more evident than in the Chicago public school system. Despite the *Brown v. Board of Education* Supreme Court decision in 1954 that separate schools for blacks and whites could not constitute equal education, the Chicago schools did nothing in the years following to change a thoroughly segregated system. Ten years after the court ruling, the Hauser Report on Chicago Public Schools made this observation: "Of 148,000 Negro elementary students, 90 percent were in schools at least 90 percent Negro. . . . Of 17,000 Negro students in upper grade centers, 97 percent were in Negro schools."[9] The Chicago Board of Education adopted the Hauser report "in principle" but took no action to implement the changes that were suggested as routes to desegregation.[10]

Other investigative reports during this period showed that less money was spent per pupil in black schools than in white. While mobile classrooms were set up to relieve overcrowding in black schools, nearby white schools had classrooms that sat empty or were assigned to "special" uses, the school board and superintendent apparently preferring these tactics to bringing integration into the classroom.

It is of little wonder that the schools and their policies became objects of severe attack by black groups and some civic associations and that groups of angry black parents orchestrated sit-ins, boycotts, and lawsuits. Strong feelings were expressed on these issues and the memories of confrontation linger on. In 1984, Dorothy Tillman, a black activist from the South Side who had been appointed by Mayor Washington to fill an aldermanic vacancy in her ward, was continually denied confirmation by the city council, at least in part because of the militant role she had played years before as a PTA leader demanding reform in her neighborhood.

But the policies of the superintendents and the Board of Education during these years were supported by many white civic associations, neighborhood groups, and politicians. Where opportunities existed in the 1960s and 1970s to integrate schools—through redrawing boundaries, busing, transfer programs, or other innovative measures such as educational parks and cluster programs—Chicago's Board of Education consistently refused to provide the creativity and leadership necessary for such massive transformation. White neighborhoods vigorously resisted the redrawing of school boundaries to relieve overcrowding when that meant the transfer of black children to classrooms in their neighborhoods. Racially changing schools were perceived as the bellwether of neighborhood change.

Again, on the issue of school desegregation, the absence of leadership from the political, business, or religious communities was strikingly evident. Mayor Daley's response to the black community's desperate but nonviolent pleas for change was not to address the injustices they called to his attention, but to claim they were "financed by outside sources for political reasons" and "caused by Communist influences."[11]

There seemed no limit to the physical and psychic brutality inflicted on Chicago's blacks during these years of wrenching change, but as the black community grew in numbers, organization, and political sophistication it began to fight back. As Chapter 3 has shown, in the 1970s blacks in Chicago grew increasingly independent in their politics and skilled in organizing. Traditional divisions in the black community had become less important by 1980. New organizational efforts, both community-based and political, created coalitions ready to act on important issues. The 1982 People's Coalition to Boycott Chicagofest was a dramatic example of this fusion of neighborhood mobilization and political consciousness. This coalition was important because in cutting across "standing fissures and leadership rivalries . . . [it] demonstrated to blacks their potential for successful action."[12]

The community-based voter registration drive that followed later that year in preparation for the mayoral primaries of early 1983 further reinforced the strength of the networks and connections among black Chicagoans. Furthermore, other new coalitions were formed to include Hispanics, liberal whites, and middle-class and poor blacks. People Organized for Welfare and Employment Rights (POWER), a coalition of 15 welfare rights, civil rights, and community groups, was credited with playing a major role in the voter registration drive that enrolled hundreds of thousands of new voters.[13]

Alinsky's Organizing Traditions

There have been strong community organizations in Chicago neighborhoods for over 40 years. Saul Alinsky began his organizing career in the Back of the Yards neighborhood on Chicago's Southwest Side in the 1930s. The Back of the Yards Neighborhood Council, although not today the force it once was, is still alive and active. A number of major community groups going strong in the 1980s were established 20 or even 30 years earlier. These include The Woodlawn Organization (TWO), organized by Alinsky and others in one of the South Side's poorest black neighborhoods; the Edgewater Community Council (ECC) and the Lakeview Citizens Council (LVCC), each representing a section of Chicago's diverse northeast lakefront community; the Northwest Community Organization (NCO) on the near Northwest Side; and the Hyde Park-Kenwood Community Conference (HPKCC) on the South Side. TWO still has a poor black constituency; ECC and LVCC still have diverse constituencies with a leadership that remains largely white; HPKCC still has an integrated middle-class constituency. Some community organizations have continued in form and name despite a complete turnover in racial composition.

The South Shore Commission (SSC) was founded in the late 1950s by white residents seeking to deal with imminent racial change in their community. A split existed in the organization at that time between those who wanted South Shore to remain white and those who sought a racially balanced community. By the late 1960s integration had become an explicit organizational goal and attracting white middle-class families to the changing community was a major priority. By 1970 about 50 percent of the Commission's membership was black; in 1972, SSC elected its first black president.[14] The South Shore Commission is now a strong and seasoned community organization with a virtually all-black membership. SSC has played an important role in eliminating some of the usual consequences of neighborhood racial transition. It worked diligently and successfully to keep the local bank from abandoning the neighborhood; it also helped save the shuttered South Shore Country Club from demolition so it could be rehabilitated as a Park District facility to provide recreational activities for the community.

In the late 1960s and 1970s community organizing reached its peak in Chicago. Many white groups began to use direct action tactics during this period, claiming they were taking their cue from the militant behavior of black groups. Lying down in front of bulldozers, disrupting meetings of the Board of Education, and staging school boycotts became routine modes of resistance to school board decisions and indecisions in the 1970s. The same issues—housing and schools—that most concerned blacks during this period concerned whites too. However, the major emphasis in the white communities was on maintaining their neighborhoods and classrooms as they were. While this meant keeping them white, it also meant keeping them intact in the face of urban development on the one hand and disinvestment on the other.

The neighborhood movement that took shape in Chicago and across the country in the 1970s was in good part an outgrowth of earlier social movements. The anti-war movement, the civil rights movement, and the women's movement had captured the allegiance of very few members of the white working class, but the impact of these movements was not lost on them. Although the neighborhood movement developed its own distinctive characteristics, it shared with these earlier movements a structure of grass-roots organizing and a propensity to question authority. It also shared a strong anti-corporate sentiment, one that, while reinforced by professional organizers, was already thriving in many neighborhoods. Events of the 1950s and 1960s laid the groundwork for the neighborhood movement both locally and nationally and created a good deal of anti-government as well as anti-corporate sentiment.[15]

Politics of Redevelopment

In 1968, responding to the city of Chicago's just released Comprehensive Plan, Hal Baron, research director for the Chicago Urban League, commented that planners rarely stop to ask, "Who is sacrificing what for whom?"[16] When all the pieces of planned development in Chicago are put together, the patterns of sacrifice and loss stand in sharp contrast to the patterns of growth, development, and gain. The groups hurt or slated to be hurt by the planned development projects of the 1950s and 1960s, however, increasingly resisted developments whose outcome would be the destruction or neglect of large segments of their communities.

In Chicago, as in urban centers around the United States, the explosion of citizen activism during this period was frequently a response to the intrusion into poor and working-class communities of new developments. Although financed through urban renewal programs, these projects offered few direct advantages to the residents and usually posed the threat of their displacement.

In the early Sixties, the city realized it had to have a campus, a Chicago branch of the University of Illinois. . . . There were several excellent areas to choose from, where people were not living: a railroad site, an industrial island near the river, an airport used by businessmen, a park, a golf course. But there was no give. The mayor looked for advice. One of his advisers suggested our neighborhood as the ideal site for the campus. . . . What shocked us was the amount of land they decided to take. They were out to demolish the entire community. . . . Though we called the mayor our enemy, we didn't know he was serving others.[17]

Florence Scala, the woman who made this statement, led a group of her neighbors, the Harrison-Halsted Community Group, in opposition to the planned destruction of their neighborhood for the new college campus. They picketed city hall and sat in at Mayor Daley's office. While they lost the battle to save their homes from being torn down, Scala and her neighbors began the movement of a whole new generation of women into leadership roles in community organizations in Chicago.[18]

When the University of Chicago's plans to expand its campus south into neighboring Woodlawn were revealed, black ministers and residents of that community came together to fight the expansion and The Woodlawn Organization was born.[19] The Northwest Community Organization was founded primarily in response to the city's designation of a large section of East Humboldt Park as a "conservation area," thus setting the stage for its future destruction.[20] The Citizens Action Program (CAP) played a major role in organizing community resistance to the Crosstown Expressway, a highway proposed to facilitate commerce and suburban commuters. According to CAP, the 22.5-mile highway would have destroyed 4,558 housing units, displacing over 14,000 persons on both the Northwest and Southwest Sides of the city.[21]

These expressions of resistance to redevelopment plans were by no means an altogether spontaneous response from the grassroots. TWO, NCO, and CAP were all founded with the assistance of organizers from Saul Alinsky's training school, the Industrial Areas Foundation, and all waged their battles with the assistance of these organizers. But the organizers were obviously tapping into feelings held by Chicagoans and held as well by low-and moderate-income families all over the country. The efforts of Chicago residents were paralleled by groups in other cities engaged in similar struggles against urban renewal or other development projects. Herbert Gans, for example, documented the losing battle of Boston's West End community, where old tenement housing for the Italian community is gone, replaced by a high-rise condominium village for middle-class professionals.[22] In San Francisco, some of the 4,000 residents who were to be displaced from their homes for a new municipal center initiated a series of lawsuits that delayed construction for years, although ultimately the center was built.[23]

Community groups, again across the nation as well as in Chicago, grew increasingly aware of the ways in which their neighborhoods paid the costs for the unbridled growth of the private sector and the prerogatives exercised by dominant institutional actors. Poor and working-class communities were neglected, if not altogether destroyed, as resources were focused on downtown commercial development, on the expansion of institutions serving the middle class, or on luxury waterfront housing. Particularly aggravating to many community leaders was the growing realization that public resources being used for the benefit of private capital reduced funds available for traditional areas of public expenditure such as education, housing, and mass transportation.

Florence Scala recently said, "What we did with the Harrison-Halsted group helped to change the political process. . . . There's a little bit more responsibility in the cities today. A *little* bit more."[24] Although it may not be due to a new sense of responsibility on the part of city officials as Scala seems to believe, others too have suggested that neighborhood activism during the 1960s and 1970s did undermine the local pro-growth coalitions. According to John Mollenkopf, "Neighborhood activism ended large-scale clearance projects, drastically revised traditional planning practices by creating citizen review and participation procedures, and created a new policy emphasis on preservation and rehabilitation."[25]

Manuel Castells has articulated a theory that formalizes the inchoate statements of thousands of community residents.[26] Since meeting essential needs is generally unprofitable to the private sector, the state must assume the role of meeting those needs. Yet the limited resources of the state are frequently targeted to assist private developers or middle-class constituencies, leaving little or nothing for the vast majority of citizens, who cannot secure the fulfillment of their needs through purchase in the private market. They must rely on housing subsidies and public schools, transportation, and recreation programs. But, as more state funds go to supplement the projects of private capital, fewer state funds are available for public services in the neighborhoods. Although urban renewal funds dried up in the 1970s and no new large-scale government-funded projects threatened neighborhoods, the unequal distribution of public burdens continued. People grew increasingly aware of this and willing to join with each other to fight the inequities.

For example, a major component of organized citizen protest against electric utility companies in the 1970s revolved around a pricing system that charged small users more per kilowatt hour than large corporate users. Small users—for example, those renting one or two rooms as a residence—often had trouble paying for the basic necessities, while large users, such as corporations with hundreds of thousands of square feet to light and heat, were paying so little per kilowatt hour they had no incentive to conserve energy. Senior citizens organizations, churches, lower-income blacks and whites, neighborhood groups, and environmentalists joined together in Chicago to protest the injustice and waste in such a system.

Similarly, a major struggle that engaged the Citizens Action Program was the unfair property tax assessment process. While homeowners paid their taxes on time, large corporations routinely ignored their assessments and then later had their lawyers arrange settlements in court, agreeing to pay a fraction of what they owed. One study showed that only 60 percent of corporate property taxes were collected in 1978, costing the Chicago schools about $75 million in that one year. "If businesses had been paying their taxes over the years, there might be no financial crisis in the schools," researcher David Moberg concluded.[27]

Coalitions built around energy or tax inequities are examples of the special-issue organizing that was able to cut across traditional class, race, and neighborhood lines in the 1970s. People could work together on issues like these without having to live together.

The perception that neighborhoods are either ignored or exploited by powerful interests has been a factor in the development of many community groups. In the 1960s, urban renewal projects, school desegregation policies, and classroom overcrowding were all equated with neighborhood destruction; in the 1970s, community disinvestment policies and the Crosstown Expressway were objects of attack by those who sought to save neighborhoods; and in the 1980s the locations of subsidized housing units and the nature of neighborhood economic development plans are debated in terms of neighborhood survival. James Greer concluded his study of urban planning in Chicago with the observation that urban planners have been "insulated from . . . , in fact, largely ignorant of . . . neighborhood activists and demands."[28] Many community groups developed a harsher assessment of motivations for decisions and believe that planners, both public and private, are willing to sacrifice some neighborhoods for the benefit of other neighborhoods or the interests of more privileged groups.

Father Francis X. Lawlor, a Catholic priest from the city's Southwest Side who organized a string of block clubs in the 1960s to resist the movement of blacks into white neighborhoods along the ghetto boundary, gave a succinct summary of how he viewed the city's development intentions in 1973:

> The powers that be have decided that the part of the city that counts is the lakefront, and they are determined to save it. The big realtors, the downtown politicians, the business community . . . are united in this situation. To them the part of Chicago that matters is the high rises of Lake Shore Drive, the high income districts in and around the Loop, and the string of institutions on the South Side running from Michael Reese Hospital to the University of Chicago. The rest of the city? Let that go to the swiftest and the strongest, be he black or blue-collar white. Provided, of course, that their squabbles do not spill over into the enclave of civilization and high property values that the smart money boys have decided to save.[29]

While Lawlor and his block clubs represented some of the most conservative, frequently racist, white ethnic enclaves in the city, his analysis could well have been presented by community leaders in Woodlawn or Pilsen or might just as well have come from a classroom lecture to organizers in training at the Industrial Areas Foundation. Despite the fact that many community leaders and organizations in the 1960s and 1970s knew their problems were due to the neglect or avarice of city officials and planners or private developers, there was usually little they could do about it.

A City of Neighborhoods

Chicago neighborhoods are defined for their residents by boundaries clearly marked in the collective consciousness; protecting those boundaries has been a major concern of many community groups in recent years.[30] As indicated earlier, at one time these neighborhoods were homes to specific ethnic groups. Some still are, but divisions among white ethnic groups have decreased in importance since the 1960s. Neighborhoods now are divided into black and white, with the emergence in recent years of more and larger Hispanic neighborhoods as well. Hispanic neighborhoods have often functioned as a kind of buffer zone between black and white residential areas. "[Hispanics have] been the first new neighbors to enter traditionally all white ethnic communities and the last to leave the same addresses as the neighborhoods resegregated a few years later to all black. During the interim, whites have treated them like para-blacks, and bitter blacks have considered them some sort of whites."[31]

Given the emphasis on the small local territory, the homogeneity of most Chicago neighborhoods, and the fact that community organization boundaries parallel neighborhood boundaries, it is not surprising that most of the groups that emerged in the 1960s and early 1970s were narrow in focus and homogeneous in membership. Only an exceedingly modest agenda could be successful under such circumstances.

Along with a growing awareness of the way in which urban politics was being played, the limits of traditional organizational structures became obvious. New organizing strategies developed and many groups shifted their concerns from purely local issues to analyses of the distribution of public resources on a broader scale. As they did so, they took on larger and stronger targets and mobilized larger and broader-based constituencies to wage their battles. Corporate and government bodies were increasingly likely to be confronted by large-scale community organizations, serving as umbrellas for numerous neighborhood-based groups. Groups realized that only in this way would they be able to take on issues that could have an effective impact on the future of their communities.

Two significant attempts to create broad-based coalitions of organizations in the 1970s were the previously mentioned Citizens Action Program and the Metropolitan Area Housing Alliance (MAHA). Both, however, were relatively short-lived. In the late 1970s and 1980s, attempts at creating larger coalition structures have been more successful in terms of longevity and suggest new possibilities for citizens' influence on policymakers. The Southwest Parish and Neighborhood Federation, the Northwest Neighborhood Federation, the United Neighborhood Organization, and the Illinois Public Action Council are all examples of such efforts.

The Disinvestment Campaign

The campaign to reverse the behavior of Chicago's lending institutions stands out as one issue of the 1970s that resulted in a victory for the neighborhoods while at the same time bringing together residents from different backgrounds and different parts of the city. As early as 1973, community leaders on the South Side of the city became aware of the difficulties people in their neighborhoods were experiencing in securing home improvement loans; relatives and friends were also finding it almost impossible to secure conventional mortgages to purchase homes in the area. The dimensions of the problem shifted quickly from the realm of the personal to that of a public issue when people became aware of just how widespread this situation was.

Local banks and savings and loan institutions were depositories for millions of neighborhood residents' dollars, yet these same institutions refused to lend that money back to the community. The Citizens Action Program took on the issue of redlining. Many of CAP's white members had previously lived in neighborhoods that had experienced racial change. Many now lived in communities that clung precariously to economic and racial stability. It was clear to these residents what the consequences would be if there were no infusion of economic resources into a community with an aging housing stock.

Community reinvestment grew as one of CAP's major themes. By 1975, the year of CAP's last annual convention, it was a key issue. That convention was attended by 2,500 delegates representing 60 affiliated community groups, civic organizations, and senior citizen groups. For CAP the fight to end redlining was part of an overall strategy to combat neighborhood deterioration. In the words of CAP's former research director, Henry Scheff, the group wanted "better city services; adequate mortgage, home improvement, and business loans; [an end to] block busting and panic peddling; [prevention of] fast foreclosures and other FHA abuses; and [an end to] the downtown favoritism of public works investments, to get better streets, parks, and police protection for the less affluent neighborhoods." [32]

CAP organizers and leaders, as well as many members of these white communities, soon learned that redlining and disinvestment by financial institutions and insurance companies was the treatment minority communities had been subjected to for years.[33] They further began to understand the institutional and political forces behind deterioration; many were able to refine their analysis and shift the blame for deterioration from "the blacks" to banks, corporate interests, and the political machine. This issue clearly had the potential for cross-racial alliances. Indeed, Scheff argues that the fight against neighborhood deterioration brought blacks and whites together for the first time in Chicago.[34] Each group, operating in its own self-interest, recognized that they were hurt by FHA abuses, realtor panic peddling, and financial disinvestment.

The strategy adopted by CAP to fight the lending institutions was called "greenlining": neighborhood residents pledged to invest their savings only in banks that agreed to reinvest in the neighborhoods. At the time of the 1975 convention, $120 million in greenlining pledges were held by CAP and three financial institutions had already signed reinvestment contracts.[35]

Simultaneously, another citywide organization, the Metropolitan Area Housing Alliance, a coalition of groups concerned with housing issues, was lobbying at both state and federal levels for legislation to end redlining abuse. As a result of the combined pressures of these two powerful Chicago-based coalitions, Illinois—along with a number of other states—passed laws prohibiting redlining and mandating tighter disclosure of mortgage lending by zip code.

At the federal level, as noted earlier, the Home Mortgage Disclosure Act (HMDA) was passed in 1975 and the Community Reinvestment Act in 1977. The latter legislation, largely a result of pressure from National People's Action (NPA), a network of community groups from around the country put together by MAHA organizers, was intended to make mortgage money available to qualified borrowers regardless of where they lived.

Despite all this legislative progress, NPA argues that the laws have not worked. In a study released in 1984, the National Training and Information Center (NTIC), the research arm of NPA, analyzed 1982 data obtained through the Home Mortgage Disclosure Act. The results of this study have already been discussed in Chapter 4. In sum, over three-fourths of the total housing loans within the metropolitan area were found to be going to the suburbs. Of the money loaned for home purchase and improvement in Chicago, 29 percent went to only three lakefront communities.[36]

In response to this persisting pattern of disinvestment, the Woodstock Institute, a small civic association focused on housing research and policy, brought together about 35 community groups active in redevelopment. They formed a coalition called the Chicago Reinvestment Alliance (CRA) and began to pressure banks to invest additional funds in the neighborhoods. By May of 1984, three major Chicago financial institutions—Harris Trust and Savings Bank, First National Bank of Chicago, and the Northern Trust—had negotiated agreements with the Alliance. In each case, the lending institution had an application before the Federal Reserve Board to either purchase another bank, be purchased by another bank, or establish a bank holding company. Thus the Alliance was able to take advantage of the legislated period for public comment. According to Gale Cincotta, executive director of NPA, this meant the threat of a challenge was present;[37] that threat was all the groups needed. Each lending institution pledged to make substantial amounts of loan money available at favorable rates for residential and commercial projects. Specifically, a total of $173 million over a five-year period was pledged to the communities. The preparation of project proposals is the responsibility of community organizations working through two "packaging agents," the Chicago Association of

Neighborhood Development Organizations (CANDO) and the Chicago Rehab Network. Final review is by a board consisting of bank officials and neighborhood representatives.

The Chicago Reinvestment Alliance is a coalition of housing groups, community organizations, and public interest research groups. The loan package is targeted to lower-income and working-class neighborhoods, both black and white. If the groups involved are able to continue functioning in concert, continually monitoring lending practices, and hammering out agreements with financial institutions, a regular flow of funds into the neighborhoods may continue.

This is a Chicago success story, a victory for poor and working-class people that resulted from the combined efforts of black and white community groups that were able to reach out not only to each other but to other groups around the country. But the effort was a decade long and involved huge amounts of volunteer time and commitment as well as staff efforts and research. Such herculean campaigns can hardly be undertaken by local groups on a regular basis.

The Citizens Action Program and Beyond

The Citizens Action Program, although relatively short-lived, was a landmark attempt to create a broad-based coalition. It represented Alinsky's major effort to organize large numbers of middle-class and working-class residents. It was the first successful attempt to build a citywide coalition of organizations representing both different geographical areas and different racial and ethnic constituencies. It also included a sizeable number of senior citizens organizations under its umbrella.

CAP began in 1969 as the Campaign Against Pollution during a summer when a weather inversion caused a dangerous cloud of pollution to hang over the city for days. A diverse group of citizens—"white collar, blue collar, ecology advocates, scientists, and a few young radicals"[38]— came together to express their concern over this pollution by launching an effort to block Commonwealth Edison's request for a rate hike, insist that the utility burn low-sulphur coal, and demand that the city pass an air pollution ordinance. The group, with the aid of Alinsky organizers, achieved success with all three goals and decided to change its name to Citizens Action Program and move on to other issues.

For the next five years CAP was a major force for drawing public attention to a series of key citizens' issues, including corporate tax underassessments, construction of the Crosstown Expressway, nuclear power plant expansion, and insurance company redlining, as well as disinvestment. At its peak CAP drew thousands to rallies and hundreds to public hearings. The focus on neighborhood deterioration helped expand CAP's white, middle-class constituency to one that included working-class white ethnics, blacks, and Hispanics.

CAP succeeded in part by using Alinsky's church-based approach to organizing. Parish priests and leaders were key actors in the organization. The first co-chairpersons of CAP were Paul Booth, a founder of Students for a Democratic Society and later a union organizer with AFSCME, and Leonard Dubi, a young activist priest from a Northwest Side parish.

CAP and its victories were an inspiration to groups around the country. But CAP, started in 1969, held its last annual convention in 1975. Several factors accounted for CAP's short life. "Almost all of CAP's success was based on smoke and mirrors," Paul Booth said, reflecting on CAP's demise. "There was almost no power. Just a scruffy bunch of a few hundred people."[39] And conflicts over internal control and program weakened the organization.

Despite CAP's short life, it marked a milestone in Chicago's organizing history. It succeeded in integrating political action with the concerns of daily life for hundreds of Chicago residents. And it brought different groups of people together in a shared struggle. CAP appeared to succeed in shifting white residents' anger and frustration away from blacks who threatened to move into all-white neighborhoods and toward those institutions— banks, savings and loan associations, HUD, insurance companies—that had systematically contributed to the community's deterioration through their housing practices. Through its greenlining and anti-disinvestment programs, CAP successfully refocused much of that anger.

One group that appeared to pick up where CAP left off was the Southwest Parish and Neighborhood Federation (SPNF). Founded in 1971 by organizers in the Alinsky tradition, SPNF was an attempt by church and community leaders in eight parish areas to stem the deterioration of the Southwest Side by targeting corporate and government practices. Its immediate goal was to halt the flight of white residents from the community. In its early years, this organization also used protest marches and the threat of boycotts to force banks to drop redlining practices and to curb unscrupulous realtors.[40]

In 1976, organizers from the Southwest Side joined with Northwest Side leaders to form a counterpart organization, the Northwest Neighborhood Federation. The Northwest Side, like the Southwest Side, was (and still is) a primarily white area beginning to see signs of racial change. The two groups have tackled similar issues; often they have worked together, thus bridging a major geographic division in the city. Combined the organizations claim a membership of thousands and have enjoyed enormous success in building a base. Most recently their shared target has been Harold Washington and his administration.

The first White Ethnic Convention in Chicago was held in the spring of 1984 with the theme: "Save Our Neighborhoods, Save Our City." It was co-sponsored by the Southwest Parish and Neighborhood Federation and the Northwest Neighborhood Federation, now formally joined in coalition. The events leading to this conference have deep roots in the city's history.

Despite the growing black population in Chicago in the 1950s and 1960s, the ethnic neighborhoods of Chicago's Southwest and Northwest Sides were able to remain almost exclusively white. Racial steering by realtors was widely condoned, no public housing was built in these neighborhoods, and open housing in the private market was only a dream for black families.

All this began to change in the late 1960s. Martin Luther King Jr. led a march for open housing in 1966 through that most ethnic of all Southwest Side neighborhoods, Marquette Park. As one observer noted, the issues ensured that "a conflict must take place between the two groups, each claiming what to them is their most important right—open housing for the blacks and, for the Lithuanians [a major ethnic group in Marquette Park], preservation of their ethnic heritage."[41]

The Southwest Side—that large residential section of the city south and west of the Loop—developed a reputation during these years for being parochial, resistant to social change, and racist. The community resisted the efforts of black families to move within their boundaries with every resource they were able to muster: organization, political leverage, intimidation, and ultimately violence. Yet the Southwest Side was in the path of inexorable black ghetto expansion. And, in the late 1960s, even without King's march, there would have been movement in the direction of racial change. Southwest Siders redefined their neighborhood boundaries as the black population pushed further west. But resistance was intense on every block that experienced change. Many white families moved west several times over a period of only a few years, staying just ahead of the black migration. Community residents were convinced that desegregation in the schools would lead to desegregation and ultimately resegregation of the neighborhoods; any attempt to integrate the schools was met with serious resistance.

It was during this time that Fr. Lawlor organized his block clubs to "hold the line" of racial change at Ashland Avenue, a major north-south thoroughfare. Lawlor, an extremely controversial figure, was perceived as a racist agitator by the black and white liberal communities, as a savior by some of the white ethnic residents, and as a polarizing, counterproductive force by many other residents. Lawlor's influence lasted long enough for him to be elected to the city council for one term in 1971. This surprising gesture of political independence by Southwest Siders—Lawlor had no support from the regular Democratic organization, to which he was an embarrassment—shows how deep and widespread was the political disaffection as well as the sentiments of fear and racism to which he spoke.

Despite the hostility and anger that he cultivated, Lawlor looked moderate compared to other groups operating on the Southwest Side during this period. The American Nazi party, for example, had its Chicago headquarters in the community for a while and periodically flexed its muscles with demonstrations in Marquette Park, the scene of many racial confrontations. At the same time, there were parish priests and community leaders concerned with defusing and redefining the racially tense situation; there was even one organization that hoped to promote peaceful integration; and there were thousands of residents who rejected the hate groups but felt they had no way of expressing their legitimate concerns about their communities.

It was into this cauldron that Alinsky-trained community organizers moved after the King march, working cautiously at first to gain the support of residents. The Catholic Church provided resources—space and staff—for these early organizing efforts, which were largely parish-based. The Southwest Community Congress (SCC) was one result of clergy joining together to hire organizers to help the community deal in a constructive way with its fears and anxieties. In 1968, SCC held its first congress with approximately 500 delegates representing churches, businesses, schools, and civic groups in the area. Even this start was not peaceful: several hundred people picketed the congress, objecting to SCC's liberal (that is, integrationist) orientation and to the Church's using funds in this way.[42]

The Southwest Community Congress still exists, now with an interracial membership and an explicit program to work for peaceful integration. It has not, however, been successful in recent years in capturing a following anywhere near the size of the Southwest Parish and Neighborhood Federation's. "My opinion is that the Federation is basically racist and that it plays on the fears of the people," says one of the leaders of SCC, suggesting that the Federation's large following is a direct result of appeals to racist sentiments. Much of the material publicizing the Save Our Neighborhoods/

Save Our City convention seemed to support this interpretation, including an inflammatory and controversial "Declaration of Neighborhood Independence" that accused Mayor Washington of exploiting racial antagonisms.[43]

The staff and leaders of the Federation deny that either their motivation or their appeal is based on racism. Their complaint, they say, is that Mayor Washington and previous mayors have ignored the problems of their neighborhoods. "We want to walk our streets without fear. We want to make sure our houses won't lose value . . . and we want to enjoy what we have striven so hard to achieve," said Jean Mayer, chairperson of the Federation, in her speech to the 750 delegates at the convention.[44]

The Southwest and the Northwest Federations have continued to exist, and indeed thrive, for a long time by community group standards. During this phase of Chicago's transition they represent a white working-class and middle-class constituency that feels itself to be the new minority group. As the black and Hispanic populations in Chicago grow in numbers and in political influence, many residents of white ethnic communities feel anew that they are struggling for their survival. A black mayor in city hall has been a powerful symbol of the shifts in political fortunes in this city. The fear of "losing" their community, whether to the migrating black community or to profit-seeking institutions, has been a part of daily life for 20 years. The fears were intensified with the election of a black mayor—who received support in 1983 from only 4.1 percent of the voting age population in these white ethnic wards[45]—and indeed many residents of these communities and members of these organizations have, as we shall see, defined Harold Washington as the enemy.

Hispanics and Coalitions

Until recently, attention to the growing Hispanic population had been notably absent from the major organizing efforts in Chicago. In 1979, the United Neighborhood Organization (UNO), however, established its first community group in Chicago under the direction of experienced organizers Mary Gonzales and Greg Galusso. By 1984, UNO had established chapters in four heavily Hispanic communities—Pilsen, Little Village, Back of the Yards, and Southeast Chicago—where it works through existing institutions, primarily local parishes, to build its base and its credibility. As a young organization in Chicago, UNO has just begun to venture into city-wide activities with a program aimed at getting the Chicago city colleges to work with local businesses and establish job-training programs relevant to the city's population and business needs.

One experienced UNO organizer claims that Chicago is "a hard city for coalitions": it has an extremely heterogeneous population and there are hundreds of distinct neighborhoods within dozens of communities.[46] Still there are coalitions that are bridging some of these enormous divides. The Chicago Alliance for Neighborhood Safety (CANS) is one such example. Initially funded with grants from the federal government and the Ford Foundation, CANS has worked to establish neighborhood-based crime prevention programs in nine neighborhoods. These neighborhoods are geographically dispersed and represent white, black, and Hispanic groups. In each neighborhood, CANS has worked through strong existing community organizations such as South Austin Community Council, Edgewater Community Council, Logan Square Neighborhood Association, Northwest Neighborhood Federation, Midwest Community Council, and the South Shore Commission. While this program has grown stronger since its start in 1981, it lives with the precarious organizational status of issue-oriented coalitions.[47]

Mayor Washington and the Neighborhoods

Harold Washington's election as mayor of Chicago coincided with a period in American history when urban neighborhoods were receiving fewer resources than they had in the past. During the first four years of his administration, President Reagan dismantled or curtailed many of the funds that were going to cities for job-training programs, community development, and housing.[48] The residents of Chicago neighborhoods see local economic decline and deterioration, in large part resulting from this absence of commitment to older cities at the national level. Some white Chicagoans, however, focus the blame on the black man in city hall who inherited the results of both a national administration oriented toward the corporate world and previous city administrations that made expedient short-run decisions with disastrous long-run consequences.

Interestingly enough, the new Save Our Neighborhoods/Save Our City coalition, which bills itself as championing "the cause of ethnic, middle income neighborhoods to reverse Chicago's 35 year trend of community economic decline and racial resegregation,"[49] may have found its strongest ally in Mayor Washington. The first SON/SOC convention made clear that many items on the agenda of the Federations were also on the agenda of the new administration. Linking downtown development opportunities with financial commitments to neighborhood development, for example, was an idea whose time had come from the perspective of both groups, equally concerned with strengthening the economies of neighborhoods.

Moderate-income housing has not been built in any substantial numbers in Chicago for years, as we saw in the preceding chapter. The Federations defined the resulting competition for decent housing as one of the major pressure points forcing black families out of the ghetto into formerly all-white neighborhoods. The administration defined the absence of such housing as a hardship for the working class of the city. Both groups support efforts to develop more moderate-income housing.

Home equity insurance is another area where the two have come together. The Federations hope to develop a plan modeled on suburban Oak Park's that guarantees home values in a community. Although this plan was originally designed to dispel white families' fears about declining property values when a neighborhood experiences racial change, the insurance concept could be applied to other situations as well.[50] In the fall of 1984, the Federations jointly received funding from HUD and the state of Illinois to conduct a study to determine if a guaranteed home equity insurance program could be adapted to Chicago neighborhoods. Mayor Washington went on record in support of the concept and the project and the coalition agreed to include black middle-class communities threatened with economic decline in the study area as well.

The Federations clashed with Mayor Washington during the early years of his term in office. Language and feelings were strong on both sides. But at the same time city hall and these neighborhoods began working together closely on a range of issues. If such an alliance can continue and achieve some successes it could be a significant force in bringing black and white moderate-income groups together to act upon shared interests.

Besides the white ethnic coalitions there are other groups in the city struggling over issues of justice or economic survival that any mayor will have to work with. The scattered site housing policy of the Washington administration in its first year served to alienate both friends and enemies.

As indicated in Chapter 4, little subsidized housing was built in Chicago during the 1970s, when the city was under court order to build new family housing units outside the existing ghetto. Resistance to such housing in neighborhoods was intense, and these were important voters. Yet the housing was desperately needed and the city was under great pressure to proceed with a plan. This was a political hot potato passed from Daley to Bilandic to Byrne to Washington.

A number of Chicago communities have for years been heterogeneous both ethnically and economically. Several of these, such as Uptown, Edgewater, and Logan Square, have accepted subsidized housing units, indeed have often welcomed them as filling a serious need for the residents of their areas. However, these several neighborhoods, because they provided the path of least resistance politically, tended to receive a disproportionate amount of such housing and some community groups began to protest. Just as the "open" white suburbs felt their willingness to accept black families might lead to ultimate resegregation, so the "open" neighborhoods feared their willingness to accept low-income families might eventuate in a serious transformation of the community resulting in loss of economic and racial balance.

A number of black communities, too, such as Garfield Park, Austin, and South Shore, have received a disproportionate number of units and are concerned about the burden this places on their local institutions and support services. Thirty-nine of the 77 communities in Chicago, however, have no public housing at all.[51]

The Chicago Housing Authority (CHA), notorious for its poor management of high-rise public housing, has also badly managed many of the scattered sites. Most troubling of all to some groups, buildings purchased by CHA for rehabilitation have sometimes sat for years, vacant and deteriorating, providing both an eyesore and a locale for criminal activities. The Washington administration's failure to deal with these issues caused it some problems. The black president of an integrated community group in Logan Square was upset when the mayor failed to appear at a meeting to hear his group's complaints about mismanagement of CHA units. His was a group that had willingly accepted scattered sites in the neighborhood. One neighborhood leader commented, "people haven't been turned off totally, but many people who worked for [Washington] here question his commitment."[52]

Not all community groups in Chicago wish to limit the number of subsidized units in their neighborhoods. Some groups, such as the Organization of the Northeast (ONE) in Uptown and Edgewater, see the need for decent, affordable housing as so great that all attempts to fill that need are welcome. While many groups believe the construction of subsidized housing will attract poor families to an area, other groups like ONE argue that the poor are already there and need the housing. "What's 'too much'?," says Joe Bute, director of ONE. "It depends on the population in a community and their needs."[53]

Throughout Chicago's history different organizations in the same geographic territory have taken different positions on issues, appealed to different constituencies, and publicly fought it out. Particularly in the more heterogeneous communities, groups that speak for the poor or ethnic minorities may have an agenda quite different from that of the middle-class groups.

The issue of subsidized housing promises to be one that will plague Chicago's city administrators for years to come. As long as the task of building housing for poor people is defined primarily as the city's job, rather than the job of the entire metropolitan region, Chicago neighborhoods will fight each other over the locations. This has been one of the most divisive issues in Chicago's recent history. Continued racial segregation and growing poverty in Chicago, the well-established practices of realtor panic peddling and block busting, and banks' disinvestment when a neighborhood's racial composition shifts, combined with the very slow pace of construction of assisted housing in the suburbs, suggest that any hopes of strong cooperative efforts to address this problem are slim.

Community Groups and the City's Future

Harold Washington demonstrated his intention to reverse the traditional procedures of government in Chicago by involving citizen and community groups more fully in the formulation and operation of city programs. During his 1983 mayoral campaign, Washington, more than any candidate in Chicago's history, drew on the input of community groups from around the city in setting his campaign goals. After his election, a broad-based team of 250 people from over 200 different public and private organizations were drawn together to prepare a transition report that would serve as the basis for a new political agenda.[54] This effort itself brought together representatives from groups—black and white, North Side, South Side, and West Side—that had seldom talked to each other in the past.

One of Washington's first efforts to develop stronger links between city hall and community organizations entailed the conversion of the Office of Neighborhoods from an information office to an advocate of local concerns. Washington's Office of Neighborhoods was to be headed by a man with good credentials among community groups and it held out the hope to neighborhoods of finally having a direct line to the mayor's office. Establishment of such an office is hardly path-breaking; in other cities offices like this have been routine for years. But many regular Democratic party alderpersons and committeepersons in Chicago saw this as a potential threat to their control over what happens in their wards. The Office of

Neighborhoods was quickly scuttled by opposition forces in city council who refused to approve its funding. Some have suggested that its establishment was merely a political maneuver, that Washington was willing to trade it away, and that it would have made little difference. Because it was never given the opportunity to function, what its role might have been remains uncertain. Washington's efforts to establish a more direct relationship with community groups, however, along with the city council majority's unwillingness to support that effort are both suggestive of what each side might have thought those changes would be.

There is a long history in Chicago of antagonism between community groups and city officials. Community organizations, especially those schooled in the Alinsky tradition, have regularly leveled personal attacks against officeholders. Although Washington demonstrated his eagerness to work more closely with communities, the city council—as long as it was dominated by Vrdolyak's allies—blocked his efforts. City planning commissioner Elizabeth Hollander—who was acting commissioner for nine months before the city council finally approved her appointment—claimed many alderpersons balked at approving planning grants to neighborhood organizations working on housing and economic development. "They're concerned we might fund community groups they don't like," she said.[55]

Despite the fact that the Office of Neighborhoods did not get off the ground, the stalemate over scattered site housing, and the recalcitrant city council, there were numerous hopeful signs during the first years of the new administration. In 1983, for the first time in Chicago's history, a neighborhood group initiated an Urban Development Action Grant for an economic development project and, with the city's support and assistance, received the funding.[56] The city also proposed the allocation of more planning grants to neighborhood groups to assist them in carrying out a variety of redevelopment projects of their own design.[57] The city and the People's Gas Company set up a $15 million low-interest loan program for energy conservation projects, to be administered by community organizations. One of the organizers of the program claimed, "If not for the Washington administration, neighborhood groups probably wouldn't have got the contract."[58]

Washington's administration, early on, took seriously the rights of citizens to have access to public information, something denied community groups under earlier mayors. The absence of access to public records—indeed, in many cases, the absence of records themselves—handicapped the work of many groups in the past. As an example, the Chicago Alliance for Neighborhood Safety fought for over two years to gain access to neighborhood crime statistics, supposedly a matter of public record.[59] The Washington administration made such information available on a routine basis and went one step further by developing a program for Affirmative Neighborhood Information designed to disseminate computerized city data on such areas as crime and housing to community groups in "a timely and understandable fashion."[60] This was indeed a break with past practice.

While there were some notable exceptions, community groups in general seemed pleased with the Washington administration's efforts. "There is a tremendous openness and accessibility that has never been there before," said one leader of a housing coalition.[61]

In addition, the Washington administration's message of change sparked some curious reactions from a city council traditionally opposed to any suggestions of political reform. One veteran community organizer claimed the political process was far more open to neighborhood groups because the regular Democrats sought to outreform the reformers. Community groups found they had access to city council members who before never recognized them.

The huge network of community organizations and special-issue groups that formed in Chicago during the years of closed machine politics is a powerful force for participatory democracy and reform in this city. But, as Len O'Conner said in his biography of Daley, "reform cannot survive in a contest with greed, unless it enjoys the absolute backing of the majority of the citizens. And Chicagoans are so conditioned to seeing the reformers fail, sooner or later, that they stand on the sidelines until the battle is over—when life goes on as usual."[62]

In the 1980s there seem to be fewer people on the sidelines and more engaged in the struggle for reform in this town. With additional resources and encouragement these groups could play a major role in building an alternative Chicago where life will go on, but not quite as usual.

6

Redevelopment Chicago Style

In a city where few new buildings had been started before him,
the sky was pierced again and again by new skyscrapers, each
bigger and more gleaming than the last.
David Halberstam[1]

Slum clearance hasn't improved it. They have substituted a more
sanitary type of squalor.
Barry Byrne[2]

Chicagoans feel a strong sense of pride in their built environment, and for
a number of reasons their city does occupy a unique place in the history of
urban design and city planning. This is the city of Louis Sullivan's inno-
vations in commercial architecture, some of Frank Lloyd Wright's most
striking residences, and Daniel H. Burnham's famous Plan of Chicago.
Yet a strong case can be made that the chief architect of contemporary
Chicago's physical environment was neither a planner nor a professional
designer, but rather the late mayor, Richard J. Daley.

During Daley's 21-year term as mayor, from 1955 to 1976, major infrastructural developments such as O'Hare Airport, the city's network of expressways, and an expanded mass transit system were constructed, private
investment in the Loop and adjoining residential neighborhoods mushroomed—following a virtual hiatus of two decades—and, perhaps most
significantly, a mutually satisfactory alliance of municipal officials, business leaders, and city planners was forged. The shared assumption of the
participants in this alliance was that the maintenance of Chicago as an
economic power among American cities turned on the reorganization of its
physical environment.

The initial portions of this chapter examine the conditions that contributed to the creation of this alliance, some of the documents and projects
by which this alliance placed its stamp on Chicago, the relationships under-
pinning planning and redevelopment in Chicago, and the physical conse-

quences of the city's postwar redevelopment. However, in the last decade the working relationships that linked municipal chief executive, business leaders, and city planners have been attenuated, and as a consequence redevelopment planning is now a less predictable process. Furthermore, the economic assumptions of the earlier redevelopment alliance have been attacked from a number of directions. This new planning environment is explored in the concluding sections of the chapter, which look in detail at the city's long-standing North Loop redevelopment project and review planning/economic development initiatives of the Washington administration.

The Reorganization of Space in
Post-World War II Chicago

The Chicago whose explosive growth in the 50 years framed by the Great Fire and the onset of the Depression variously fed the imaginations and assaulted the sensibilities of observers the world over was a classic product of the industrial age. Although food production was its first great industry, by the beginning of the twentieth century the manufacture of machinery and farm implements and the fabrication of steel were also among Chicago's economic bulwarks. The variety and scale of its productive activities were, of course, enhanced by its dominant place in the national rail system, which had developed in the same period. The spatial requirements of the city's manufacturing and railroad facilities combined to produce a sprawling core area, whose expansion was so rapid as to render obsolete some residential neighborhoods in little more than a generation from their founding.

In most respects this exploding Chicago was not a physically pleasant community, and by the turn of the century business and civic leaders began to take action. Their concerns were most dramatically registered through the Commercial Club's sponsorship of the Plan of Chicago in 1909.[3] In the ensuing years a concerted drive resulted in the city's reclaiming the lakefront from industry via a network of parks, the location of several cultural edifices in Grant Park east of the Loop, and the consolidation of a municipal park system. Following the Second World War—and accompanied by several signs that the city's great burst of growth was spent—the planning agenda shifted from civic beautification to economic growth. As described in Chapter 2, manufacturing employment in Chicago began to decline immediately following the cessation of hostilities. Furthermore, the railroads' loss of passengers to the automobile and airplane and loss of freight to the trucking industry did not bode well for Chicago. In each instance, jobs were lost by the city and large tracts of abandoned factories, warehouses, and railhead littered the vicinity of the downtown. The physical decay identified with such districts and their proximity to the Loop were sufficient in themselves to trouble local leaders. Yet the direct impact on the Loop of railroad decline was mitigated by several factors that allowed the city to retain a substantial share of the national convention and tourism trade.[4] The building of a huge exposition hall, McCormick Place, promoted Chicago as a location for trade shows and conventions, regardless of how one traveled to the city. Additionally, the construction of O'Hare Airport sustained the city as a major junction for travelers, and, of course, Chicago's central geographic location placed it well for individuals traveling by automobile.

More directly discouraging for downtown businesses were trends in retail trade. In 1948 stores in the Loop accounted for 13 percent of the entire metropolitan area's retail sales, but during the next 15 years not only did their share of metropolitan sales decline but their absolute volume of sales diminished as well.[5] During this time the city's population began to decrease. With white middle-class families representing the bulk of the population loss, suburban towns grew dramatically, and dozens of shopping complexes were erected on the periphery of the city and in outlying suburbs. As we shall see, firms with large investments in Loop retailing such as Marshall Field and Company have played an important role in promoting downtown redevelopment in Chicago.

A final component of the organization of space in central Chicago that was critical in establishing the context for downtown rebuilding was not so clearly tied to immediate economic changes, but was especially visible to Chicago's political, business, and civic leaders. This was physical dilapidation on the city's near South Side. Running south from Roosevelt Road and from Lake Michigan west to State Street was the upper edge of Chicago's Black Belt. Its northernmost portion had been the point of arrival for many of the city's immigrant southern blacks since the First World War. Not only did this area include some of the city's oldest residential blocks, but its history of racial segregation had also resulted in horrific overcrowding. The wear and tear on residential quarters, which were often haphazardly converted single-family homes in the first place, had, over a generation, produced some of the worst slum housing in the city. In addition, much of the northern part of this area was occupied by the sort of residential-manufacturing-warehousing mixture of land uses that was anathema to professional planners and civic leaders. In short, the Loop was perceived to be at the edge of a threatening sea of residential blight.

The Environmental Requisites of a New Central Chicago

During the first decade following World War II business leaders and municipal officials of big cities across the country sounded the alarm in behalf of urban redevelopment.[6] Their fascination with the eradication of physical blight, per se, in contrast to examination of the underlying processes producing blight, suggests that their comprehension of just what was occurring to their cities was not thoroughgoing. The call for redevelopment was likewise heard in Chicago; nonetheless, there were clear signs during this period that Chicago had not begun an unremitting cycle of economic decline and physical deterioration. The city was becoming the leading convention site in the country, favored by its location, transportation accessibility, a variety of facilities for meetings and trade shows, and substantial hotel accommodations. Furthermore, Chicago's growth as an industrial center had also made it a center for corporate headquarters. In 1957 the Chicago area housed the central offices of 54 Fortune 500 firms, a number that was exceeded only by New York and that more than doubled the number of headquarters in any other U.S. city. In addition, the banks, law firms, accountants' offices, and media professionals servicing the management of these corporations accounted for an increasing share of the downtown work force.[7] Chicago has a very fixed image of itself as a blue-collar city of "broad shoulders," but as these developments suggest, very soon after the Second World War the city's economic evolution was working to transform its occupational structure, and soon enough its physical structure.

Fitful efforts to plan a new Chicago began in the mid-1940s, when several downtown business leaders and a planning-oriented civic group, the Metropolitan Housing and Planning Council, began to explore the possibility of rebuilding portions of the central city.[8] Their efforts led to identifying areas of prime redevelopment potential, including the near South Side, and the Illinois state legislature's enactment in 1947 of the Blighted Areas Redevelopment Act. This legislation closely anticipated the provisions of the U.S. Housing Act of 1949. Subsequently, the city and two major South Side institutions, Michael Reese Hospital and the Illinois Institute of Technology (IIT), implemented the demolition and reconstruction of a large area south of the Loop and bounding their respective facilities. Investment dollars were provided by the New York Life Insurance Company, and the ultimate result was two huge, middle-income high-rise residential developments, Lake Meadows and Prairie Shores. These were classic examples of early postwar urban renewal. Glass and concrete towers arranged in a park setting, only their architectural details and more ample facilities distinguish them from public housing projects of the same era. Their intent was also very much of the time: a large, decayed tract of dwellings was eliminated; two institutions of metropolitan prominence "anchored" their sites. Their success in attracting tenants served to demonstrate the previously untested premise that congenial near-downtown residential quarters could prove popular among the city's middle-income, professional and managerial population, a group whose place in the central area work force would become increasingly important.

The aborted Fort Dearborn project of the same period, however, indicated the uncertain nature of Chicago's initial redevelopment efforts. In 1949 a leading local real estate manager and developer, Arthur Rubloff, proposed a massive, mixed-use complex on the city's near North Side just across the Chicago River from the Loop. Emulating the premises of the South Side redevelopment model, Rubloff sought the erection of a new government center, including federal, state, and county offices in addition to a new city hall, as the anchor for surrounding residential and commercial structures. His site, overlooking the river and within easy walking range of the northern end of the traditional downtown center of Chicago, was auspicious. Furthermore, given careful site drawing there seemed little question that the Fort Dearborn project could qualify for federal urban renewal funding. But unlike Lake Meadows, which was a largely residential project flanked by institutions already in place, Rubloff's development would entail a substantial relocation of local government facilities. This move promised to be costly and was opposed by many attorneys, whose offices were near the existing city/county complex. Finally, important South Loop retailers, among them Carson, Pirie, Scott, apparently feared that this project would favor competitors such as Marshall Field, which was located nearer the proposed site. Thus, Rubloff's effort to ensure the success of his plan as a real estate venture elicited political resistance from downtown interests of considerable economic and political import. Faced with this opposition to the Rubloff plan, Mayor Daley announced that municipal offices were best left in their present location. Other government officials and agencies followed suit, and with only a huge residential project in the works, Rubloff was unable to obtain financial backing for his venture.[9]

Aside from the questionable proposition that development in one portion of central Chicago should be focused, in part, by drawing institutions and tenants from another part of the core area, the extensive political infighting that greeted Rubloff's Fort Dearborn plan resulted from real uncertainty among business leaders regarding the future of the Loop. Indeed, for many retailers whose primary competitive efforts had been directed at wresting as many customers as possible from local peers, the prospect of downtown cooperation in meeting an external threat must have seemed extraordinary. Yet by the mid-1950s a new, downtown-oriented civic organization had been founded, the Chicago Central Area Committee (CCAC), which drew its members from most of the leading corporations operating in and around the Loop. The collective perspective of this group was well served when the city's Department of City Planning released its "Development Plan for the Central Area of Chicago" in 1958.[10] Although produced by a city agency, this document clearly reflects a new vision for the city emanating from the headquarters of Chicago's major corporations. Indeed, the CCAC is listed first among the private groups consulted by the planning department in preparing this report. By reviewing its contents we can identify with some precision the main dimensions of the new Chicago to be promoted jointly by the city government and leading private enterprises.

The Development Plan devotes itself exclusively to the physical restructuring of downtown Chicago—an orientation not at all unusual among city planning documents of the late 1950s—and is quite direct in its preference for a shift in activities and land uses away from the sort that had typified Chicago's core. For instance, the city's railway facilities, once the lifeline of its economic dynamism, are now viewed as a threat to their surroundings: "The present railroad terminals on the South Side, which were constructed more than fifty years ago, have contributed to the growth of blight, and decreased property values in adjacent areas."[11] The heart of this plan's recommendations is the concentration of office development in a dense core. A complex expressway network is to link this core with surrounding areas, while an array of garages on the periphery of the downtown is to accommodate the automobiles used to drive in and out of the Loop. Certain physical design improvements such as outdoor plazas, beautification of the riverfront, and the construction of a downtown subway system are also recommended. The particular facilities specified by the document—a new civic center, a transportation center, and a University of Illinois campus—are all congenial with a downtown given over to management, finance, retailing, and services. Finally, there is discussion of near-downtown housing, eventually enough on the South and North Sides to provide residences for 50,000 families. Not only did this housing, as well as the university campus, imply the absorption of substantial space then given over to other uses, but the creation of a series of new residential communities would hardly be congenial with adjoining industry.

In short, Chicago's first downtown planning document in the post-World War II era posited a substantial shift in central area economic functions, general activity patterns, and land use. Its vision of the Chicago to come is, to use a latter-day term, strikingly post-industrial. The fabrication of products is largely absent from the urban core, and the provision of residences for downtown professional and managerial workers is quite complementary with economic and lifestyle trends that indeed came to fruition in the next generation. Furthermore, a substantial proportion of the particular projects recommended in this document have been completed. Thus, it seems safe to conclude that the 1958 Development Plan represents an emergent consensus among governmental officials and business leaders regarding the future of Chicago and that an era of successful collaboration in fulfilling its prescriptions followed in its wake.

The Institutional Arrangement of Redevelopment in Chicago

Two features of these early postwar redevelopment efforts continued to characterize redevelopment planning and implementation throughout the Daley administration. The first was the primacy of private influence in generating models of Chicago's future. Quite routinely, representatives of leading Loop corporations and the organizations that speak for these firms collectively were consulted first when municipal officials considered planning and redevelopment issues. We have already noted evidence of this tendency in the 1958 Development Plan, and in succeeding years this dynamic of business-municipal cooperation became, if anything, more established.[12] Second, the city government's planning and redevelopment operations throughout this period were remarkably fragmented. Various components of the city's redevelopment activities were apportioned to separate agencies, and particular initiatives often seem to have been carried out with little reference to one another. This is in considerable contrast to the practice of other cities such as New York, Boston, and San Francisco, where planning and redevelopment were consolidated under the aegis of redevelopment "czars" Robert Moses, Edward Logue, and Justin Herman, respectively.[13] Although the consequences of this more centralized arrangement have been much criticized, the Chicago record is none too favorable either. In effect, the absence of coordinated agency action resulted in an overall "shape" to Chicago redevelopment that was arrived at for the most part in Mayor Daley's office, on the basis of his consultations with but a few trusted advisers.[14]

Concern with the maintenance of the Loop and its environs as a safe and environmentally congenial locale for business activities, cultural institutions, and affluent residents was central to the recommendations made by the 1958 Development Plan. In the next decade and a half, the city's formal planning for the downtown area was turned over to the CCAC. Burnham's 1909 Plan of Chicago, itself privately sponsored though later endorsed by the city council, had not been revised or superseded in the subsequent half-century. Indeed, with the exception of a residential survey done in the 1940s and a flurry of studies required to qualify for urban renewal funds, the city's planning activities were moribund until the production of the 1958 Development Plan. Then, with a new Department of City Planning created under the direction of Ira J. Bach, the city proceeded in the 1960s to draw up a comprehensive plan. Its overall agenda was described in reports released in 1964 and 1966; these were followed by a series of sixteen "development area" studies focusing on particular locales within the city.

The last of these local studies was entitled "Chicago 21: A Plan for the Central Area Communities," and it discussed the Loop and the adjoining near North, West, and South Sides.[15] Remarkably enough, it was published not by the city planning department, but by the CCAC. Its provisions were congruent with the 1958 Development Plan: Loop beautification, riverside and lakefront improvement, and the erection of near-downtown residential districts.[16] However, the "central area" covered by this document included some predominantly residential, working-class neighborhoods on the fringe of Chicago's core area. The prospects of redevelopment for middle-class residents spawned objections from these blue-collar neighborhoods. Though physically decayed, areas such as East Humboldt Park and Pilsen sport some strong local organizations, and their leaders contended that their neighborhoods were viable communities and, more generally, that the city's continued demolition of central area low-cost housing was not in the interest of the incumbent residents of such locales.[17] Far less controversial—and very dear to the hearts of State Street merchants— was the Chicago 21 document's recommendation of a State Street pedestrian mall running from Wacker Drive to the Congress Parkway.

A decade following the release of the Chicago 21 plan, an updated central area plan was released, this time jointly, by the city and the CCAC. Its goals are quite consistent with its 1958 and 1973 predecessors and also once more reflective of what city planning commissioner Elizabeth Hollander terms Chicago's "unusual private role for planning."[18] These are, specifically, to support and encourage economic growth, to provide a high-quality urban environment, to provide for supporting and enriching land uses, and to provide for linkages between major activities.[19] It is also a document given over exclusively to physical planning considerations, and it bears noting that its very vision of the future Chicago originated in the city's private sector. Just as was the case with the 1958 and 1973 central area plans, design consultation and graphic presentations were the work not of the city planning department, but of the Chicago-based architectural firm Skidmore, Owings and Merrill.

It is equally evident that in addition to the privatistic substance of down-town planning and redevelopment in Chicago, decision-making mechanisms have been decidedly weighted in the direction of corporate and other mobilized private influence. For instance, Arnold Hirsch in his study of early redevelopment efforts in Chicago, *Making the Second Ghetto*, identifies the crucial role played by two individuals, Milton C. Mumford and Holman D. Pettibone, executives with Marshall Field and Chicago Title and Trust, respectively, in promoting the state enabling legislation and initial redevelopment projects sponsored by the city.[20] Mumford and Pettibone, as authors of the state redevelopment statutes, sponsors of downtown land use studies via the Metropolitan Housing and Planning Council, and intermediaries between institutional redevelopment sponsors and investors, established the redevelopment process in Chicago.

During the same period state legislation was approved that allowed private redevelopment at the neighborhood level in Chicago. In this case, private redevelopment corporations could exercise eminent domain within renewal sites if owners of 60 percent of the site's area agreed to sell. This specifically allowed the University of Chicago-sponsored South East Chicago Commission (SECC) to proceed with redevelopment of the Hyde Park neighborhood.[21]

This decision-making pattern, by which a few leading institutions and their representatives consistently define the substantive agenda for redevelopment, and nearly as frequently exercise direct control over planning efforts and the execution of projects, has been fundamentally based on the close personal contacts between business leaders and Chicago chief executives. In an interview in 1978, John H. Perkins, then head of Chicago's largest bank, Continental Illinois Bank and Trust Company, contended that business-government cooperation in Chicago ought to be emulated in other cities.[22] In the course of this discussion, he indicated that frequent informal meetings with Chicago mayors Bilandic and Daley defined his sense of this cooperation. Two years later, real estate developer Arthur Rubloff characterized his early participation in the controversial North Loop redevelopment project in this fashion: "I was led to believe under Mayor Daley that I was going to be the developer of this project."[23] In this instance Mayor Daley personally asked Rubloff to begin project plans and negotiations with potential project participants—and indeed independently of city planning and redevelopment agencies. Similarly, when Sears, Roebuck and Company executives determined that construction of their new headquarters in the West Loop necessitated the closing off of a city street, chairman of the board Gordon Metcalfe simply approached Mayor Daley and the transfer of the thoroughfare to the firm was accomplished.[24]

One might infer from these examples that Daley was a pawn of the business community and at the same time that he exercised total control of the city's planning bureaucrats. By considering the institutional fragmentation of planning and redevelopment in Chicago we can identify evidence of a somewhat different decision-making relationship. By breaking up the planning and redevelopment functions into a number of separate, specialized units, Daley channeled the energies of most city planners in the direction of rather narrowly gauged project design and management. The planners who directed these staffs, unlike their subordinates, had access to Mayor Daley. However, these men—Ira Bach, James Downs, Phil Doyle, and Lewis Hill—took a view of planning and redevelopment quite congruent with the mayor's and the business elite's. Thus, a fragmented planning apparatus, directed by a nucleus of Daley aides, executed the city's privatistic redevelopment program.

The institutional fragmentation of city planning and redevelopment in Chicago has deep roots, which can be traced to the very genesis of city planning in the city, the Burnham Plan of 1909. This document, whose vision of a monumental arrangement of urban space, impressive civic edifices, and regional integration was to influence city planning across the country, was initially sponsored by a private group, the Commercial Club.[25] In addition, a group of civic leaders was appointed to promote the city government's endorsement of the Burnham Plan, and this latter group, the Chicago Plan Commission, became in 1939 the city's official planning body. However, its quasi-private character has remained. Its membership is drawn from the city's business, political, and civic sectors, although its review of land use issues is of course dependent on recommendations from its professional staff.

Once Chicago became involved in the construction and management of public housing, and then urban redevelopment, a series of new institutional agents was created. The first of these was the Chicago Housing Authority, established in 1937, which, due to state legislators' hostility to public housing, was bypassed when state urban redevelopment legislation was enacted in 1947. At that time a Land Clearance Commission was established to authorize large-scale redevelopment plans; its powers were extended to include local oversight of redevelopment under the 1949 U.S. Housing Act. In 1953 a Community Conservation Board was empowered to review neighborhood redevelopment such as in Hyde Park. Thus, by the middle 1950s Chicago possessed a civic-dominated planning commission, a public housing agency, and redevelopment commissions for large redevelopment projects and neighborhood renewal efforts. Not surprisingly, the city also had a housing and redevelopment coordinator whose role was to impart some continuity to this array of agencies.

In the next two decades, this arrangement was regularly adjusted, but it is difficult to conclude that enhanced planning autonomy was the result. In 1957 a Department of City Planning was created, apparently in order to increase the influence of the professional planning staff vis à vis the Plan Commission's appointed members.[26] In 1962, three redevelopment-oriented bodies were merged—the Land Clearance Commission, the Community Conservation Board, and the Tenants Relocation Bureau—into a Department of Urban Renewal. Yet matched against this consolidation of planning and redevelopment functions was the establishment of the Mayor's Committee for Economic and Cultural Development. Its members were recruited from the business and civic communities, while a staff produced economic development studies. In 1976 its functions were assumed by the new Economic Development Commission, but by this time another group, the Mayor's Council of Manpower and Economic Advisors, also worked in this area. In 1978 the Department of Planning, City and Community Development assumed control of city planning, development, and urban renewal functions; however, even this consolidation was partial. The Commercial District Development Commission, which dated from 1975, was not included, and in 1982 a new Department of Economic Development was established. More significantly, the Washington administration's economic development commissioner, Robert Mier, noted that, so far as he could judge, the various planning and development agencies in previous administrations had not consistently communicated or otherwise coordinated their activities.[27]

From the mid-1950s to the mid-1970s the hinge linking Chicago's mobilized business community and its fragmented public planning apparatus was Richard J. Daley. Daley was the funnel for business opinion on municipal policy, and once he was convinced of the utility of a particular redevelopment plan, achieving coordinated action was expected. The mayor from Bridgeport seems at first glance an anomalous exponent of downtown economic growth and extensive neighborhood demolition, and one must suppose that he himself felt some misgivings in this role. Long-time city planner Ira Bach recalled that Daley was "disabused of there being any slums. How could Chicago have slums?" Even after Bach and other planners confronted Daley with figures demonstrating the blight in a particular area, the mayor accepted them "ungracefully." [28] But accept them, he did. On one side was a business elite for whom a rebuilt Chicago was a paramount goal, and on the other was an acquiescent planning and redevelopment bureaucracy whose executives shared the business elite's vision of a new Chicago. By all accounts this same vision compelled Mayor Daley. Achieving the "highest and best use" for particular parcels is a dictum espoused by both business leaders and planners in Chicago, and it has consistently been employed to justify increasing the density of the downtown, upgrading near-downtown residential areas, and, by doing so, diverting resources from other available courses of action.

Rebuilding Post-World War II Chicago: Underpinnings and Consequences

The period from 1948, when negotiations for the South Side Lake Meadows project began, to 1976, when Richard Daley died, may be viewed as a single era in terms of redevelopment in Chicago. Further, we can summarize it from three vantage points: the functional directions of redevelopment, the conditions promoting redevelopment in Chicago, and the spatial effects of the redevelopment initiatives.

Modes of Redevelopment   Three modes of redevelopment have been prominent in postwar Chicago, and by focusing on the degree of local government participation in each we can readily delineate them. In the first of these, infrastructural expansion, the city and allied local governments have directly constructed massive new facilities—though in several instances substantial fiscal resources have been derived from the federal government. Notable examples of such projects have been the construction of the city's expressway system (which was wholly accomplished during this period), the expansion of the city's fixed rail mass transit system, the erection of O'Hare Airport, and the construction of McCormick Place as a convention and trade show site. With the exception of expressway siting, these have been relatively uncontroversial projects whose very construction has represented an important stimulus for the local economy and whose long-term purpose has been to modernize the city's transportation system and cater to emerging economic patterns.

Second, the city has been involved in a variety of cooperative ventures with private groups. These have generally involved neighborhood and residential development. In the 1950s and 1960s, the city's primary role in these efforts turned on the designation of urban renewal sites, and—if operating under the mandate of federal statutes—the acquisition, demolition, preparation, and sale of such sites. In the last decade, the use of Community Development funds and Urban Development Action Grants (the latter for commercial projects) to improve sites or otherwise support private investments has become commonplace. In an empirical analysis of public and private redevelopment investments in Chicago, political scientist James Greer found that public expenditures have tended to follow private spending—that is, where private redevelopers have sensed lucrative investments, the city has been willing to further sweeten their pie.[29]

One can readily ascertain this tendency in reference to neighborhood planning in Chicago. Hyde Park-Kenwood surely set the tone for later neighborhood projects across the city. With its organized community group, the Hyde Park-Kenwood Community Conference, and development corporation, the SECC, the University of Chicago took full advantage of redevelopment statutes and, with the city's endorsement, proceeded to reshape its locale substantially.[30] In the case of the huge Sandburg Village residential development on the near North Side, the city operated under urban renewal provisions to acquire and turn over a tremendously valuable parcel to developer Arthur Rubloff, who then put up an array of high-rises and townhouses whose intended audience was clearly not the population unhoused by the original demolition of the site.[31] Just to the north in Lincoln Park, organized community support for urban renewal designation was focused in the Lincoln Park Conservation Association (LPCA). In this instance—and probably due to the obvious potential of this neighborhood for individual owner property upgrading and small site new construction—neither the LPCA nor a commercial developer such as Rubloff were required to sponsor wholesale renewal.[32] Nonetheless, over the course of a decade a startling transformation of the neighborhood was accomplished—and in the general direction of single-family and multiple dwelling units for white-collar professionals. In contrast, despite the 15 development area plans produced in conjunction with the 1966 Comprehensive Plan, only a trickle of public investment has flowed into the West Side and South Side neighborhoods in which private investment has virtually disappeared.[33]

The third functional component of Chicago's rebuilding has been essentially private. This is the construction of new headquarters complexes such as the Sears and Standard Oil (Indiana) towers, shopping-tourist facilities such as Water Tower Place on the near North Side, and numerous speculative office buildings. Again, the erection of these facilities has represented a boon for local building trades, and their predominance in the Loop and its environs demonstrates the city's shift from a manufacturing-based to a management- and services-anchored economy. Nor have such projects been carried out wholly without local government support, as the Sears Tower case illustrates, but for the most part this construction has been financed by the private resources of their sponsors.

The postwar private rebuilding of central Chicago has been paralleled by major corporate investments and relocations in a cluster of suburban locations. A huge assemblage of hotels, office complexes, and light manufacturers has settled in the vicinity of O'Hare Airport, northwest of the city. Running north and west of the city along the Kennedy and Eisenhower Expressways are dozens more campus-style business complexes. Suburban Oak Brook, along the interstate west of the Eisenhower Expressway, is the home of McDonalds' and United Airlines' world headquarters as well as the main offices of numerous smaller corporations and another concentration of hotels. Somewhat less impressive development has occurred on other links in the metropolitan expressway system.

However, the location of these development nodes has resulted not from the efforts of the region's ostensible planning body, the Northeastern Illinois Planning Commission, but in consequence of the airport and highway construction programs intended to upgrade the region's transportation network. These commercial developments have in turn played a major role in defining the residential character of surrounding communities. Although there is room for debate regarding the objectives and techniques of planning in the city of Chicago, the processes affecting the pattern of suburban development—though also quite visible—have not been explicitly directed by any public agency. And for a sizeable share of the metropolitan region's population, the private building of suburban Chicago is the predominant shaper of their physical environment.

Conditions for Redevelopment   There have been three requisites for the postwar rebuilding of central Chicago, and in the foregoing discussion we have already intimated their interrelation. The city government has consistently directed its formal planning efforts in a trajectory congenial with the interests of large corporations and downtown-oriented business. As we have noted, downtown planning was in effect transferred from the city to the CCAC. More substantively, the city's major infrastructural investments have primarily sought to enhance the environmental quality of the downtown and link it with outlying facilities such as O'Hare Airport and the suburban communities housing much of the corporate work force. Finally, discussions of particular redevelopment projects and even private construction are rife with incidents of the pliant attitude adopted by city officials (from the mayor down) in negotiating with private developers, corporate heads, and the like.

The Daley regime was marked by cordial relations with federal redevelopment officials as well, and federal financial support for renewal efforts in Chicago represents the second major requisite for Chicago's rebuilding. Especially during the Kennedy and Johnson presidencies, Chicago projects generated a steady stream of federal aid. Indeed, a city report in 1969 boasted, "To date, the city has received federal grants totalling $120,324,079 or 65.8% of the total reservation. Such percentage of grants collected (perhaps indicative of program accomplishment) is the highest of all cities with grant reservations of $100 million or more."[34] The significance of this aid should not be underestimated, especially during a time in which the city's fiscal resources were increasingly strapped. Also, because this money was furnished under provisions of urban renewal legislation, its principal purpose was the city's acquisition and then transfer into private hands of sites for redevelopment.

The third requisite for Chicago's rebuilding was investor confidence, and it is safe to say that this required the momentum of the foregoing two in order to be activated. Like a number of Eastern industrial cities, Chicago was virtually abandoned by downtown real estate investors from the Great Depression until the 1950s.[35] This absence of downtown construction was clearly one of the primary factors leading to the organization of the CCAC in the 1950s, and it also prodded the city's early forays into redevelopment. By the late 1960s, however, this development trough had been passed, with major building spurts in the early and, again, late 1970s. A 1982 city planning document reports: "With 80 million square feet of office space (17 million added over the past five years) and an estimated 14 million to be added during the next five years, Chicago's downtown contains a broad cross-section of first-class space and support facilities."[36] In short, city planning directed toward downtown reconstruction and the acquisition of large sums of federal redevelopment dollars have been joined, since sometime in the late 1950s or early 1960s, by an equally impressive investment of private dollars in the city's central area.

The Effects of Redevelopment   The physical results of this generation of public-private reconstruction are in broad outline comparable with the reordering of cities undergoing similar economic transformations, such as Boston, New York, and Philadelphia, although Chicago's particular cultural and political milieu has made its mark on many of the details of the new city. Concentrated development in the Loop over the last generation has virtually exhausted available sites; as a result, office construction in hitherto undesirable or unavailable locations has proceeded—west of the Loop across the Chicago River and on the south bank of the river east of Michigan Avenue and north of Grant Park. Although the State Street retail district has been revamped with a pedestrian mall, it has been supplanted as the city's prestige shopping area by Michigan Avenue north of the Chicago River.

The increased concentration of core activities and the spatial expansion of the new Chicago downtown have had two auxiliary effects. First, there has been a vast increase in demand for residential space convenient to downtown employment centers. Second, older entertainment districts such as Rush Street and residential neighborhoods such as the Gold Coast and Old Town are now contiguous to the expanded commercial center of Chicago. Although the Gold Coast never ceased to be a prestige community, Old Town's rundown but intact rowhouses and small apartment buildings have been subject to a thoroughgoing restoration since the mid-1960s. In turn, adjoining neighborhoods to the north and along the lakefront such as Lincoln Park and Lakeview have undergone parallel renovation, and by the same sorts of people—younger professionals with small families, singles, and gays.

In the foregoing neighborhoods considerable in-fill construction has also been in evidence, but more dramatically, substantial residential construction has taken place in some areas within walking distance of the Loop itself. The harbingers of this were a series of high-rise apartments and condominiums built just off the lake and east of the downtown. More recently, large industrial buildings have been converted to residences on the near North and South Sides (the latter area known as Printing House Row in commemoration of its industrial past), and Dearborn Park, a complex of townhouses and medium-rise structures, has been built on abandoned railhead south of the Loop.

Outside Chicago's central area there has been no concerted redevelopment policy. The urban renewal program in Hyde Park is attributable not to the city's initiative, but rather to the University of Chicago's desire to insulate its campus. No other part of Chicago away from the Loop and the near north lakefront has been subject to a comparable expenditure of public or private resources. In recent years commercial redevelopment of neighborhood shopping districts has been pursued in a few locations; the abandoned Union Stockyards on the near Southwest Side have been cleared for reuse as an industrial park. Some city funds have also flowed to the neighborhoods for housing rehabilitation. All in all the record is extremely slight.

Yet for non-central portions of Chicago the indirect effects of postwar planning and redevelopment have been profound. South Side and West Side urban renewal set in motion huge migrations of displaced residents, for the most part black, into neighborhoods more removed from the central city. Arnold Hirsch contends that this exodus on the South Side played a large role in generating the preservationist neighborhood movement in that part of Chicago, and there are signs of a comparable process on the West Side. Concurrent with Chicago's early urban renewal efforts was a huge program of public housing construction by the Chicago Housing Authority (CHA). Hirsch has demonstrated that much of this CHA housing was used to absorb the human spillover from central area urban renewal. As we have seen, in Chicago's white neighborhoods opposition to public housing was substantial, and thus the CHA built the vast majority of its units in several predominantly black neighborhoods on the South and West Sides.[37] This concentration of thousands of units of public housing— much of it the bleakest of 1950s-style high-rise project—disrupted neighborhoods and probably played its own part in diminishing property values and maintenance practices in the adjoining, privately held housing stock. And aside from the consequences of central area displacement, the city's emphasis on downtown, affluent neighborhood, and transportation network reconstruction has represented a tremendous opportunity cost in terms of foregone neighborhood improvements in most parts of the city. Commercial districts, housing, and infrastructure away from the center of Chicago have suffered from long-standing neglect, whose magnitude serves to justify continued inattention.[38] Interestingly, outside Chicago a ring of older communities has been bypassed by recent growth on the suburban periphery, and in a number of respects—especially their aging infrastructure—the physical condition of these towns parallels that of many of the city's neglected neighborhoods.[39]

In a city in which neighborhood organization is such an important part of the political fabric, and where such organizations have become an important agent of dissent from the prevailing ways of carrying on politics, it should not be surprising that the planning and redevelopment record of the last generation is highly suspect. In addition, with the passing of Mayor Daley, the smooth behind-the-scenes management of redevelopment lost its director. Thus, city planning and redevelopment issues in general, as well as particular projects, have come under increased scrutiny in recent years. In the next section, we will examine the evolution of the city's North Loop redevelopment project, which is exemplary of the emerging character of the redevelopment process and redevelopment politics in contemporary Chicago.

Redeveloping Chicago's North Loop

The North Loop project straddles the Daley era and the more recent period of flux in Chicago redevelopment. As such, the project's physical vision and economic rationale were rooted in the conventional wisdom of the Daley-orchestrated redevelopment alliance. However, in the years following Richard J. Daley's death the city's capacity for quick project execution declined. Consequently, plans for the North Loop were subject to far more public scrutiny than past city-sponsored redevelopment initiatives. The concerns of preservationist groups for sustaining the historical character of the Loop, as well as resource allocation issues raised by neighborhood organizations, postponed execution of the North Loop project and to some degree recast its physical character and likely economic impact. By examining in detail the evolution of the North Loop project we can outline the new political context of redevelopment in Chicago and make some predictions about the character of future redevelopment initiatives.

In its infancy, the North Loop project did not seem likely to produce such an interesting chain of events. Mayor Daley appears to have asked developer Arthur Rubloff to scout locations for a new central library for the city. Rubloff returned with a proposal to clear a large area west of State Street, south from Wacker Drive overlooking the river, down to Randolph and Washington Streets, and west to Clark and LaSalle Streets —and of course including the library in the new construction.[40] The Department of Urban Renewal prepared a preliminary study of the area in the latter part of 1973, and at this time as well legislation was introduced to the city council to establish a Commercial District Development Commission under whose auspices projects such as the North Loop would be carried out. In 1975 this board was formed.

Through the mid-1970s preliminary work on the North Loop project proceeded without much public notice. Mayor Daley died in 1976, but Arthur Rubloff was intent on pursuing his unofficial mandate to orchestrate total demolition and reconstruction of the North Loop site. In early 1978 the city prepared an Urban Development Action Grant (UDAG) application for the Department of Housing and Urban Development. By the summer of that year the North Loop emerged as a significant public issue. In August, Arthur Rubloff released his redevelopment plan, in conjunction with an agreement with Hilton Hotels, Inc. to build a large convention hotel on the northeast corner of the redevelopment area.[41] Coincidentally, Rubloff and Governor James Thompson held a press conference to announce the construction of a State of Illinois Building (to consolidate state offices in the city) on the westernmost North Loop block. In Rubloff's view, the location of these anchors at either end of the project greatly enhanced the redevelopment potential of the intermediate blocks. To punctuate the year's flurry of North Loop activity, fall of 1978 brought an amended UDAG proposal, the revised document seeking aid only for the block to be sold to Hilton.[42] A month later the Commercial District Development Commission approved the North Loop project, thus granting the city authority to exercise eminent domain in the project area.

Although 1978 was a year in which formal progress was substantial, by early 1979 countervailing forces were set in motion that arrested the preceding year's advances. First, Rubloff's total demolition plan did not sit well with the city's preservationist groups. In previous years they had witnessed the razing of structures such as the Chicago Stock Exchange, and much better organized than in the past, they were vocally critical of the intended fate of several architecturally significant commercial structures in the North Loop area. Furthermore, Mayor Michael Bilandic, who was apparently quite acquiescent to the Rubloff plan, was surprisingly swept from office by Jane Byrne in February 1979. Preceding the election, Byrne had expressed reservations regarding the North Loop plan; once in office "she had her own real estate advisors," and from this time Arthur Rubloff's informal direction of North Loop planning ceased.[43]

The next step in project planning indicated its suddenly ambiguous status. In April 1979 the Chicago Plan Commission held hearings as part of the project authorization process, and though it decided in favor of the project, substantial opposition was voiced.[44] Notably, a local preservationist group, the Landmarks Preservation Council of Illinois, the Metropolitan

Housing and Planning Council, and a representative of the National Trust for Historic Preservation spoke against the development plan. Their common complaint was that the city documents did not sufficiently specify general design guidelines or particular buildings to be preserved. The timing of this decision was also peculiar. Byrne was by then mayor-elect and out of town on vacation when the Chicago Plan Commission reached its decision.

In the following months concerted opposition to the North Loop plan took shape. Among the structures threatened with demolition were Chicago's oldest and grandest movie house, the Chicago Theatre, on the east side of State Street, and two former legitimate theatres, the Harris and the Selwyn, on the corner of Dearborn and Lake Streets. From 1978 the Chicago Theatre Trust, Inc. was at work on studies to preserve the Chicago Theatre and ensure its future economic viability.[45] In corresponding fashion, the Landmarks Preservation Council and the Performing Arts Center of Chicago commissioned an architect to produce a renovation plan for the Harris and the Selwyn, which these groups envisioned as performance spaces to be shared by several local theatre and dance companies.[46]

By the summer of 1979 Mayor Byrne dropped her objections and named a formal project coordinator, Charles Shaw, like Rubloff a private real estate developer. Shaw was to oversee project negotiations and also participate in site development. In the following months the financial details of the project began to emerge: Mayor Byrne seeking approximately $50 million (to be raised by notes issued to a consortium of local banks) as the city's direct expenditure, and tax abatement legislation approved by the Cook County Board to reduce the initial property levy on redevelopment sites in "blighted commercial areas."[47] Then in the spring of 1980 new development guidelines were submitted by the city, this document seeming to mandate the preservation of several of the landmark buildings.[48] Also, the city signed a development contract with Hilton Hotels, the provisions of which would prove highly controversial. Not only was Hilton granted a substantial tax abatement, but in addition the hotel chain was granted power of approval over redevelopment around its hotel site.[49]

The latter months of 1980, though, brought more trials for the project. By late summer the city's "sweet" deal with Hilton was reported in the press, and by virtue of one of the frequent political battles that rocked her administration, Mayor Byrne's ability to deliver on this contract was also undermined. The city's proposal of a 13-year, $70 million tax reduction for the Hilton site was subject to approval by the Cook County tax assessor, Thomas Hynes. Hynes was associated with a rival faction in the Democratic party, and it was widely supposed in August—when he refused to review the city's abatement request without detailed information on each North Loop block—that he was balancing past scores with the mayor. Hynes' ruling, nevertheless, was strictly advisory. He rejected the form of the city's proposal and not necessarily its substance, but over the next year, until his formal rejection was offered, this cast a cloud over the entire project.[50]

Furthermore, and probably due to their cognizance of civic opposition to the planning of the North Loop project, HUD officials began to signal doubts concerning the UDAG proposal.[51] By reducing its request from $25 million to $7.9 million, the city had also reduced the area for which it sought federal aid. Excluded were those portions of the original North Loop site in which historic structures were located (by this time seven such buildings were on the National Register of Historic Places). UDAG funds cannot be used to raze buildings so designated, but HUD suspected the city of site "segmentation" and the intent to go ahead with the demolitions using only local funds. If this were so the reduced UDAG might be withheld. This, too, must have caused city officials to pause.

Finally, in November 1980 Charles Shaw released his plan for the North Loop, which, though it salvaged several historic structures and greatly increased the residential composition of the project, was met with mixed reviews. Some reactions characterized the designs as "Buck Rogersish," and Shaw's references to creating a consolidated cultural center were unsatisfactory to the management of existing facilities such as Orchestra Hall and the Civic Opera House.[52]

Nineteen eighty-one brought more reversals for the North Loop project. In late winter Shaw withdrew as project coordinator and, in so doing, scotched the development plan released months before. He was replaced by Miles Berger, another local developer but, as chairman of the Chicago Plan Commission, presumably more attuned to city decision-making processes. In the following months the city's development model shifted considerably. Unlike Shaw and Rubloff, whose coordination was tantamount to personal development rights, Berger only oversaw city planning for the project and negotiations with prospective developers. He had no direct financial stake in the proceedings, and under his direction, competitive bidding for individual blocks was inaugurated—with developers' plans then subject to comprehensive guidelines set by the city.[53]

A new political barrier was emerging, also. The details of the Hilton contract were eliciting opposition on two fronts: first, neighborhood groups objected to the size of the subsidy and further advocated increased municipal attention to neighborhood planning, redevelopment, and services; second, downtown businesses, presumably jealous, objected to this much city largesse directed at a single firm. The former, comprised of neighborhood groups such as the Lakeview Citizens Council, the South Shore Commission, and the Northwest Community Organization, called meetings and submitted petitions to County Assessor Hynes under the banner of the Campaign Against the North Loop Tax Break. The financially well-heeled business opposition formed the Property Conservation Council and commissioned Jared Shlaes, a prominent real estate analyst, to prepare a study of the Hilton deal's real cost and prospective benefits for the city. This report was readied in time for the assessor's hearings on the tax abatement in December 1981.[54]

Given County Assessor Hynes' political quarreling with Mayor Byrne and noisy opposition from business leaders and neighborhood groups, his overturning the Hilton contract was not startling. However, Hynes' counterproposal was a neatly judicious blend of political and substantive considerations. In effect, although refusing to approve the contract as negotiated between the city and Hilton, Hynes indicated his willingness to support a contingent tax abatement. Reductions in local property tax obligations would be scaled to the degree of the hotel's profitability: if it did well, then the tax considerations would be less.[55] Hilton officials, who all along had taken an inflexible posture in the face of criticism of their arrangement with the city, reviewed Hynes' counterplan and rejected it. For a few more weeks they insisted that they would find alternative, private financing even in the absence of the tax abatement, but by March 1982 the Hilton corporation withdrew from any participation—subsidized or unsubsidized—in the North Loop project.[56]

In the wake of what numerous city officials characterized as a catastrophic setback for the North Loop project, there was some headway made in 1982. Rehabilitation of some of the threatened historic structures in the project area was underway, and by late 1982 construction of the Transportation Center was underway—a structure to consolidate airline ticketing in the Loop, concentrate cab and limousine services, and provide parking. The city had accepted independent bids on this site in 1981. Development specifications for individual blocks, in anticipation of developer bidding, were prepared, and in what was becoming a nearly annual process, new guidelines for overall development were drawn up.[57]

In December 1982 a single bid was made on what had been the Hilton site, but it was attractive enough to be approved. This proposal, by a consortium of local developers and Americana Hotels, was for a smaller hotel than had been previously sought. However, the consortium was willing to accept the city's development guidelines for the site, and in other respects, the smaller facility offered many of the advantages of the earlier Hilton proposal.[58] Thus, when Harold Washington assumed the mayoralty in April 1983, he took on the stewardship of a huge redevelopment site whose decade-long history was just beginning to make the step from design to concrete and reinforced steel.

Like his predecessor, as a candidate for mayor Harold Washington expressed skepticism of the North Loop plan, but also like Jane Byrne, he accepted its inevitability. During the first two years of the Washington administration a series of development firms and hotel operators was offered the option to buy the pivotal block abandoned by Hilton. Each in turn was unable to deliver the cash for purchase, but the city remained committed to a hotel development on the site.[59] Similarly, the Washington administration convinced the city council to approve a tax increment financing arrangement to raise the funds necessary to pay for future public improvements in the North Loop district.[60] In late 1984 the city also arranged for the sale of the Chicago Theatre to a local investment group planning to rehabilitate the old movie palace and convert it to a performing arts center.[61]

The politics of redevelopment in Chicago have taken a decided turn in the direction of increased complexity. Downtown-oriented businesses and major corporations continue to exercise primary control of what enters the redevelopment agenda. Moreover, due to the fragility of municipal finances and the subtle but powerful need to sustain a "favorable business climate," mayors, including reformers such as Harold Washington, must to some degree collaborate in the promotion of environmental enhancement of the central area. However, development at any cost—the credo many Chicagoans associate with Arthur Rubloff and his development packages— generates opposition today even within the business community. Both the Rubloff plan and the Hilton deal generated "insider" opposition in Chicago, in part from competitive impulses but also from a sense that the central city as a residential and cultural environment can absorb only so much homogenized high-rise office/commercial development.

Preservationists and their organizations also played a substantial role in directing discussion of various North Loop proposals. Indeed, by rallying support for the old commercial structures threatened by Arthur Rubloff, these groups transformed the North Loop from just another redevelopment scheme to a prime public policy issue. Their tenacity in reacting to new city plans, monitoring hearings, and making counterproposals is also noteworthy. Yet their objections to North Loop planning mainly focused on aesthetic and physical planning matters. They did not seem so concerned with the planning process and resource allocation issues raised by other North Loop opponents.

After 1980, neighborhood organizations, whose members frequently reside miles from the Loop and presumably seldom so much as visit the central area, became increasingly prominent participants in the political debate—and their concerns were of an entirely different cast from those of the preservationists. They were concerned with equity questions: Just how large was the Hilton subsidy? Would such a large commitment to one block's development drain off resources from neighborhood redevelopment throughout the city? Assessor Hynes had his own reasons for heeding these arguments, and division within the downtown business community also undermined the Hilton deal. Nonetheless, by introducing these economic equity issues the neighborhood opposition to the Hilton deal added an entirely new dimension to discussions of redevelopment in Chicago. Formally speaking, little now remains of the Campaign Against the North Loop Tax Break, although a similar movement greeted and ultimately helped block plans to stage a Chicago World's Fair in 1992. Whether a neighborhood agenda for the city can evolve from these particular discussions, and from the experience of the individuals and organizations involved, remains to be seen. However, it is quite unlikely that organized neighborhood participation in city redevelopment planning will diminish in the future.

The central lesson of the North Loop is that the days are past in Chicago when the city government can, without risk and under cover of urban renewal or state redevelopment legislation, exercise eminent domain and fiscally underwrite what under other circumstances would simply be termed real estate deals. The local political and planning apparatus no longer moves quickly and quietly enough. Mobilized community groups monitor city operations and can marshal considerable opposition to particular proposals. Still, the question remains whether a positive process of neighborhood planning and economic development is being fostered in this city. This was part of the promise of the Washington administration, so to its record we now turn.

Neighborhood and Economic Development Planning

Before the mid-1970s, Chicago's city government was reluctant to acknowledge the wishes and activities of neighborhood-based organizations, and as we have seen, it concentrated planning and redevelopment initiatives in the central area and a few other locations where there was major institutional support. However, in the last decade—and in advance of the Washington administration—several factors joined to effect a marginal shift in the city's attitude toward neighborhood planning and redevelopment. Most evidently, the large number of active neighborhood groups in Chicago—and their willingness to criticize city government policy—wore down the city's resistance to their plans. Furthermore, as neighborhood planning councils and development corporations sprang up through their own initiative, and then developed communication lines with federal officials, local lending institutions, and neighborhood groups in other cities, they became an evident means by which the city could leverage its resources and attract additional private investment or aid from non-local governmental sources. With the tightening of municipal finances in the mid-1970s, it is reasonable to suggest that many municipal officials began to see spontaneously organized neighborhood groups and corporate/community partnerships as an opportunity as well as a nuisance. Finally, since the mid-1960s city planners in Chicago as in other cities have become more sensitive to the failed promise and abuses characteristic of large-scale urban renewal. Although professional planners do not control redevelopment policy in Chicago, they have been in a position to reorient agency activities to some degree, and a gradual movement toward neighborhood collaboration has been evident.

By considering some of the particular projects that have emerged during this recent period of increased city-neighborhood-corporate collaboration, we can establish the parameters of this policy shift. For instance, both the Bilandic and Byrne administrations issued large blocks of municipal bonds to generate funds for home purchase and improvement loans.[62] During the high-interest period of the late 1970s, these programs represented, for qualifying families, an attractive alternative to conventional financing. Moreover, both administrations trumpeted these initiatives to generally approving local newspaper and television coverage. In practice, however, the number of families supported by these efforts was miniscule, totaling just a few thousand. Much of the money was channeled to already gentrifying neighborhoods, and less affluent households participated far less frequently than those whose incomes were near the upper end of the qualifying range.[63]

The city government has also taken an interest in collaborative planning with local development corporations, particularly those oriented toward improving neighborhood commercial strips around the city. In the far North Side Albany Park neighborhood, a local planning group, the North River

Commission, has worked with the city on a variety of tasks. By way of community meetings and consultation with city planners, a neighborhood plan was first developed. The Lawrence Avenue Development Corporation, which is affiliated with the North River Commission and focuses on upgrading the neighborhood's primary shopping district, has packaged loans by way of local banks, the Small Business Administration, and the city's Facade Rebate Plan to help merchants expand their facilities, buy new equipment, and upgrade the exteriors of their shops. The North River Commission has also worked to consolidate the hearing of housing court cases pertinent to the neighborhood. Local residents seem pleased with the results of these initiatives, and city officials have accepted their share of the praise as well.[64]

Nonetheless, systematic neighborhood planning of this sort has not been instituted in Chicago. The city's most recent comprehensive planning document specifies that local planning boards will be established, but the document has not been formally approved and no action has been taken to establish the neighborhood boards.[65] In effect, neighborhood planning has sprung up when local groups have persistently demanded it and when city government insiders—especially elected officials such as the alderperson—have felt enough heat themselves to demand a response from city agencies. The programs that Chicago has carried out citywide have been directed at individuals, families, and particular enterprises. These include the home loan programs and the Economic Development Commission's Facade Rebate Plan. The latter provides shopowners grants up to $5,000 with which to make external improvements on their facilities.[66]

Viewed in the context of past city administrations' attitudes toward urban redevelopment, the Washington administration's 1984 Chicago Development Plan represents a substantial shift in course.[67] Principal among its objectives are job creation as the central criterion for assessing the worth of particular projects, the balancing of downtown and neighborhood development, and the mobilization of neighborhood groups as agents for development activities. In effect, the Washington administration sought to move away from a simple bricks-and-mortar strategy of redevelopment to consider questions such as the human consequences of projects and their impact on the overall physical fabric of the city. The Development Plan connects an array of particular techniques to these general objectives: assistance to businesses to be determined explicitly in terms of the prospects of job generation, a city commitment to rely more on contractors and suppliers from within Chicago and from among minority populations, assistance for large-scale and downtown developers to be contingent on their agreeing to contribute to neighborhood development projects, increased infrastructure investment for neighborhoods, and cooperation with existing neighborhood groups to work on local projects.

However, there are constraints that are implicit in these programmatic ends and means and that in the long run could serve to dilute this new redevelopment emphasis. The most fundamental of these is fiscal. The city does not have the financial resources to upgrade neighborhood infrastructure systematically. Its decision to redistribute available resources is laudable, but in reality many neighborhoods will not experience its benefits for some time, if ever. Similarly, the commitment to link downtown development to neighborhood programs will generate some center-to-periphery spillovers. Yet one cannot anticipate major private developers' committing to neighborhoods more than a fraction of the funds they seek to plow into the Loop and its environs. Finally, the recognition of indigenous neighborhood organizations is noteworthy, but in Chicago an even more revolutionary action would be to establish neighborhood planning councils, which could review an array of city and private initiatives and might even oversee specific redevelopment projects. At present it appears that, once again, the city's financial situation prevents it from taking on this scale of local planning innovation.[68]

Redevelopment in the 1980s

In the mid-1980s, redevelopment in Chicago proceeds along two tracks. The first and more visible one carries through many of the assumptions that have governed urban redevelopment across the country since World War II. The central city is viewed as the linchpin of urban progress, and the lion's share of municipal and federally derived redevelopment resources are channeled toward this locale. This view of redevelopment has been somewhat tempered by preservationist considerations in recent years; thus, the conversion of older commercial structures and the maintenance of some semblance of historic continuity of the urban fabric are more evident. Also, the simple-minded project execution strategy that dictated the total clearance of sites followed by their hastily negotiated resale to private developers characteristic of early urban renewal has been replaced by a more thoroughgoing process of city-investor dialogue through which each seeks fairly specific guarantees and commitments from the other. Program objectives in urban redevelopment are more explicitly directed at economic development (that is, tax base expansion and job creation) as opposed to the eradication of blight and the erection of middle-income housing. This shift is due in part to changing federal government priorities, as well as the strength of unassisted private development in gentrifying neighborhoods, which has made it less of a direct priority for local government in Chicago, as elsewhere.

Through the operations of the first redevelopment track Chicago has managed to transform the Loop and surrounding neighborhoods, from a polyglot of industry, retailing, banking, and residential districts running the gamut from port of entry to Gold Coast, to a more homogeneous environment of corporate offices, business services, and elite residences. This was accomplished in part by the city's aggressive urban renewal program, but as we have emphasized in the preceding pages city officials have in various ways paid close attention to the views and plans of Chicago's business leaders. Not only the city's land clearance but also its infrastructure investments, location of new public facilities, and provision of tax abatements have been employed to spur and reinforce private investment. Thus, contemporary Chicago possesses one of the most impressive downtown cores in America and, stretching north along the lake and more recently west and south of the Loop, some of the most attractive upper-income urban residential districts. Among the latter, some, such as Sandburg Village and Lincoln Park, were reclaimed for the middle class via urban renewal. Others, such as Dearborn Park just south and Presidential Towers just west of the Loop, are primarily private ventures occupying former industrial sites. Yet both Presidential Towers and Dearborn Park were expedited by the efforts of city government.[69]

Away from its core Chicago is a city of neighborhood stasis and decay. Apart from a few areas where major institutions have promoted redevelopment, notably Hyde Park-Kenwood, neighborhood quality seems to depend mainly on the commitment of property owners and the aggressiveness of local politicians in prodding decent city service delivery. On Chicago's South and West Sides the concentration of high-rise public housing and the Chicago Housing Authority's indifferent management of these projects have undoubtedly contributed to neighborhood decay.

In sum, Chicago's primary redevelopment track has rebuilt the downtown and made central Chicago a good place to live for its growing managerial and professional populations. Its impact on the remainder of the city is ambiguous. The majority of the city's neighborhoods have been affected by it hardly at all, except as a diversion for resources that might have been invested in their maintenance. To the west and south of the Loop the residential dislocation associated with central area redevelopment has cost these neighborhoods, and the city, dearly.

Beside this primary central area redevelopment track is a second, neighborhood, track. The groups that participate in it, by virtue of example and more direct political action, have made some inroads on the first track. City government now assists their operations to a limited degree, and there is an emerging sense that the ethos of neighborhood preservation has been one of the humanizing strains evident in some recent downtown redevelopment in Chicago. Yet this second track is tiny, particularly in regard to the fiscal resources it can muster. Many of its participants—especially the various development corporations—are consistently on the verge of fiscal expiration. The foundation support, community development funds, and private lending money that fuel them is continually subject to reduction or disappearance. In short, the sensitivity and imagination one observes in so many of these operations must be balanced against their scale, which at present cannot hope to work substantial changes in the overall development pattern in Chicago, unless, of course, the policy redirection beginning to take shape in city hall is matched by analogous reorientations of thinking and funding in Springfield and Washington, D.C.

7

Chicago's Future

I'm also predicting that one day the sons and daughters of those
who permitted race to determine their votes for and against
Washington in 1983 will come together to commemorate Washington's first mayoral election as a phenomenon that launched
Chicago in the direction of becoming an authentic City of Hope
—for everybody.

Vernon Jarrett[1]

The city of Chicago, its suburbs, and the region are in a precarious state.
Political conflict, social strife, and uneven economic development are defining characteristics of the community. Predictions are tenuous under the
best of circumstances. The trajectory of developments in just the immediate future may present too much of a challenge for even the most omni-
scient seer. After all, in the spring of 1982 nobody could have predicted
Harold Washington's victory one year later, and made a credible claim to
sanity at the same time.

Cloudiness of the crystal ball should not be confused, however, with
predestination. Citizens of the Chicago community can and will shape
their future. Nevertheless, the parameters within which they will be able to
act may well be limited by developments beyond their control. For example, adoption and implementation of a national industrial policy could
determine which industries will grow and which ones will further decline.
A sudden increase in the price of an essential natural resource, like the jolt
OPEC gave the United States in the mid-1970s, could cause further, and
unpredictable, disruption. A world war, or the launching of a limited and
"winnable" nuclear protection strike, cannot be ruled out altogether.

More probable threats to the welfare of Chicago, however, are local
cleavages that, if exacerbated, would further political paralysis, social dis-
integration, and economic decline. Historically, Chicago has been severely
scarred by racial prejudice, labor unrest, and a variety of conflicts between
the city and its suburbs and between the Loop and surrounding neighbor-

hoods. The ability of the city to ameliorate these tensions will go a long way toward determining the fate of the community.

If precise prediction is improbable, the types of issues on which the future will be decided are not so inscrutable. Chicago's past, present, and future turn far more on political and social conflict than on technical or administrative processes. (Observers have long admired the efficacy of Chicago's political machine, but it is the power relations embodied by that organization, not its technical efficiency, that has given the Democratic party its authority.) Values rather than technique still predominate. The end of ideology has not been reached. Pursuit of "more" in the absence of explicit acknowledgment of what it is that will be pursued, who will be included in the decision-making, and how the "product" will be distributed ultimately will prove to be a losing formula for the vast majority of Chicagoans.

Chicago has reason for optimism. As indicated at the outset of this book, it is a regional headquarters that also contains the home base of several national corporations and non-profit organizations. It is the hub of several transportation networks linking raw materials, manufacturers, markets, and other resources nationally and internationally. The city has an abundant supply of water, power, and other natural resources. Entrepreneurship abounds and there is a large skilled and unskilled work force from which business may draw. In recent years the city has had an experienced administration that has at least attempted to provide services and employment on an equitable basis and to implement a balanced and progressive economic development agenda. Over the years a strong network of neighborhood organizations has evolved that is vital for meaningful citizen participation in a genuinely democratic community.[2]

Putting the Growth Machine on Hold

If Chicago has cause for optimism, however, it is a cautious optimism. The threshold question is this: Will Chicago continue to operate as a growth machine, or will it adopt a public balance sheet? That is, will the city and the wider community be exploited as a vehicle for private capital accumulation whereby all efforts are geared toward the creation of the proverbial "good business climate" in hopes that anticipated economic growth will automatically lead to the enrichment of all?[3] Or will public and private benefits and costs be explicitly weighed through a democratic process by which equity as well as growth becomes a conscious objective of public policy? Will the alternative Chicago be realized?[4] The former vision avows acquiescence to elitism and the experts, faith in technocracy, and allegiance to the market. It also constitutes the road to further destructive, uneven development for the city and the region. The latter vision advocates participation, belief in democratized structures and procedures, and tempering of market forces where human needs so dictate. Such values provide the basis for more balanced economic and community development.

Simply put, Chicago must shed its growth ideology. As a veteran local journalist, M. W. Newman, artfully stated:

> It will be a welcome hour, indeed, when our officials quit prostrating themselves before any hack commercial developer who flashes a bank note, and begin to talk back:
>
> "Look here, you want to build? Fine, the city needs it. But we don't need another dead-weight office building unless it has stores on the street. We want life in our streets, not just stone and plastic. And put up some housing, too, if you want to build offices."[5]

None of this is meant to deny the need for economic growth. The litany of ills in Chicago and every other major metropolitan area is far too extensive and well known to deny the contribution that growth can make. But growth for growth's sake will not necessarily be responsive to those ills. Chicago needs to stimulate economic activity but it must be activity responsive to social need, not just market signals. As Derek Shearer advised the national Democratic party in 1984:

> The political program we adopt must emphasize values rather than techniques; the proposals we advocate must be democratic and we must be able to implement them at the community level; the message we offer must be spoken in an American idiom. *Above all, we must talk about quality of life, not simply quantity of output.*[6] (Emphasis added.)

Shedding the growth ideology also does not mean the total rejection of the market. What it does mean is that planning is essential to assure that the community can enjoy the benefits of competitive markets while minimizing the havoc of unrestrained market forces and more equitably distributing the costs and benefits. Achieving these objectives requires the creation of participatory democratic structures and procedures so that those affected by economic development policies can have a say in how such decisions are made.

Since most of the nation's wealth resides in the private sector, creation of such a program cannot be restricted to public expenditures. While public services like education and transportation are important in preparing people for and getting them to work, they are of far less value if no jobs are available. Public assistance in the forms of unemployment compensation and welfare keep many families from starving, but they are at best insufficient efforts to mitigate the damage inflicted on communities after the fact of disinvestment. If participatory democratic structures are to be created in order to achieve "quality" as well as "quantity" objectives, those structures must encompass private investment decision-making as well as government policy-making. As Joshua Cohen and Joel Rogers forcefully argued:

> Investment is effectively the only guarantee of a society's future. If that future is not available as a subject of social deliberation, then social deliberations are fundamentally constrained and incomplete. [A democratic order] cannot proceed under free and equal conditions if some of its members have a restrictive monopoly on decisions over the disposition of social surplus. The democratic conception therefore requires that formal political freedom, public funding of party competition, and distributional measures of the sort described be accompanied by public control of investment.[7]

In Chicago, there has been some movement in this direction. The city has issued an economic development plan that emphasizes balanced growth and broader participation in its implementation so that city and suburban residents, of all racial and economic groups, can have more voice in those decisions that shape their futures. Fairness is frequently mentioned as a priority in economic development and virtually all other initiatives of city government.

In recent years several redevelopment projects sponsored (either formally or informally) by downtown business interests have been blocked or altered by community groups that have organized effectively to protect their neighborhoods' interests. Direct negotiations between neighborhood organizations (white and non-white) and major corporations, particularly banks, savings and loans, and insurance companies, have led to substantial reinvestment programs in many of the city's older communities. Partnerships involving the city, local businesses, and community groups—frequently representing multi-racial and multi-ethnic constituencies—have generated new resources and new hope for declining neighborhoods.

Increasing numbers of workers threatened with unemployment have been able to purchase businesses on the verge of closing, saving those businesses and their jobs. Cooperatives have been established that provide goods and services previously unavailable or unaffordable for their members. Local unions and other labor organizations have been instrumental in aiding many of these efforts, despite the absence of enthusiastic support from key government and private sector leaders.

If a combination of city planning efforts incorporating the concept of a public balance sheet, effective community organizations, and the emergence of employee-owned and cooperative enterprises constitutes the outlines of a new vision and force for development in Chicago, at the current time it remains a somewhat blurred vision and a relatively weak force. Yet the terms of debate are changing. Participation in policy-making is expanding. But the fundamental assumptions underlying the Chicago growth machine and the social relations that have framed the structure of that machine still hold sway.

Even assuming that redevelopment initiatives will be pursued along an increasingly progressive track, that city-suburban conflicts can be minimized, and that the city's racial and ethnic animosities can be ameliorated, in the forseeable future the resources devoted to such an approach will be minimal compared to those controlled by traditional financial and other private sector institutions. As more Chicago suburbs practice the traditional politics of growth, the potential for more progressive politics is further limited. The question also arises as to what will happen should private capital feel threatened by public sector and community-based efforts to guide private investment and capital allocation decision-making. Such infringements on what is firmly believed to be management prerogatives will, of course, be strongly resisted. Will the financial community threaten to undermine the solvency of the city as happened to Cleveland under Dennis Kucinich?[8] Will more businesses simply choose to leave Chicago? Can capital go on strike?

That private capital would resist, and long has resisted, whenever traditional privileges of wealth have been challenged, cannot be denied. But such challenges have been forged, and won, in the past. When Congress debated and subsequently passed the Wagner Act in the 1930s granting working people the right to form unions and bargain collectively with their employers, the business community objected strenuously (occasionally with violence) in part on the grounds that unions unfairly interfered with essential management prerogatives. Civil rights legislation in the 1960s placed further restrictions on whom employers could hire and fire and the terms of employment they were permitted to provide. Occupational safety and environmental legislation in the 1970s placed some restrictions on how employers could allocate private capital. In these and many other instances private prerogatives were circumscribed because of broader public benefits that were anticipated, and were in fact obtained. Any progressive changes that threaten the privileges of private capital will be resisted. But the anticipated resistance need not prohibit successful efforts to advance the public balance sheet.

Among the essential ingredients for such success are similar initiatives in other communities and at the national level. No city, including Chicago, can single-handedly overcome the power of private capital. The Washington administration indicated its awareness of the city's limitations. One of the five central goals of the economic development plan it proposed in 1984 was to pursue a state, regional, and national legislative agenda to assist Chicago, its suburban communities, and other urban areas.[9]

The election of Harold Washington, though an important event in and of itself, is most appropriately viewed as a continuation of a historical struggle toward a more progressive politics and away from the debilitating politics of growth. If the ascendancy of Harold Washington constituted a major victory, it clearly remains an extension rather than culmination of that struggle. In chronicling the early years of another black reform mayor in a large city—Richard Hatcher of Gary, Indiana—former Hatcher aid Edward Greer concluded:

> There is no realistic prospect of overcoming the urban crisis without the implementation of government policies to achieve full employment and to compel the investment of private capital in ways that are contrary to free market forces. As long as such dramatic national reforms are not on the political agenda, it is meaningless to discuss whether or not a particular city or its government is "successful." The best that can be said for either is the degree to which the inexorable slide downward of urban conditions is retarded.[10]

If Greer's pessimism is overstated, he has articulated the critical structural constraints with which every mayor—black, white, or Hispanic, male or female—must contend.

A City of Hope

There is no quick fix for Chicago. No technological breakthrough can resolve the city's fundamental social problems. Though high-technology industries may be part of the city's future, they will produce only a fraction of the jobs that are needed. Further tax breaks or related financial inducements that mandate no public quid for the private quo will simply perpetuate the destructive economic competition between the city and its suburbs, and among all regions of the nation. More efficiency in city government would certainly help, but at best would only tangentially address the central causes of Chicago's fiscal crisis. The next rise in the business cycle might aid selected sectors of the community but will not bail the city out of its economic troubles.

Unfortunately, some of the city fathers are not convinced. The *Chicago Tribune* recently claimed "it's been obvious what has to be done" and proceeded to advocate precisely these kinds of actions that brought the city to its current condition. According to the *Tribune* Chicago must "revive the fading downtown, create an attractive climate for industrial expansion and neighborhood improvement, . . . rewrite obsolete codes that obstruct growth, . . . trim the city's work force, . . . hire professional managers to assure its efficiency, . . . market the city's high-technology capabilities." The *Tribune* believes the city's business and civic groups "are primed to get involved in all of these projects and more . . . what they need is a welcome mat at City Hall in the form of consistent, reliable, cooperative leadership."[11] And the business community agrees. In articulating its support for a long-term strategic plan for economic development, the Commercial Club—a coalition of prominent business leaders in Chicago—expressed "an equally strong willingness to personally participate in such a project."[12] A first step, according to the Commercial Club, is to "improve the business climate by correcting such weaknesses as the high cost of doing business."[13]

Taken literally, in and of themselves these propositions sound reasonable. Reviving anything that is faded, including downtown, makes sense. Certainly an attractive climate for expansion and growth is better than an unattractive one. Eliminating obsolescence should be no loss. Efficiency is something almost all people value. And nobody will argue with reliability, cooperation, or lower costs. But in their most cogent expositions of the growth ideology, the *Tribune* and the Commercial Club have coupled apparently neutral values and universally held objectives in a manner that masks critical ideological issues and real conflicts. What such statements, and the growth ideology generally, conceal are questions regarding who pays, who benefits, and who decides. In Chicago and elsewhere terms like "revival," "growth," "efficiency," and "cooperation" have been attached to those developments that aid private capital, white affluent communities, and other already privileged sectors at the expense of labor and the unemployed, minority communities, and other exploited groups. Similarly, the term "costs" tends to be associated with those activities that benefit the latter groups. The Commercial Club candidly notes that "two of the most onerous costs of doing business . . . are Workers' Compensation (WC) and Unemployment Insurance (UI)."[14] For years city hall has been a welcome mat for business and annointed civic groups, and the city has suffered as a result.

Chicago's economic problems are rooted in political and social struggles among diverse and conflicting interests. Those conflicts are real and will not be eliminated with patriotic slogans about a city that works or by outcompeting other communities in efforts to lure more private capital. Ceasing the economic hemorrhaging of Chicago, ameliorating racial prejudice, and setting the city on an even course of development (economic and otherwise) demands policies premised on a different set of values from those the growth advocates hold, yet they are traditional values that are firmly rooted in the history of American culture. These values include participation, self-reliance, entrepreneurship in the production and distribution of goods and services (as opposed to paper entrepreneurialism), control and responsibility over one's fate. In a word: democracy.

There are alternatives to hierarchy and elitism, to private capital accumulation via unrestrained growth, and to privilege amidst poverty. Accommodation to established social systems and power relations is not inevitable. The capability to imagine new social forms and to act on popularly chosen values is one of the most precious human gifts. If Chicago is to realize its hope, it must make the democratic choice.

Notes

Chapter 1

1. Nelson Algren, *Chicago: City on the Make* (New York: McGraw-Hill, 1983), p. 56.

2. Stanley Ziemba, "City Loses 123,500 Jobs, Study Shows," *Chicago Tribune*, June 12, 1983.

3. From its analysis of 1980 census data the Chicago Urban League found that socio-economic disparities between blacks and whites were far greater than in any of the 11 metropolitan areas in the United States with a population over 2.5 million (Chicago Urban League, "A Perspective on the Socio-Economic Status of Chicago Area Blacks," report, Nov. 1983). See also Ben Joravsky, "A Moment of Truth," *Chicago*, Aug., 1986, 97–101, 124–125.

4. R. C. Longworth, "How Much Time Do We Have? . . . No Time," part of a series entitled "Chicago: City on the Brink," *Chicago Tribune*, May 10, 1981.

5. According to the Current Population Survey—which provides population estimates between decennial censuses—the city of Chicago population grew from 3,005,000 in 1980 to 3,083,000 in 1985 (John Herbers, "New Jobs in Cities Little Aid to Poor," *New York Times*, Oct. 22, 1986).

6. Mike Royko, *Boss: Richard J. Daley of Chicago* (New York. E. P. Dutton, 1971), p. 210.

7. Eugene Kennedy, *Himself: The Life and Times of Mayor Richard J. Daley* (New York: Viking Press, 1978); Len O'Connor, *Clout: Mayor Daley and His City* (New York: Avon, 1975); Len O'Connor, *Requiem: The Decline and Demise of Mayor Daley and His Era* (Chicago: Contemporary Books, 1977); Milton Rakove, *Don't Make No Waves . . . Don't Back No Losers: An Insider's Analysis of the Daley Machine* (Bloomington: Indiana University Press, 1975); Milton Rakove, *We Don't Want Nobody Nobody Sent: An Oral History of the Daley Years* (Bloomington: Indiana University Press, 1979); Ward Heeler, *The Election Chicago Style* (Chicago: Feature Group, 1977); Royko, *Boss*.

8. William I. Thomas and Florian Znaniecki, *The Polish Peasant in Europe and America* (New York: Alfred A. Knopf, 1927); Robert E. Park and Ernest W. Burgess, *The City* (Chicago: University of Chicago Press, 1923); Nels Anderson, *The Hobo: The Sociology of the Homeless Man* (Chicago: University of Chicago Press, 1923); Frederic M. Thrasher, *The Gang* (Chicago: University of Chicago Press, 1927); Louis Wirth, *The Ghetto* (Chicago: University of Chicago Press, 1928); Harvey W. Zorbaugh, *The Gold Coast and the Slum* (Chicago: University of Chicago Press, 1929); Gerald Suttles, *The Social Order of the Slum: Ethnicity and Territory in the Inner City* (Chicago: University of Chicago Press, 1968); Gerald Suttles with Albert Hunter, *The Social Construction of Communities* (Chicago: University of Chicago Press, 1972).

9. Suttles, *Social Order of the Slum*, p. 234.

10. Metropolitan Housing and Planning Council, "Directory of Economic Development Organizations in the Chicago Metropolitan Area," brochure, 1983.

11. National Training and Information Center, "Insurance Redlining: Organizing to Win" (2d ed.), brochure, 1981, pp. 178–230; Midwestern Regional Advisory Committees to the U.S. Commission on Civil Rights, *Insurance Redlining: Fact, Not Fiction* (Washington, D.C.: U.S. Government Printing Office, 1979), pp. 40–57; Gregory D. Squires, Ruthanne DeWolfe, and Alan S. DeWolfe, "Urban Decline or Disinvestment: Uneven Development, Redlining, and the Role of the Insurance Industry," *Social Problems* 27 (Oct. 1979): 79–95; National Association of Insurance Commissioners Task Force and Advisory Committee on Urban Reinvestment, "Final Report," June 8, 1982.

12. Kennedy, *Himself*, pp. 252–255.

13. Richard Wright, *Native Son* (New York: Harper and Row, 1940); James T. Farrell, *Studs Lonigan* (New York: New American Library, 1965); Theodore Dreiser, *The Financier* (New York: New American Library, 1967); Theodore Dreiser, *The Titans* (New York: Thomas Y. Crowell, 1981); Theodore Dreiser, *The Stoic* (New York: New American Library, 1981).

14. Rakove, *We Don't Want Nobody Nobody Sent*, p. x.

15. Gelvin Stevenson, "Insurance Redlining: A New Front in the Battle to Save People's Homes," *The Progressive* 43 (March 1979): 49–50.

16. Rose Helper, *Racial Policies and Practices of Real Estate Brokers* (Minneapolis: University of Minnesota Press, 1969), p. 201.

17. American Institute of Real Estate Appraisers, *The Appraisal of Real Estate* (Chicago: The Institute, 1967), cited in Michael S. Holewinski, "Mortgage Redlining: Are Neighborhoods Losing the Battle They Thought Was Won?," unpub. report, Aug. 3, 1977, pp. 5–6.

18. Frances E. Werner, William F. Frej, and David M. Madway, "Redlining and Disinvestment: Causes, Consequences, and Proposed Remedies," *Clearinghouse Review* 10 (Oct. 1976): 501–542.

19. Holewinski, "Mortgage Redlining"; Karen Orren, *Corporate Power and Social Change: The Politics of the Life Insurance Industry* (Baltimore: Johns Hopkins University Press, 1974); Woodstock Institute, "Partners in Need," brochure, 1986.

20. James L. Greer, "The Politics of Decline and Growth: Planning, Economic Transformation, and the Structuring of Urban Futures in American Cities," Ph.D. diss., University of Chicago, 1983.

21. Charles Bowden and Lew Kreinberg, *Street Signs Chicago: Neighborhood and Other Illusions of Big-City Life* (Chicago: Chicago Review Press, 1981), p. 146.

22. Chicago Economic Development Commission, "Chicago: One Town That Won't Let You Down," brochure, n.d.

23. Algren, *Chicago*, pp. 68–69.

24. City of Chicago, "Chicago 1992 Comprehensive Plan: Goals and Policies and Ten-Year Capital Development Strategies," report, Oct. 1982; TRUST, Inc., "Negotiating Chicago's Future," report, 1983.

25. Daniel Bell, *The End of Ideology* (New York: Free Press, 1960).

26. Harvey Molotch, "The City as a Growth Machine: Toward a Political Economy of Place," *American Journal of Sociology* 82 (Sept. 1976): 483–499; G. William Domhoff, *Who Rules America Now?* (Englewood Cliffs, N.J.: Prentice-Hall, 1983).

27. "The Reindustrialization of America," special issue of *Business Week*, June 30, 1980, pp. 24–27.

28. "Summary Fact Sheet: The President's Economic Program," brochure, Feb. 18, 1981.

29. "A Guide to Understanding the Supply-Siders," *Business Week*, Dec. 22, 1980.

30. Roger E. Alcaly and David Mermelstein (eds.), *The Fiscal Crisis of American Cities* (New York: Vintage Books, 1977), p. 8.

31. *Ibid.*, p. 7.

32. *Ibid.*, p. 9.

33. R. C. Longworth, "City on the Brink," *Chicago Tribune*, May 12, 1981.

34. Washington Transition Committee, "Towards a Prosperous, Compassionate, and Efficient Chicago: Policy Recommendations for Mayor Harold Washington," report, 1983, p. 135.

35. Chicago Economic Development Commission, "Chicago's Economic Incentives for Business," report, n.d.

36. Longworth, "How Much Time Do We Have?," May 10, 1981.

37. "Growth Plans Need a Push," *Chicago Tribune*, April 9, 1984.

38. William S. Singer and William J. Mahin, "Chicago's Fiscal Crisis," lecture series on the future of Chicago, Department of Political Science, University of Illinois at Chicago Circle, 1983.

39. Alan Wolfe, *America's Impasse: The Rise and Fall of the Politics of Growth* (Boston: South End Press, 1981).

40. Lester C. Thurow, *The Zero-Sum Society: Distribution and the Possibilities for Economic Change* (New York: Penguin Books, 1981), pp. 7–10; Ira C. Magaziner and Robert B. Reich, *Minding America's Business: The Decline and Rise of the American Economy* (New York: Vintage Books, 1982), pp. 41–63; Samuel Bowles, David M. Gordon, and Thomas E. Weisskopf, *Beyond the Wasteland: A Democratic Alternative to Economic Decline* (New York: Anchor/Doubleday, 1983), pp. 34–61.

41. Barry Bluestone and Bennett Harrison, *The Deindustrialization of America: Plant Closings, Community Abandonment, and the Dismantling of Basic Industry* (New York: Basic Books, 1982), p. 26.

42. Robert G. Sheets, Russell L. Smith, and Kenneth P. Voytek, "Corporate Disinvestment and Metropolitan Manufacturing Job Loss," report, Labor Market Information Service, Center for Governmental Studies, Northern Illinois University, 1984.

43. President's Commission for a National Agenda for the Eighties, *A National Agenda for the Eighties* (Washington, D.C.: U.S. Government Printing Office, 1980), p. 65.

44. Bluestone and Harrison, *Deindustrialization*, p. 42.

45. *Ibid.*, pp. 140–190.

46. Robert Sherrill, "Mergermania Reigns: The Decline and Fall of Antitrust," *The Nation* 321 (March 19, 1983): 336–339.

47. Robert B. Reich, *The Next American Frontier* (New York: Times Books, 1983), p. 157.

48. Robert H. Hayes and William J. Abernathy, "Managing Our Way to Decline," *Harvard Business Review* 58 (July/Aug. 1980): 67–77.

49. Jack Newfield and Paul DuBrul, *The Abuse of Power: The Permanent Government and the Fall of New York* (New York: Viking Press, 1977).

50. Mark Laubacher and Woods Bowman, "Illinois Business: Charity Begins at Home," *Illinois Issues*, May 1982; Michael Kieschnick, *Taxes and Growth: Business Incentives and Economic Development* (Washington, D.C.: Council of State Planning Agencies, 1981); David M. Gordon, *The Working Poor: Towards a State Agenda* (Washington, D.C.: Council of State Planning Agencies, 1979); Thomas A. Pascarella and Richard D. Raymond, "Buying Bonds for Business: An Evaluation of the Industrial Revenue Bond Program," *Urban Affairs Quarterly* 18 (Sept. 1982): 73–89.

51. Illinois Advisory Committee to the U.S. Commission on Civil Rights, *Industrial Revenue Bonds: Equal Opportunity in Chicago's Industrial Revenue Bond Program?* (Washington, D.C.: U.S. Government Printing Office, 1986).

52. Michael I. Luger, "Some Micro-Consequences of Macro-Policies: The Case of Business Tax Incentives (BTIs)," *Proceedings of the National Tax Association* (Columbus, Ohio: The Association, 1981).

53. Harvey Brenner, "Estimating the Social Costs of National Economic Policy: Implications for Mental and Physical Health and Clinical Aggression," report, Joint Economic Committee of the Congress of the United States, 1976.

54. Stephen S. Mick, "Social and Personal Costs of Plant Shutdowns," *Industrial Relations* 14 (May 1975): 203–208; C&R Associates, "Measuring the Community Costs of Plant Closing: Overview of Methods and Data Sources," report, Federal Trade Commission, n.d.

55. Sidney Cobb and Stanislav V. Kasl, *Termination: The Consequences of Job Loss* (Washington, D.C.: National Institute for Occupational Safety and Health, U.S. Department of Health, Education and Welfare, 1977), p. 134.

56. C&R Associates, "Indicators for Measuring the Community Costs of Plant Closings," report, Federal Trade Commission, 1978.

57. Illinois Advisory Committee to the U.S. Commission on Civil Rights, *Shutdown: Economic Dislocation and Equal Opportunity* (Washington, D.C.: U.S. Government Printing Office, 1981).

58. Thomas C. Nowak and Kay A. Snyder, "Women's Struggle to Survive a Plant Shutdown," *Journal of Intergroup Relations* 11, no. 4 (Winter 1983): 25–44.

59. Alfred Watkins, "Felix Rohatyn's Biggest Deal," *Working Papers* 8 (Sept./Oct. 1981): 44–52.

60. William E. Connolly, "Progress, Growth, and Pessimism in America," *democracy*, Fall 1983, pp. 23–24.

61. Bluestone and Harrison, *Deindustrialization*, pp. 82–107; Joe R. Feagin, "The Social Costs of Houston's Growth: A Sunbelt Boomtown Reexamined," *International Journal of Urban and Regional Research* 9 (1985): 164–185.

62. Survey Research Center, Institute for Social Research, University of Michigan, *Employee Ownership Report to the Economic Development Administration, U.S. Department of Commerce* (Ann Arbor: University of Michigan, 1977); Daniel Zwerdling, *Workplace Democracy* (New York Harper Colophon, 1980); Frank Lindenfeld and Joyce Rothschild-Whitt, *Workplace Democracy and Social Change* (Boston: Porter Sargent, 1982); Corey Rosen, Katherine J. Klein, and Karen M. Young, *Employee Ownership in America: The Equity Solution* (Lexington, Mass.: D. C. Heath, 1986). For additional information contact The National Center for Employee Ownership, 4836 South 28th Street, Arlington, Va. 22206.

63. Ana Gutierrez Johnson and William Foote Whyte, "The Mondragon System of Worker Production Cooperatives," *Industrial and Labor Relations Review* 31 (Oct. 1977): 18–30; Center for Community Economic Development, "Community Development Corporations," (The Center, 1975); Stewart E. Perry, *Building a Model Black Community: The Roxbury Action Program* (Cambridge, Mass.: Center for Community Economic Development, 1978).

64. Joe R. Feagin, *The Urban Real Estate Game: Playing Monopoly with Real Money* (Englewood Cliffs, N.J.: Prentice-Hall, 1983), pp. 191–208.

65. Reich, *Next American Frontier*, p. 20.

66. C. Wright Mills, *The Sociological Imagination* (New York: Oxford University Press, 1968).

67. David Smith and Patrick McGuigan, *Towards a Public Balance Sheet* (Washington, D.C.: National Center for Economic Alternatives, 1979).

Chapter 2

1. Anthony Massaro, "Child of Steel," *Mill Hunk Herald* (Pittsburgh), Spring 1985.

2. In talking about the Chicago area we will look at three geographic groupings. When we refer to the "Chicago metropolitan area," we will be looking at the city of Chicago and its suburbs, also known as the Chicago Standard Metropolitan Statistical Area (SMSA). References to "Chicago" or the "city" will exclude the suburbs. Finally the "Chicago region" or "urban area" will refer to Chicago, its Illinois suburbs, and the contiguous Northwest Indiana urban industrial area. (See Map 2.1.) Although politically divided from Chicago and Illinois, the economy of Northwest Indiana — specifically Hammond, East Chicago, and Gary — is interwoven with Chicago's industrial roots. The relationship between these two metropolitan areas is recognized by the U.S. Bureau of the Census, which has combined the 7,163,624 residents of the Chicago SMSA with the 642,781 inhabitants of the Gary-Hammond-East Chicago, Indiana SMSA and the 123,137 residents of the Kenosha, Wisconsin SMSA to create the Chicago-Gary-Kenosha Consolidated Statistical Area. (For more information on the rationale used by the U.S. Census Bureau in defining the relationship between these metropolitan areas, see U.S. Department of Commerce, *1980 Census Users' Guide* [Washington, D.C.: U.S. Government Printing Office, 1981].)

3. John F. McDonald, *Employment Location and Industrial Land Use in Metropolitan Chicago* (Champaign, Ill.: Stipes Publishing Co., 1984), table 1.4, p. 10.

4. The 1977 figure is from *ibid.*, table 1.4, p. 10.

5. Lake County, Indiana also experienced a reduced share of manufacturing employment during this period — a drop from 9.8 percent in 1947 to 7.9 percent in 1982. In 1977 Lake County's share was 9.0 percent; the precipitous drop in steel employment in 1977–1982 undoubtedly contributed to the employment share decline in this very short time period.

6. The Cook County figure from 1982 actually represents a decline from 322,000 in 1977, so Cook County manufacturing employment increased until 1977, but is now declining.

7. McDonald, *Employment Location*, p. 11.

8. Disinvestment refers to a pattern of investment that functions to reduce or eliminate capital investment in the region. Disinvestment often involves a pattern of not using profits to maintain and upgrade machinery and plant facilities; instead, profits are channeled to other industries or other regions. The term has been used most recently in books studying deindustrialization: Lester C. Thurow, *The Zero-Sum Society: Distribution and the Possibilities for Economic Change* (New York: Basic Books, 1980), p. 77, and Barry Bluestone and Bennett Harrison, *The Deindustrialization of America: Plant Closings, Community Abandonment, and the Dismantling of Basic Industry* (New York: Basic Books, 1982).

9. Chicago Department of City Planning, *Industrial Movements and Expansions, 1947–1957* (Chicago: The Department, 1961), cited in James S. deBettencourt, untitled study on small business in the Chicago area completed for Continental Bank, 1984, p. 7., n. 2.

10. Patrick Ashton, "Urbanization and the Dynamics of Suburban Development Under Capitalism," in William K. Tabb and Larry Sawers (eds.), *Marxism and the Metropolis*, 2d ed. (New York: Oxford University Press, 1984), pp. 54–81; Paul A. Baran and Paul M. Sweezy, *Monopoly Capital* (New York: Monthly Review Press, 1966); John Kramer (ed.), *North American Suburbs: Politics, Diversity, and Change* (Berkeley, Calif.: Glendessary Press, 1972); Bennett Harrison, *Urban Economic Development: Suburbanization, Minority Opportunity, and the Condition of the Central City* (Washington, D.C.: Urban Institute, 1974); John D. Kasarda, "The Implications of Contemporary Redistribution Trends for National Urban Policy," *Social Science Quarterly* 61 (Dec. 1980): 373–400.

11. Robert G. Sheets, Russell L. Smith, and Kenneth P. Voytek, "Corporate Disinvestment and Metropolitan Manufacturing Job Loss," report, Labor Market Information Service, Center for Government Studies, Northern Illinois University, 1984.

12. *Ibid.*, p. 19.

13. R. C. Longworth, "How Much Time Do We Have? . . . No Time," *Chicago Tribune*, May 10, 1981.

14. DeBettencourt, Continental Bank study, p. 14.

15. McDonald, *Employment Location*, p. 12.

16. Illinois Advisory Committee to the U.S. Commission on Civil Rights, *Shutdown: Economic Dislocation and Equal Opportunity* (Washington, D.C.: U.S. Government Printing Office, 1981).

17. R. C. Longworth, "Holding Actions," *Chicago Tribune Magazine*, April 15, 1984.

18. Joseph Persky's research is cited in Dan Swinney, "Documenting the Social Costs of Unemployment," *Labor Research Review* 1 (Summer 1983): 50–51. Persky's research was part of a 1983 research project completed by David C. Ranney, Joe Persky, and Susan Rosenblum for the Center for Urban Economic Development, University of Illinois at Chicago.

19. James L. Greer, "The Politics of Decline and Growth: Planning, Economic Transformation, and the Structuring of Urban Futures in American Cities," Ph.D. diss., University of Chicago, 1983, pp. 107–108.

20. For example, research completed by Tom DuBois for the Midwest Center for

Labor Research has shown that, while regional steel industry employment has dropped since the late 1970s, annual steel production has remained stable or has increased.

21. Among those criticizing USX have been Monsignor Owen Rice (Western Pennsylvania), Staughton Lynd (a Youngstown, Ohio lawyer and labor activist), and Ron Wiesen (president of USWA Local 1397, representing workers at the shutdown USX steel works in Homestead, Pennsylvania). The California Newsreel film *Business of America* includes interviews with these critics. The Midwest Center for Labor Research has argued the same point, most recently in *Labor Research Review* 1 (Winter 1983).

22. Steven Greenhouse, "U.S. Steel's Long Road Back," *New York Times*, June 5, 1984; Richard I. Kirkland Jr., "Big Steel Recasts Itself," *Fortune*, April 6, 1981, pp. 28–34.

23. Daniel Rosenheim and James Warren, "Layoff Study Shows Costly Human Toll," *Chicago Tribune*, Oct. 21, 1984.

24. *Ibid.*

25. Northeastern Illinois Planning Commission, *Spatial Distribution of Employment* (Chicago: The Commission, 1981), table 2C, p. 15.

26. The 1985 figure is based on the March 1985 employment figure published in the Indiana Employment Security Division *Labor Market Letter* and provided by the Northwest Indiana Regional Planning Authority, Highland, Indiana.

27. This is based on an estimate of regional employment published by the Illinois Department of Labor. In 1972, they reported that there were 222,600 employees in the CBD; in 1982 there were 240,200. There was actually a drop below the 223,000 level for a number of the years, but there has been a steady increase since 1975. These figures are also slight underestimates of employment since they do not include state and local government employees (Illinois Department of Employment Security, *Where Workers Work, 1982* [Springfield, Ill.: The Department, 1983], p. 59).

28. Interview with Robert Palmer, staff member, Planning Division of the DuPage County Development Department, Wheaton, Ill., Jan. 8, 1986.

29. *Ibid.*

30. *Ibid.*

31. This is based on data from the "Economic Profiles" of each SMSA county published by the Illinois Department of Commerce and Community Affairs, n.d.

32. Interview with Donald Klein, executive director, Greater Barrington Council of Governments, Barrington Hills, Ill., Jan. 8, 1986.

33. *Ibid.*

34. Interview with Beth Benoit, senior economic development specialist, Lake County Department of Planning, Zoning, and Environmental Quality, Waukegan, Ill., Jan. 3, 1986.

35. Based on data from "The Fortune 500," *Fortune*, April 30, 1984, pp. 274–322.

36. Longworth, "How Much Time Do We Have?"

37. "The City That Survives," special issues of *The Economist*, March 29–April 4, 1980.

38. Robert A. Bennett, "U.S. Will Invest $4.5 Billion in Rescue of Chicago Bank," *New York Times*, July 27, 1984.

39. Greg David and David Snyder, "Biggest U.S. Banks Targeting Chicago,

Threaten Hot Battle," *Crain's Chicago Business*, May 14, 1984, pp. 1 and 87; "Chicago: The Enigma of Banking," *Chicago Tribune*, Oct. 28, 1984.

40. John Coulter, director of economic development, Chicago Association of Commerce and Industry, comments to American Demographics conference, Chicago, March 6, 1984.

41. Commercial Club of Chicago, "Economic Plan: Jobs for Metropolitan Chicago, Economic Scan," data prepared by Federal Reserve Bank of Chicago for a subsequent report published as Commercial Club of Chicago, *Make No Little Plans: Jobs for Metropolitan Chicago* (Chicago: The Club, 1984).

42. Chicago Department of Economic Development, "Chicago's Assets for Business and Industry," report, 1983, p. 15.

43. Commercial Club, "Economic Plan," p. I-3.0.

44. *Ibid.*, p. I-22.0.

45. *Ibid.*, p. I-4.0.

46. *Ibid.*, p. I-3.0.

47. Quoted in R. C. Longworth, "Fewer Firms, Fewer Jobs, Less Revenue," part of series entitled "Chicago: City on the Brink," *Chicago Tribune*, May 11, 1981.

48. Commercial Club, "Economic Plan," p. I-9.0.

49. *Ibid.*, pp. I-10.0–I-15.0.

50. McDonald, *Employment Location*, pp. 98–99.

51. Commercial Club, "Economic Plan," p. I-8.0.

52. Palmer interview.

53. Patrick Reardon, "Suburban Saga: Rich Town, Poor Town," *Chicago Tribune*, Dec. 15, 1985.

54. *Ibid.*

55. Klein interview.

56. "State and Metropolitan Area Employment and Unemployment," U.S. Bureau of Labor Statistics *News*, March 1984 (preliminary figure for Gary-Hammond-East Chicago SMSA).

57. Commercial Club, "Economic Plan," p. E-32.0.

58. Estimates from Richard B. Freeman and James L. Medoff, "New Estimates of Private Sector Unionism in the United States," *Industrial and Labor Relations Review* 32 (Jan. 1979): 167–168.

59. U.S. Bureau of Labor Statistics, *Directory of National Unions and Employee Associations*, Bulletin 2044 (Washington, D.C.: The Bureau, 1977), p. 63.

60. Bill Granger and Lori Granger, *Fighting Jane: Mayor Jane Byrne and the Chicago Machine* (New York: Dial Press, 1980), pp. 92–93.

61. James Warren, "City, County Stay a Step Ahead on Union-Voting Law," *Chicago Tribune*, May 27, 1984.

62. This is, in part, because of labor's weak foothold in the suburbs. It is also due to the fact that newer suburban manufacturing firms tend to be smaller, and small firms have traditionally been difficult to organize. Although no government agency or union body maintains accurate figures on city-to-suburb unionization differentials, a few studies have confirmed the impression that the unionization rate is lower in the suburbs. A survey of small business firms found that 50 percent of the city manufacturing firms were unionized compared to only 25 percent of the suburban manufacturing

firms (cited in deBettencourt, Continental Bank study, p. 30). Newer suburban businesses are also less likely than older city businesses to be unionized since major industrial unions have either not been aggressive in such workplaces or have been frustrated by a more anti-union environment in the suburbs. Union organizers in the service sector have recognized that the suburbs have usually been more hostile to organized labor (interview with Bonnie Ladin, staff member, District 925 of the Service Employees International Union in Chicago, Chicago, Nov. 14, 1984).

63. Interview with Robert Mier, commissioner, Chicago Department of Economic Development, Chicago, Feb. 28, 1984.

64. Interview with Paul Booth, staff member, American Federation of State, County, and Municipal Employees in Chicago, Chicago, Nov. 16, 1984.

65. *Ibid.*

66. *Shakman v. Democratic Organization of Cook County*, 435 F.2d 267 (7th Cir. 1970).

67. Ladin interview.

68. More details on the Chicago-based rank-and-file reform movement in the steelworkers union is contained in Philip W. Nyden, *Steelworkers Rank-and-File: The Political Economy of a Union Reform Movement* (New York: Praeger/Bergin and Garvey, 1984).

69. "State Business Climate Still Rests Near Bottom," *Chicago Sun-Times*, Feb. 7, 1983; Joe Cappo, "Grant Survey Needs More Stuff, Less Fluff," *Crain's Chicago Business*, April 30, 1984, p. 6.

70. Within the Chicago metropolitan area there is another distinction regarding business climate. While Alexander Grant has not rated city and suburb, *Crain's Chicago Business* has. In a 1984 survey of 841 area business executives, on a scale of 1 (poor) to 10 (excellent), Chicago ranked a low 3.9 while the suburbs received a 6.2 (Sandra Conn, "Survey Reveals Anger at Business Climate," *Crain's Chicago Business*, April 30, 1984, pp. 1–46).

While the suburban score does not indicate that the executives view the white-collar communities as a businessperson's heaven, it certainly does show a preference for the growing suburbs. The same survey found a Catch 22 for Chicago city planners: when a city firm *is* successful and starts to look around for room to expand, the suburbs look better because of lower taxes, lower real estate costs, a more favorable political climate, and a lower unionization rate (Conn, "Survey"). Therefore, in the eyes of those who look at business climates, the city is completely overcast while the suburbs are only partly cloudy. The city-suburban business climate contrast, while not unique to Chicago, poses a challenge to those seeking to save the city's economic base.

71. Bluestone and Harrison, *Deindustrialization*, p. 133.

72. Cappo, "Grant Survey."

73. Bluestone and Harrison, *Deindustrialization*, p. 182.

74. George Cloos and Philip Cummins, "Economic Upheaval in the Midwest," Federal Reserve Bank of Chicago *Economic Perspectives* 8, no. 1 (Jan./Feb. 1984): p. 11.

75. John Herbers, "Vast Shift Seen in U.S. Grants to States and Municipalities," *New York Times*, Dec. 20, 1983.

76. James R. Anderson, *Bankrupting American Cities: The Tax Burden and Expenditures of the Pentagon by Metropolitan Area* (Lansing, Mich.: Employment Research Associates, 1983).

77. Stanley J. Hallett and G. Alfred Hess Jr., "The Future of Chicago: Technological Innovation," speech no. 5, in series ed. Dick Simpson, Department of Political Science, University of Illinois at Chicago, 1981? (n.d.), no page numbers.

78. Sandra Conn, "Small Business Boom: Chicago-Area Firms Predict Big Gains in Sales, Profits," *Crain's Chicago Business*, April 23, 1984, p. 1.

79. There is a further argument that small employers are more labor intensive than large corporations and more likely to provide significant numbers of new jobs (David Birch, "The Job Generation Process," paper, MIT Program on Neighborhood and Regional Change, 1979).

On the other hand, other researchers have questioned some of Birch's assumptions and have cautioned that small businesses may be more likely than larger businesses to provide part-time and lower-paying jobs (Catherine Armington and Margarie Odle, "Small Business—How Many Jobs?," *Brookings Review* 1 [Winter 1982]: 14–17; Mark Maier, "Is Small Beautiful?: Few Jobs, Poor Conditions in Small Firms," *Dollars & Sense* 103 [Jan. 1985]: 12–14). Nevertheless, in the present discussion of the impact of small business, it is important to point out that small businesses are more likely to develop in neighborhoods rather than in the central business district.

80. Illinois Bureau of Employment Security, *Where Workers Work*, p. 58. This is actually an underestimate since these figures do not include state and local government employment, which is heavily concentrated in Chicago's CBD.

81. Longworth, "How Much Time Do We Have?"

82. Tim Franklin and Carol Oppenheim, "Block Grant in City Tug of War," *Chicago Tribune*, May 13, 1984.

83. David Moberg, "Will Neighborhood Jobs Win 'War' for Washington?," *In These Times*, May 2–8, 1984.

84. Thom Shanker, "Washington, Assessing Mayor's First Year in Office," *Chicago Tribune*, April 29, 1984.

85. Moberg, "Will Neighborhood Jobs Win 'War'?"

86. City of Chicago, "Chicago Works Together: 1984 Chicago Development Plan," report, May 1984, p. 1.

87. Although there are different understandings of which industries are "high-tech," the U.S. Bureau of Labor Statistics (BLS) defines "high-tech" industries as those with much higher than average research and development expenditures and a well above average number of technical employees (*Business Week*, March 28, 1983). Generally, this industrial group includes makers of drugs, computers, electronic components, aircraft, and laboratory equipment. Service industries such as computer programming, data processing, and research laboratories are also considered to be in this sector.

The BLS includes in the "high-tech" category those industries with twice the national average of research and development expenditures and technical employees. It does have another classification of "high-tech intensive," which includes industries not included in the first category but above average on these two dimensions. This latter category covers most of the chemical industry, the petroleum refining industry, and makers of textile, printing, electrical, and medical equipment.

88. Some economic planners have also questioned the high-tech solution; for ex-

ample, see the special issue of the *American Planning Association Journal*, Summer 1984.

89. "America Reaches to High Tech for Growth," *Business Week*, March 28, 1983, pp. 84–90.

90. *Ibid.*

91. Interview with David B. Mirza, professor of economics, Loyola University of Chicago, Chicago, Feb. 25, 1983. While Chicago does have research universities that do some work in a range of high-tech fields—for example, the Illinois Institute of Technology, the University of Illinois at Chicago, Northwestern University, and the University of Chicago—these universities have not been providing the support network and critical mass of personnel needed to stimulate high-tech industries.

92. "America Reaches to High Tech for Growth."

93. "What Sent Atari Overseas," *Business Week*, March 14, 1983, pp. 102–103.

94. "America Reaches to High Tech for Growth."

95. Subcommittee on Monetary and Fiscal Policy of the Joint Economic Committee, U.S. Congress, *Location of High Technology Firms and Regional Economic Development* (Washington, D.C.: U.S. Government Printing Office, 1982), p. 29.

96. Chicago Department of Economic Development, "Chicago's Enterprise Zones," pamphlet, 1984? (n.d.).

97. Longworth, "Holding Actions."

98. Bluestone and Harrison, *Deindustrialization*, pp. 18, 19, 91, 195.

99. Based on data from Barry Bluestone and Bennett Harrison, *Capital and Communities: The Causes and Consequences of Private Disinvestment* (Washington, D.C.: Progressive Alliance, 1980), table 31, p. 225.

100. Birch, "Job Generation Process," p. 8; Ralph Nader and Jerry Jacobs, "Battle to Lure Industry Costly," *Chicago Tribune*, Nov. 12, 1979; William Street, "Better Late Than . . .: Myths of Economic Development," *Plant Closings Bulletin*, Summer 1981.

101. Bluestone and Harrison, *Deindustrialization*, p. 228.

102. William W. Goldsmith, "Bringing the Third World Home," *Working Papers* 9 (March/April 1982): 25–30.

103. Kathleen McCourt, Sheryl Knight, and Philip W. Nyden, "Survey of Agencies Offering Employment Services for Women," report, Midwest Women's Center, Chicago, 1983.

104. Interview with Dan Swinney, director, Midwest Center for Labor Research, Chicago, Nov. 19, 1984.

105. Interview with Tom DuBois, staff member, Midwest Center for Labor Research, Chicago, Nov. 19, 1984.

106. The city issued a $1 million low-interest industrial revenue bond (IRB) to help Playskool buy new machinery. Between 1980 and 1984 this probably saved the company $200,000 in interest compared to the level of interest that would have been charged by other sources of such loans. In the IRB agreement, Playskool promised to increase employment and the city's tax base. Playskool was later bought by Hasbro Bradley, which decided to consolidate operations elsewhere in the United States (David Moberg, "After Playskool," *In These Times*, Dec. 5–11, 1984).

107. R. C. Longworth, "Toymaker Cuts Deal with City on Closings," *Chicago Tribune*, Jan. 29, 1985. As a result of Playskool's actions, the city of Chicago, as well

as the suburbs, is exploring ways to attach tighter strings to economic incentives that they provide to business (Ray Gibson, "Playskool Defection Has Cities Thinking Twice," *Chicago Tribune*, Jan. 29, 1985).

108. Merrill Goozner, "Workers Fund Study to Save Chicago Tannery," *Crain's Chicago Business*, Aug. 20–27, 1984; "Neighborhood Notes," *The Reader* (Chicago), Jan. 25, 1985, p. 3.

109. Goozner, "Workers Fund Study."

110. For example, in Wierton, West Virginia, steelworkers bought their plant when National Steel announced plans to shut it down. After months of planning and co-operation from community leaders, by 1986 Wierton Steel had become the largest employee-owned firm in the nation and ranked among the Fortune 500 industrial corporations. While the employee stock ownership plan (ESOP) used to finance the takeover plan has been criticized as not allowing for true workers' control, the scheme has certainly been a shot in the arm for an otherwise declining industrial area.

There are scores of examples of successful employee or community buyouts in the United States. See Frank Lindenfeld and Joyce Rothschild-Whitt, *Workplace Democracy and Social Change* (Boston: Porter Sargent, 1982); William Foote Whyte, Tove Helland Hammer, Christopher B. Meek, Reed Nelson, and Robert N. Stern, *Worker Participation and Ownership: Cooperative Strategies for Strengthening Local Economies* (Ithaca, N.Y.: ILR Press, 1983); Daniel Zwerdling, *Workplace Democracy* (New York: Harper Colophon, 1980).

111. Interview with Scott Bernstein, executive director, Center for Neighborhood Technology, Chicago, Nov. 13, 1984.

112. *Ibid.*

Chapter 3

1. Interview with Nicholas von Hoffman on "Morning Edition," National Public Radio, Jan. 7, 1985.

2. For example, see Thom Shanker and William Presecky, "Mayor Stumps in Test of His Own Machine," *Chicago Tribune*, March 18, 1984.

3. Allan H. Spear, *Black Chicago: The Making of a Negro Ghetto, 1890–1920* (Chicago: University of Chicago Press, 1967), pp. 186–192.

4. Raymond E. Wolfinger, "Why Political Machines Have Not Withered Away and Other Revisionist Thoughts," *Journal of Politics* 34 (May 1972): 374–375.

5. John M. Allswang, *A House for All Peoples: Ethnic Politics in Chicago, 1890–1936* (Lexington: University of Kentucky Press, 1971), pp. 15–36.

6. Spear, *Black Chicago*, p. 192.

7. Alex Gottfried, *Boss Cermak of Chicago* (Seattle: University of Washington Press, 1962), pp. 98–198; Harold F. Gosnell, *Machine Politics Chicago Model* (Chicago: University of Chicago Press, 1977), pp. 91–126; Allswang, *A House for All Peoples*, p. 45.

8. Gosnell, *Machine Politics*, pp. 75–76.

9. *Ibid.*, pp. 27–50.

10. *Ibid.*, pp. 51–68. For a contemporary discussion of these variations, see William

Kornblum, *Blue Collar Community* (Chicago: University of Chicago Press, 1974), pp. 141–156.

11. Milton Rakove, *Don't Make No Waves... Don't Back No Losers: An Insider's Analysis of the Daley Machine* (Bloomington: Indiana University Press, 1975), pp. 117–128; Thomas R. Guterbock, *Machine Politics in Transition: Party and Community in Chicago* (Chicago: University of Chicago Press, 1980), pp. 173–207.

12. Interview with Aloysius Majerczyk, Chicago, Feb. 21, 1984.

13. Len O'Connor, *Clout: Mayor Daley and His City* (New York: Avon, 1975), pp. 239–251.

14. O'Connor, *Clout*, pp. 50–63; Martin Meyerson and Edward C. Banfield, *Politics, Planning, and the Public Interest: The Case of Public Housing in Chicago* (Glencoe, Ill.: Free Press, 1955), pp. 61–88.

15. O'Connor, *Clout*, p. 61; Meyerson and Banfield, *Politics*, p. 80.

16. O'Connor, *Clout*, pp. 87–88; Mike Royko, *Boss: Richard J. Daley of Chicago* (New York: E. P. Dutton, 1971), pp. 61–63. Also see Ira J. Bach's comments in Arnold R. Hirsch, *Making the Second Ghetto: Race and Housing in Chicago, 1940–1960* (New York: Cambridge University Press, 1983), p. 130.

17. O'Connor, *Clout*, pp. 1–82.

18. Rakove's estimate of the amount of available patronage was probably the most reliable. He set the number of jobs in all local governments in Cook County at 30,000 (*Don't Make No Waves*, p. 112).

19. According to the 1976 and 1977 *Municipal Yearbooks* (the *Yearbooks* are published annually in Washington, D.C. by the International City Management Association), among cities with more than one million residents Chicago led in entry-level salaries for firemen and refuse workers. Only Los Angeles' police officers were paid more (see pp. 102 and 107, respectively). In 1954, the year before Daley became mayor, Detroit and Los Angeles paid policemen more, and Los Angeles paid firemen more than did Chicago (*Municipal Yearbook, 1955*, pp. 376, 413).

20. O'Connor, *Clout*, p. 131.

21. In 1954, the year before Richard Daley assumed the mayoralty, the city planning staff numbered 24. Ten years later this figure was 84. City planning expenditures increased from $149,500 to $914,500 annually during this same period. See the *Municipal Yearbooks* for 1954 (p. 296) and 1965 (p. 318) for these figures. At the end of 1954 the city counted seven urban renewal projects (four in the execution stage). By 1956 this number was 19; by 1959 it was 25—with 22 completed or in the execution stage (Housing and Home Finance Agency, *Annual Reports* for 1955, 1957, and 1960 [Washington, D.C.: U.S. Government Printing Office], pp. 460, 253, and 278 respectively).

22. William Gruber, "Close Ties to Business 'Vital' to Cities," *Chicago Tribune*, Sept. 17, 1978; Paul E. Peterson, *School Politics Chicago Style* (Chicago: University of Chicago Press, 1976), pp. 90–96.

23. O'Connor, *Clout*, pp. 172–174; Royko, *Boss*, pp. 119–123.

24. Metropolitan Housing and Planning Council, "Chicago Area Public Capital Investments: Toward the Year 2000," report, Dec. 1982, p. 4.

25. Rakove, *Don't Make No Waves*, p. 254.

26. Charles J. Orlebeke, *Federal Aid to Chicago* (Washington, D.C.: Brookings Institution, 1983), p. 15.

27. Steve Bogira, "Drawing the Lines," *The Reader* (Chicago), March 5, 1982.

28. Study Commission on Metropolitan Government, Illinois City Managers Association, "Governmental Structure in the Chicago Metropolitan Area," report, May 1966, pp. 29–38.

29. For example, see Edward C. Banfield, *Political Influence* (New York: Free Press, 1965), pp. 57–90.

30. John Gorman, "Tax Foes Move to Ban Home Rule in 15 Suburbs," *Chicago Tribune*, Nov. 1, 1979.

31. Carole Goodwin, *The Oak Park Strategy: Community Control of Racial Change* (Chicago: University of Chicago Press, 1979); Ray Gibson, "Oak Park Backs Idea of Integration Plan," *Chicago Tribune*, Aug. 21, 1984. Oak Park's strategy of managed integration is discussed in Chapter 4.

32. Robert Benjamin, "Gun Control Catching On in the Suburbs," *Chicago Tribune*, July 15, 1981.

33. George Papajohn, "13 Suburbs Sue to Block O'Hare Plan," *Chicago Tribune*, Dec. 5, 1984.

34. Metropolitan Housing and Planning Council, "Infrastructure Planning and Financing Survey: Preliminary Results," report, Nov. 30, 1984.

35. Banfield, *Political Influence*, pp. 190–231; David Gilbert, "RTA Plan Approved," *Chicago Tribune*, Dec. 2, 1973.

36. Joe Kolman, "RTA: The Monster That Hates Chicago," *The Reader* (Chicago), June 6, 1980.

37. Gary Washburn and Philip Lentz, "Fares Top New RTA's Agenda," *Chicago Tribune*, Nov. 3, 1983; Daniel Engler and Tim Franklin, "'Build Illinois' Nailed Down," *Chicago Tribune*, July 9, 1985; R. Bruce Dold, "Chicago, Cook Cut into 'Build Illinois' Pie," *Chicago Tribune*, July 9, 1985.

38. For the general statement of the Alinsky strategy, see Saul D. Alinsky, *Reveille for Radicals* (New York: Vintage Books, 1969). On the development of TWO, see John Hall Fish, *Black Power/White Control: The Struggle of the Woodlawn Organization in Chicago* (Princeton, N.J.: Princeton University Press, 1973).

39. Hirsch, *Making the Second Ghetto*, pp. 135–211.

40. *Ibid.*, pp. 212–258. Also see Meyerson and Banfield, *Politics*, pp. 91–251. The consequences of this practice will be discussed in Chapter 4.

41. Interview with Richard Barnett, political organizer, Chicago, Jan. 8, 1984.

42. Ann Grimes, "UNO: Catholic Clergy Up Front in Back of the Yards Organizing Effort," *The Reader* (Chicago), April 1, 1983.

43. John McCarron, "Study Charges City Gets Short End of Tax Break for Hilton," *Chicago Tribune*, Nov. 8, 1981.

44. Majerczyk interview.

45. James Q. Wilson, *The Amateur Democrat* (Chicago: University of Chicago Press, 1966).

46. *Ibid.*, pp. 65–95.

47. Dick Simpson and George Beam, *Strategies for Change* (Chicago: Swallow Press, 1976), pp. 188–203.

48. Greta Salem, *The Forty-Fourth Ward Assembly* (Chicago: Center for Urban Policy, Loyola University, 1980); Dick Simpson, Judy Stevens, and Rick Kohnen

(eds.), *Neighborhood Government in Chicago's 44th Ward* (Champaign, Ill.: Stipes Publishing Co., 1979).

49. O'Connor, *Clout*, p. 121; Paul Kleppner, "Chicago Elects a Black Mayor: An Historical Analysis of the 1983 Election," report, American Jewish Committee, Chicago Chapter, July 1983.

50. Kleppner, "Chicago Elects a Black Mayor," p. 35.

51. Gary Rivlin, "Edward the Second," *The Reader* (Chicago), Jan. 20, 1984.

52. O'Connor, *Clout*, p. 254.

53. Len O'Connor, *Requiem: The Decline and Demise of Mayor Daley and His Era* (Chicago: Contemporary Books, 1977), p. 121.

54. Peterson, *School Politics*, pp. 186–216.

55. Gilbert, "RTA Plan Approved."

56. Sanford J. Ungar, "Chicago A.D. (After Daley)," *The Atlantic*, March 1977, pp. 4–18.

57. Kleppner, "Chicago Elects a Black Mayor," p. 42; Joseph Zikmund II, "Mayoral Voting and Ethnic Politics in the Daley-Bilandic-Byrne Era," in Samuel K. Gove and Louis H. Masotti (eds.), *After Daley: Chicago Politics in Transition* (Urbana: University of Illinois Press, 1982), p. 45.

58. A third consequence was that the Washington administration, which far more than its two predecessors was inclined to systematically replace Daley-era personnel, was constrained from doing so.

59. Guterbock, *Machine Politics in Transition*, p. 38.

60. James Q. Wilson, *Negro Politics* (New York: Free Press, 1965), pp. 111–132.

61. O'Connor, *Clout*, pp. 194–195; David Halberstam, "Daley of Chicago," *Harper's*, Aug. 1968, pp. 32–33.

62. O'Connor, *Clout*, p. 204.

63. *Ibid.*

64. Michael B. Preston, "Black Politics in the Post-Daley Era," in Gove and Masotti (eds.), *After Daley*, p. 99; Kleppner, "Chicago Elects a Black Mayor," pp. 34–42.

65. Preston, "Black Politics," p. 109.

66. Tim Franklin, "Black Voter Sign-Up Far Exceeds '79 Level," *Chicago Tribune*, Feb. 16, 1983.

67. Kleppner, "Chicago Elects a Black Mayor," pp. 76–81.

68. Douglas Frantz, "Daley Calls Campaign Leaflet a 'Filthy' Attempt to Split City," *Chicago Tribune*, Feb. 20, 1983.

69. Election figures appear in the *Chicago Tribune*, Feb. 23, 1983.

70. *Chicago Tribune*, April 14, 1983.

71. Kleppner, "Chicago Elects a Black Mayor," pp. 133–134.

72. O'Connor, *Clout*, p. 40.

73. E. R. Shipp, "Chicago Mayor Loses on Budget to Council Foes," *New York Times*, Dec. 18, 1983, p. 16; Thom Shanker, "City Budget Compromise Is Approved," *Chicago Tribune*, Dec. 23, 1983.

74. R. Bruce Dold and John Kass, "Mayor Vetoes O'Hare, 'L' Work," *Chicago Tribune*, Aug. 30, 1984.

75. Hank De Zutter, "So Far, Not Bad: Community Leaders Rate Washington Administration," *The Reader* (Chicago), Dec. 25, 1983.

76. John McCarron, "Navy Pier Talks Lose Council Vote," *Chicago Tribune*, May 1, 1983.

77. Gary Washburn, "Developers on Hold since Mayoral Race," *Chicago Tribune*, May 1, 1983; John McCarron, "City Projects Stuck on Drawing Board," *Chicago Tribune*, Dec. 11, 1983; interview with Robert Mier, commissioner, Chicago Department of Economic Development, Chicago, Feb. 28, 1984.

Chapter 4

1. *Chicago Real Estate Board Bulletin* 25, no. 4 (April 1917): 315–317, cited in Rose Helper, *Racial Policies and Practices of Real Estate Brokers* (Minneapolis: University of Minnesota Press, 1969), p. 225.

2. Pierre deVise, "Chicago's Spreading Gold Coast: Shifts in the Chicago Area's Geography of Wealth, 1970–1980," Chicago Regional Inventory Working Paper no. II.76, April 1984.

3. Chicago Fact Book Consortium, Department of Sociology, University of Illinois at Chicago (eds.), *Local Community Fact Book: Chicago Metropolitan Area, 1984* (Chicago: The Consortium, 1984).

4. Stanley Ziemba, "10 of Poorest U.S. Areas in CHA: Study," *Chicago Tribune*, May 23, 1984.

5. Tom Brune and Eduardo Camacho, *Race and Poverty in Chicago: A Special Report* (Chicago: *Chicago Reporter* and Center for Community Research and Assistance, 1983), p. 14.

6. Gary Orfield, Albert Woolbright, and Helene Kim, "Neighborhood Change and Integration in Metropolitan Chicago," report, Leadership Council for Metropolitan Open Communities, July 1984.

7. Chicago Urban League, "A Perspective on the Socio-Economic Status of Chicago Area Blacks," report, Nov. 1983.

8. Robert E. Park, "Introduction," in Harvey W. Zorbaugh, *The Gold Coast and the Slum* (Chicago: University of Chicago Press, 1976; orig. pub. 1929), p. xix.

9. Paul Taylor, *Mexican Labor in the United States: Chicago and the California Region* (Berkeley: University of California Press, 1932), p. 52.

10. Sterling D. Spero and Abram L. Harris, *The Black Worker* (New York: Atheneum, 1972; orig. pub. 1931), p. 163.

11. The job-skills mismatch of earlier decades is still a serious problem in the metropolitan area. See, for example, Stanley Ziemba, "Home and Jobs Often Worlds—and Miles—Apart, Study Finds," *Chicago Tribune*, Oct. 30, 1983.

12. Gary Orfield and Ricardo M. Tostado (eds.), *Latinos in Metropolitan Chicago: A Study of Housing and Employment*, Monograph No. 6 (Chicago: Latino Institute, 1983).

13. Roger Fox and Deborah Haines, *Black Homeowners in Transition Areas* (Chicago: Chicago Urban League, 1981), p. 158.

14. Kevin B. Blackistone, "Racial Violence and Harassment Escalate in Chicago Area," *Chicago Reporter* 14, no. 1 (Jan. 1985).

15. Paul Kleppner suggests this in "Chicago Elects a Black Mayor: An Historical

Analysis of the 1983 Election," report, American Jewish Committee, Chicago Chapter, July 1983.

16. The activities surrounding this conference are discussed at more length in Chapter 5.

17. Thomas Lee Philpott, *The Slum and the Ghetto: Neighborhood Deterioration and Middle-Class Reform, Chicago, 1880–1930* (New York: Oxford University Press, 1978), p. 116.

18. St. Clair Drake and Horace Cayton, *Black Metropolis: A Study of Negro Life in a Northern City*, rev. ed. (New York: Harcourt, Brace and World, 1962), p. 65.

19. Perry R. Duis, "A Clean, Well-Lighted Place: Reformers Do Battle with Slums That Will Not Go Away," *Chicago*, Jan. 1984, pp. 82–85.

20. Drake and Cayton, *Black Metropolis*, p. 77.

21. William Kornblum, in *Blue Collar Community* (Chicago: University of Chicago Press, 1974), demonstrates how this operated in the steel mills in southeast Chicago.

22. Devereux Bowly, Jr., *The Poorhouse: Subsidized Housing in Chicago, 1895–1976* (Carbondale: Southern Illinois University Press, 1978), p. 17.

23. Bowly, *The Poorhouse*, p. 18.

24. Arnold R. Hirsch, *Making the Second Ghetto: Race and Housing in Chicago, 1940–1960* (New York: Cambridge University Press, 1983), ch. 2.

25. Richard Pollenberg, *One Nation Divisible: Class, Race and Ethnicity in the United States since 1938* (New York: Penguin Books, 1980), p. 34.

26. Martin Meyerson and Edward C. Banfield, *Politics, Planning, and the Public Interest: The Case of Public Housing in Chicago* (Glencoe, Ill.: Free Press, 1955), p. 126.

27. Hirsch, *Making the Second Ghetto*, ch. 2.

28. *Ibid.*, ch. 3.

29. Blackistone, "Racial Violence."

30. Bowly, *The Poorhouse*, p. 77.

31. *Ibid.*, p. 84.

32. Meyerson and Banfield, *Politics*, p. 156.

33. Bowly, *The Poorhouse*, p. 125.

34. *Local Community Fact Book*, p. xvi.

35. Hirsch, *Making the Second Ghetto*, p. 27.

36. Leonard Rubinowitz, "Chicago, Illinois," in Paul R. Dommel et al., *Case Studies in Community Development: Decentralizing Urban Policy* (Washington, D.C.: Brookings Institution, 1982), ch. 5.

37. Ashley A. Foard and Hilbert Fefferman, "Federal Urban Renewal Legislation," in James Q. Wilson (ed.), *Urban Renewal: The Record and the Controversy* (Cambridge, Mass.: MIT Press, 1966), pp. 71–125.

38. Foard and Fefferman, "Federal Urban Renewal Legislation," p. 109.

39. *Ibid.*, p. 113.

40. Pierre deVise, "Chicago's Widening Color Gap," report no. 2, Interuniversity Social Research Committee, Dec. 1967.

41. Chester Hartman, "The Housing of Relocated Families," in Wilson (ed.), *Urban Renewal*, p. 310.

42. Hirsch, *Making the Second Ghetto*, p. 124.

43. Brian J. L. Berry, *The Open Housing Question: Race and Housing in Chicago, 1966–1976* (Cambridge, Mass.: Ballinger Publishing Co., 1979), p. 4.

44. *Ibid.*, p. 9.

45. The segregation index ranges from 100, when every city block is either 100 percent black or 0 percent black, to zero when every city block has the same ratio of blacks to its total population as does the entire city. Karl Taeuber, who has constructed indices based on census data from 1940 to 1980, reports on the current figures in "Racial Residential Segregation, 28 Cities, 1970–1980," Center for Demography and Ecology Working Paper no. 83-12, University of Wisconsin, Madison, n.d.

46. Otis Dudley Duncan and Beverly Duncan, *The Negro Population of Chicago* (Chicago: University of Chicago Press, 1957).

47. Harvey Luskin Molotch, *Managed Integration: Dilemmas of Doing Good in the City* (Berkeley: University of California Press, 1972), p. 15.

48. Molotch, *Managed Integration*, p. 19, and Carole Goodwin, *The Oak Park Strategy: Community Control of Racial Change* (Chicago: University of Chicago Press, 1979), pp. 54–55.

49. Deborah L. Haines, "Race Discrimination in Real Estate Advertising," Fall 1981, Chicago Urban League *Research Notes*, pp. 1–6.

50. Helper, *Racial Policies*, p. 201.

51. Robert W. Lake, *The New Suburbanites: Race and Housing in the Suburbs* (New Brunswick, N.J.: Rutgers University Press, 1981), p. 232.

52. Helper, *Racial Policies*, p. 42.

53. Orfield, Woolbright, and Kim, "Neighborhood Change," p. 17.

54. Dennis R. Marino, "Mortgage Lending, Blacks and Hispanics: From the Dual Housing Finance Market to Reinvestment to Unitary Unsatisfactory Market for All," in "Housing: Chicago Style," papers presented at a consultation sponsored by the Illinois Advisory Committee to the U.S. Commission on Civil Rights, Chicago, Oct. 1982, pp. 23–29.

55. Roger Fox and Amy Goldman, "Marquette Park: A Descriptive History of Efforts to Peacefully Resolve Racial Conflict," report, Chicago Urban League, Fall 1979. Other FHA-backed buyers were not able to assume the financial responsibilities of homeowners, but the mortgage lenders facilitated their purchase of houses nonetheless, since there were quick, substantial, and guaranteed profits to be made through foreclosures.

56. Marino, "Mortgage Lending," p. 26.

57. Rubinowitz, "Chicago," p. 133.

58. *Disclosure: Newsletter of the National Training and Information Center* (Chicago), Jan.–March 1984. Figures in the next paragraph are also from this document.

59. Orfield and Tostado (eds.), *Latinos*, p. 22.

60. *Ibid.*, p. 24.

61. *Ibid.*, p. 37.

62. Gerald William Ropka, *The Evolving Residential Pattern of the Mexican, Puerto Rican, and Cuban Population in the City of Chicago* (New York: Arno Press, 1980), pp. 125–126.

63. Stanley Ziemba, "Census Shows Suburbs are Ethnic Smorgasbord," *Chicago Tribune*, Mar. 13, 1984.

64. Michael N. Danielson, *The Politics of Exclusion* (New York: Columbia University Press, 1976).

65. Housing Abandonment Task Force, "An End to Housing Abandonment: Saving Affordable Housing in Chicago Neighborhoods," report, July 1984.

66. Lisa Goff, "Mike Pensack Fights Landlords, Makes Evanston Apartment Law Work," *Crain's Chicago Business*, May 14, 1984.

67. William K. Tabb, *The Long Default: New York City and the Urban Fiscal Crisis* (New York: Monthly Review Press, 1982), p. 91.

68. There is, of course, another housing class, the homeless. According to a report from Mayor Harold Washington's Task Force on the Homeless, in 1984 there were between 12,000 and 25,000 people in Chicago who had no permanent residence.

69. George Curry and Jerry Thornton, "When It Comes to Crises, the CHA Is a High-Rise," *Chicago Tribune*, March 11, 1984.

70. *Ibid.*

71. William Julius Wilson, "The Black Underclass," *Wilson Quarterly*, Spring 1984, pp. 88–99.

72. Hirsch, *Making the Second Ghetto*, p. 266.

73. *Ibid.*

74. *Ibid.*, p. 265.

75. *Ibid.*

76. Kale Williams, "The Dual Housing Market in the Chicago Metropolitan Area," in "Housing: Chicago Style," p. 41.

77. Hirsch, *Making the Second Ghetto*, p. 226.

78. J. S. Fuerst and Roy Petty, "Bleak Housing in Chicago," *Public Interst*, July 1978.

79. Memorandum to Judge Marvin E. Aspen from Nancy Jefferson, vice chair, and Ed Marciniak, chair, Advisory Committee to the Chicago Housing Authority, Feb. 6, 1984, p. 4.

80. Section 8 of the Housing and Community Development Act of 1974 allows not only for new housing to be built and existing housing to be rehabilitated but also for individual persons and families who are qualified to receive certificates of eligibility for government rental assistance in housing they find themselves that meets HUD's criteria.

81. Curry and Thornton, "When It Comes to Crises."

82. Williams, "Dual Housing Market," p. 39.

83. DeVise, "Chicago's Spreading Gold Coast."

84. Elizabeth Warren, *Subsidized Housing in Chicago Suburbs*, Urban Insights Series (Chicago: Loyola University Press, 1981), apps. A and D.

85. Alan P. Henry and Don Wycliff, "Blacks Seek Gains in Public Services," *Chicago Sun-Times*, Oct. 18, 1983.

86. City of Chicago, "Chicago Works Together: 1984 Chicago Development Plan," report, May 1984, p. 10.

87. Goodwin, *Oak Park Strategy*, and Roberta Raymond, "Racial Diversity: A Model for American Communities," in "Housing: Chicago Style," pp. 85–93.

88. Goodwin, *Oak Park Strategy*, p. 167.

89. Ray Gibson, "Oak Park: Architect of Racial Unity," *Chicago Tribune*, Oct. 7, 1984.

90. "Illinois Village Sets Housing Integration Plan," *New York Times*, Nov. 11, 1984.

91. Gibson, "Oak Park."

92. Catherine Collins, "Doggedness of Cicero May Prevail Against Its Newest Problem—Old Age," *Chicago Tribune*, June 15–16, 1984.

93. Hugh Hough, "Population Boom in Suburbs Seen," *Chicago Sun-Times*, Jan. 31, 1984.

94. Collins, "Doggedness."

95. F. Peter Model, "Up Front," *Perspectives: The Civil Rights Quarterly* 15, no. 3 (Summer 1983): 3. In 1984, Cicero made some effort to exclude children from the housing for the track employees. Given that this housing is an almost permanent residence for the adults who care for the horses, excluding children would essentially mean separating parents from their children. The reasons given by the city were overcrowding and unsafe conditions. However, Cicero's schools have been the object of several civil rights suits because of their unwillingness to enroll black children.

96. Hirsch, *Making the Second Ghetto*, p. 200.

97. Glen Elsasser, "U.S. Will Press Civil Rights Suit Against Cicero," *Chicago Tribune*, June 2, 1984.

98. Warren, *Subsidized Housing*.

99. Northeastern Illinois Planning Commission, "Regional Data Report," June 30, 1978, table EC-8, p. V-25.

100. Brian J. L. Berry, Carole A. Goodwin, Robert W. Lake, and Katherine B. Smith, "Attitudes Toward Integration: The Role of Status in Community Response to Racial Change," in Barry Schwartz (ed.), *The Changing Face of the Suburbs* (Chicago: University of Chicago Press, 1976), p. 225.

101. "William J. Phillips and Dorothy R. Phillips vs. Hunter Trails Community Association in the United States Court of Appeals for the Seventh Circuit, No.81-2372, argued April 8, 1982 and decided August 3, 1982."

102. Andrew Fegelman, "Court Clears DuPage in Housing Bias Case," *Chicago Tribune*, June 27, 1984.

103. Andrew Fegelman, "DuPage Board Oks Open Housing," *Chicago Tribune*, May 30, 1984.

104. Fegelman, "Court Clears DuPage."

105. *Ibid.*

106. Irving Cutler, *Chicago: Metropolis of the Mid-Continent*, 2d ed. (Dubuque, Iowa: Kendall/Hunt, 1976), p. 192.

107. Don Wycliff and Alan P. Henry, "Selective 'Steering' Integrates Suburbs," *Chicago Sun-Times*, Oct. 16, 1983.

108. *Ibid.*

109. *Ibid.*

110. Donald L. Demarco, "Promoting and Preserving Racial Residential Diversity: The Park Forest Case," in "Housing: Chicago Style," p. 83.

111. Warren, *Subsidized Housing*, p. 18.

112. *Ibid.*, p. 20.

113. John Atlas and Peter Dreier, "Mobilize or Compromise?: The Tenants' Movement and American Politics," in Chester Hartman (ed.), *America's Housing Crisis* (Boston: Routledge and Kegan Paul, 1983), pp. 151–185.

114. "Drafting a National Low-Income Housing Policy," *Neighborhood Works*, May 1984, pp. 14–17.

Chapter 5

1. Charles Bowden and Lew Kreinberg, *Street Signs Chicago* (Chicago: Chicago Review Press, 1980), p. 33.

2. Len O'Conner, *Clout: Mayor Daley and His City* (New York: Avon, 1975), p. 44.

3. Harry Golden Jr., "4 Wards Hold 20% of City Jobs," *Chicago Sun-Times*, Dec. 21, 1982.

4. Tom Brune, "Chicago Park District Shortchanges Black and Latino Wards," *Chicago Reporter* 7, no. 5 (May 1978).

5. In 1950 blacks numbered 492,265 and constituted 13.6 percent of Chicago's population; by 1960, the black population was 812,637, 22.9 percent of the city's total population.

6. Roger Fox and Amy Goldman, "Marquette Park: A Descriptive History of Efforts to Peacefully Resolve Racial Conflict," report, Chicago Urban League, Fall 1979, p. 46.

7. Commissioner Quinn is quoted in Thomas Brune (ed.), "Neglected Neighborhoods: Patterns of Discrimination in Chicago City Services," (Chicago: Community Renewal Society, 1981), p. 11.

8. Mayor Daley is quoted in Mike Royko, *Boss: Richard J. Daley of Chicago* (New York: E. P. Dutton, 1971), p. 134.

9. Mary J. Herrick, *The Chicago Schools: A Social and Political History* (Beverly Hills, Calif.: Sage Publications, 1981), p. 324.

10. Herrick, *Chicago Schools*, p. 325.

11. *Ibid.*, p. 337.

12. Paul Kleppner, "Chicago Elects a Black Mayor: An Historical Analysis of the 1983 Election," report, American Jewish Committee, Chicago Chapter, July 1983, p. 68.

13. Editorial, *Chicago Sun-Times*, Oct. 9, 1982.

14. Brian J. L. Berry, *The Open Housing Question: Race and Housing in Chicago, 1966–1976* (Cambridge, Mass.: Ballinger Publishing Co., 1979), p. 108.

15. For a fuller discussion of the neighborhood movement and its relationship to earlier social movements, see Harry Boyte, *The Backyard Revolution: Understanding the New Citizen Movement* (Philadelphia: Temple University Press, 1980).

16. Hal Baron is quoted in Edwin C. Berry and Walter W. Stafford, *The Racial Aspects of Urban Planning: Critique of the Comprehensive Plan of the City of Chicago* (Chicago: Chicago Urban League, 1968).

17. Studs Terkel, *Division Street: America* (New York: Pantheon Books, 1967), pp. 5–6.

18. For more on the role of women in neighborhood groups, see Kathleen McCourt, *Working-Class Women and Grassroots Politics* (Bloomington: Indiana University Press, 1977).

19. John Hall Fish, *Black Power/White Control: The Struggle of the Woodlawn Organization in Chicago* (Princeton, N.J.: Princeton University Press, 1973).

20. Ed Marciniak, *Reviving an Inner City Community* (Chicago: Loyola University Press, 1977).

21. David Emmons, unpub. MS. "Community Organizing and Urban Policy: Saul Alinsky and Chicago's Citizens Action Program."

22. Herbert Gans, *The Urban Villagers* (New York: Free Press, 1962).

23. Chester Hartman and Rob Kessler, "The Illusion and Reality of Urban Renewal: San Francisco's Yerba Buena Center," in William K. Tabb and Larry Sawers (eds.), *Marxism and the Metropolis* (New York: Oxford University Press, 1978), pp. 153–178.

24. Florence Scala is quoted in Robert Cross, "Neighborhood Crusader: Saluting the Lady Who Took On City Hall," *Chicago Tribune*, Oct. 15, 1984.

25. John H. Mollenkopf, *The Contested City* (Princeton, N.J.: Princeton University Press, 1983), p. 210.

26. Manuel Castells, *The City and the Grassroots: A Cross-Cultural Theory of Urban Social Movements* (Berkeley: University of California Press, 1983).

27. David Moberg, "Introducing the Three Bs: Bankers, Businessmen, and Bankruptcy," *The Reader* (Chicago), Feb. 1, 1980.

28. James L. Greer, "The Politics of Decline and Growth: Planning, Economic Transformation, and the Structuring of Urban Futures in American Cities," Ph.D. diss., University of Chicago, 1983, p. 96.

29. Lawlor is quoted in Ronald Grossman, *Chicago Journalism Review*, Feb. 1973, p. 14; reprinted in Berry, *Open Housing Question*, p. 189.

30. For theoretical and empirical insights into the ways in which Chicago residents construct their neighborhood boundaries, see Gerald D. Suttles, *The Social Construction of Communities* (Chicago: University of Chicago Press, 1972), and Albert Hunter, *Symbolic Communities: The Persistence and Change of Chicago's Local Communities* (Chicago: University of Chicago Press, 1974).

31. Debbie Nathan, "On Panic and Puerto Ricans: Is Blockbusting Back on the South Side?," *The Reader* (Chicago), June 8, 1984.

32. Henry Scheff, "Issues and Communities: The CAP Model of Organizing," *Focus/Midwest* 11, no. 69 (n.d.): 14–17.

33. Gregory D. Squires, Ruthanne DeWolfe, and Alan S. DeWolfe, "Urban Decline or Disinvestment: Uneven Development, Redlining, and the Role of the Insurance Industry," *Social Problems* 27 (Oct. 1979): 79–95.

34. Scheff, "Issues and Communities," p. 16.

35. Ron Dorfman, "Greenlining Chicago: The Citizens Action Program," *Working Papers* 3 (Summer 1975): 32–36.

36. *Disclosure: Newsletter of the National Training and Information Center* (Chicago), Jan.–March 1984.

37. *Ibid.*

38. Joan Lancourt, *Confront or Concede: The Alinsky Citizen Action Organizations* (Lexington, Mass.: Lexington Books, 1979), p. 26.

39. David Moberg, "Citizens Action Program: Dead Before Its Time," *In These Times*, Nov. 30–Dec. 6, 1977.

40. Ben Joravsky and Jorge Caruso, "City's Ethnics Charge Neglect Despite Mayoral Charm," *Chicago Reporter*, Feb. 1984.

41. Jonas Dovydenso, "Right Against Right," *Chicago*, March 1977, p. 218.

42. McCourt, *Working-Class Women*, p. 48.

43. Ann Grimes, "Community Organizing in Black and White: The 'New Victims' Raise Their Voices," *The Reader* (Chicago), May 4, 1984.

44. *Ibid.*

45. Kleppner, "Chicago Elects a Black Mayor," p. 99.

46. Interview with Phil Mullins, organizing director, Southeast UNO, April 15, 1985.

47. Interview with Warren Friedman, director, Chicago Alliance for Neighborhood Safety, Feb. 14, 1985.

48. Kirsten Grønbjerg and her colleagues conclude that the Chicago agencies most adversely affected by government retrenchment in the Reagan administration are "those providing employment, training and income support, housing and community development, or advocacy and legal services"; these lost 12 percent in real government support between 1981 and 1982 Urban Institute, *The Chicago Nonprofit Service Sector in a Time of Governmental Retrenchment* (Washington, D.C.: The Institute, 1984), p. 2.

49. This quotation is from a flyer, "Urban Problems; Neighborhood Solutions," that was distributed to advertise Seminar Day for the Save Our Neighborhoods/Save Our City coalition, Sept. 29, 1984.

50. Little has been published on the home equity insurance program. Those interested might consult Michael A. Murray, "Reassuring the Small Homeowner in Oak Park: An Interim Report on the Equity Assurance Plan," report, Village of Oak Park, Jan. 1976, or Arthur Lyons, Kathleen McCourt, and Philip Nyden, "Preserving Home Values in Chicago through a Home Equity Guarantee Program," report, Chicago Neighborhood Organizing Project Jan. 31, 1986. The latter report explores the feasibility of a home value guarantee program in selected Chicago communities.

51. Arsenio Oleroso Jr., "Scattered Sites Concentrated in Edgewater and Uptown: Report," *Lerner Newspaper* (Chicago), Nov. 21, 1984.

52. David Moberg, "Will Neighborhood Jobs Win 'War' for Washington?," *In These Times*, May 2–8, 1984.

53. Bute is quoted in Oleroso, "Scattered Sites."

54. City of Chicago, "Chicago Works Together: 1984 Chicago Development Plan," report, May 1984.

55. Lucia Mouat, "Neighborhoods Are Top Priority for Chicago Planner," *Christian Science Monitor*, July 18, 1984.

56. Moberg, "Will Neighborhood Jobs Win?"

57. "Chicago Works Together," p. 14.

58. Moberg, "Will Neighborhood Jobs Win?"

59. Friedman interview.

60. "Chicago Works Together," p. 50.

61. Telephone interview with Jerry Altman, director, Housing Agenda, Chicago, Ill., June 13, 1984.

62. O'Conner, *Clout*, p. 6.

Chapter 6

1. "Daley of Chicago," *Harper's*, Aug. 1968, p. 25.

2. Byrne, a Chicago architect, is quoted in Studs Terkel, *Division Street: America* (New York: Pantheon Books, 1967), pp. 260–261.

3. Carl W. Condit, *Chicago, 1910–29: Buildings, Planning, and Urban Technology* (Chicago: University of Chicago Press, 1973), pp. 59–85, 178–234.

4. Chicago Municipal Reference Library, "Facts About Chicago," brochure, May 1983; Dennis R. Judd, *The Politics of American Cities* (Boston: Little, Brown, 1979), p. 378.

5. Brian J. L. Berry, Irving Cutler, Edwin H. Draine, Ying-cheng Kiang, Thomas R. Tocalis, and Pierre deVise, *Chicago: Transformations of an Urban System* (Cambridge, Mass.: Ballinger Publishing Co., 1976), pp. 73–75; Robert Enstad, "Mall Ends Slump in State Street Sales," *Chicago Tribune*, June 30, 1981.

6. Mark I. Gelfand, *A Nation of Cities: The Federal Government and Urban America, 1933–1965* (New York: Oxford University Press, 1975), pp. 118–152; Mel Scott, *American City Planning since 1890* (Berkeley: University of California Press, 1969), pp. 415–429.

7. R. B. Cohen, "The New International Division of Labor, Multinational Corporations, and Urban Hierarchy," in Michael Dear and Allen J. Scott (eds.), *Urbanization and Urban Planning in Capitalist Society* (London: Methuen, 1981), p. 305. However, the growth of white-collar jobs in Chicago's Loop has not resulted in a significant increase in employment. Rather, these job gains have in part compensated for declines in traditional occupations. See R. C. Longworth, "How Much Time Do We Have? . . . No Time," *Chicago Tribune*, May 10, 1981.

8. Arnold R. Hirsch, *Making the Second Ghetto: Race and Housing in Chicago, 1940–1960* (New York: Cambridge University Press, 1983), pp. 100–134.

9. Edward C. Banfield, *Political Influence* (New York: Free Press, 1965), pp. 126–158.

10. Chicago Department of City Planning, "Development Plan for the Central Area of Chicago," report, Aug. 1958.

11. *Ibid.*, p. 19.

12. See Sam Bass Warner Jr., *The Private City: Philadelphia in Three Periods of Its Growth* (Philadelphia: University of Pennsylvania Press, 1968), esp. pp. 3–4, for Warner's discussion of privatism. In the following pages we will expand this approach by emphasizing the cooperative decision-making pattern linking Chicago's public and private sectors.

13. See Robert A. Caro, *The Power Broker: Robert Moses and the Fall of New York* (New York: Vintage Books, 1975), pp. 707, 1005–1025; Walter McQuade, "Urban Renewal in Boston," in James Q. Wilson (ed.), *Urban Renewal: The Record and the Controversy* (Cambridge, Mass.: MIT Press, 1966), pp. 259–277; Chester Hartman, *Yerba Buena: Land Grab and Community Resistance in San Francisco* (San Francisco: Glide Publications, 1974), pp. 48–51.

14. For example, see George Rosen's *Decision-Making Chicago-Style* (Urbana: University of Illinois Press, 1980), pp. 61–93, for an account of the discussions resulting in site location for the University of Illinois-Chicago campus.

15. Chicago Central Area Committee, "Chicago 21: A Plan for the Central Area

Communities," report, Sept. 1973.

16. For a discussion of the latter, see David Emmons, *Dearborn Park/South Loop New Town: A Project in the Chicago 21 Plan* (Chicago: Citizens' Information Service, 1977).

17. James L. Greer, "The Politics of Decline and Growth: Planning, Economic Transformation, and the Structuring of Urban Futures in American Cities," Ph.D. diss., University of Chicago, 1983, pp. 154–158; Ed Marciniak, *Reviving an Inner-City Neighborhood* (Chicago: Loyola University Press, 1977), pp. 25–47; Kit Scruggs, "Area Groups Rap Chicago 21 as 'Plot' to Oust Poor," *Chicago Sun-Times*, Nov. 14, 1976.

18. The Hollander quote appears in Ann Grimes, "Future Tension: Scrutinizing the Central Area Plan," *The Reader* (Chicago), Oct. 21, 1983.

19. Chicago Central Area Committee and City of Chicago, "Chicago Central Area Plan: A Plan for the Heart of the City," report, March 1983, pp. 29–31.

20. Hirsch, *Making the Second Ghetto*, pp. 101–102.

21. *Ibid.*, p. 151. For a different perspective, see Peter H. Rossi and Robert A. Dentler, *The Politics of Urban Renewal* (Glencoe, Ill.: Free Press, 1963).

22. William Gruber, "Close Ties to Business 'Vital' to Cities," *Chicago Tribune*, Sept. 17, 1978.

23. Arthur Rubloff, letter to *Chicago Tribune*, June 20, 1980.

24. Len O'Connor, *Clout: Mayor Daley and His City* (New York: Avon, 1975), pp. 137–140.

25. Scott, *American City Planning*, pp. 100–109.

26. Interview with Ira J. Bach, director of City Development, Chicago, Dec. 21 and 23, 1983.

27. Interview with Robert Mier, commissioner, Chicago Department of Economic Development, Chicago, Feb. 28, 1984.

28. Bach interview.

29. Greer, "The Politics of Decline and Growth," pp. 164–182.

30. Hirsch, *Making the Second Ghetto*, pp. 135–170.

31. Denise DeClue, "The Siege of Sandburg Village," *The Reader* (Chicago), Jan. 20, 1978.

32. Chicago Department of Urban Renewal, "Lincoln Park General Neighborhood Renewal Plan," report, 1962.

33. On the 1966 Comprehensive Plan and Chicago's neighborhoods, see Carl W. Condit, *Chicago, 1930–70: Buildings, Planning, and Urban Technology* (Chicago: University of Chicago Press, 1974), pp. 275–277.

34. City of Chicago, "HUD Federally Aided Programs," report, Feb. 1969, p. 2.

35. Berry et al., *Chicago*, p. 76.

36. City of Chicago, "Chicago 1992 Comprehensive Plan: Goals and Policies and Ten-Year Capital Development Strategies," report, Oct. 1982, p. 21.

37. Hirsch, *Making the Second Ghetto*, pp. 130–132, 185–210; Martin Meyerson and Edward C. Banfield, *Politics, Planning, and the Public Interest: The Case of Public Housing in Chicago* (Glencoe, Ill.: Free Press, 1955), pp. 91–118, 153–222; Robert Bailey Jr., *Radicals in City Politics* (Chicago: University of Chicago Press, 1974), pp. 4–11, 27–41.

38. Donald H. Haider, "Capital Budgeting and Planning in the Post-Daley Era,"

in Samuel K. Gove and Louis H. Masotti (eds.), *After Daley: Chicago Politics in Transition* (Urbana: University of Illinois Press, 1982), pp. 159–174; Stevenson O. Swanson, "Reports Say City May Be Wearing Out," *Chicago Tribune*, Feb. 25, 1982.

39. Metropolitan Housing and Planning Council, "Infrastructure Planning and Financing Survey: Preliminary Results," report, Nov. 30, 1984.

40. Interview with Charles Wolf, vice-president, Rubloff Redevelopment Corp., Chicago, May 9, 1983; Rubloff letter; Chicago Department of Urban Renewal, "Staff Report: North Loop Study Area," Oct. 2, 1973, p. 5.

41. Rubloff Redevelopment Corp., "North Loop Redevelopment," report, n.d.; Rubloff letter; Richard Christiansen, "Chicago at the Crossroads: A Report on the Redevelopment of the North Loop," *Chicago Tribune*, Nov. 9, 1980.

42. Paul Gapp, "Failure to Guarantee Preservation of Buildings Perils N. Loop Funds," *Chicago Tribune*, Aug. 3, 1980; Joe Kolman, "The Trial of the Chicago 12," *The Reader* (Chicago), Oct. 10, 1979.

43. Wolf interview.

44. Ed McManus, "Chicago Plan Unit OKs North Loop Renovation," *Chicago Tribune*, April 12, 1979.

45. George Papajohn, "The Chicago Theatre Tug-of-War," *Chicago Tribune*, March 14, 1982.

46. Christiansen, "Chicago at the Crossroads."

47. Robert Davis, "Banks to Put Up $50 Million to Aid North Loop," *Chicago Tribune*, July 21, 1979; Lillian Williams, "Co. Panel Approves 'Blighted' Tax Break," *Chicago Sun-Times*, Feb. 26, 1980.

48. John McCarron, "Good, Bad News for North Loop Project Backers," *Chicago Tribune*, April 7, 1980.

49. John McCarron and Stanley Ziemba, "Contract Lets Hilton Corp. Control North Loop Plan," *Chicago Tribune*, Aug. 17, 1980.

50. William Juneau, "Assessor Rejects N. Loop Tax Break Bid as 'Incomplete,'" *Chicago Tribune*, Aug. 20, 1980.

51. Gapp, "Failure to Guarantee Preservation."

52. Christiansen, "Chicago at the Crossroads;" Paul Gapp, "Good Show, But Questions Remain," *Chicago Tribune*, Nov. 14, 1980; Richard Christiansen, "Arts, Not Edifices Come First," *Chicago Tribune*, Nov. 14, 1980.

53. Stanley Ziemba, "City Gets Its N. Loop Act Together," *Chicago Tribune*, Oct. 21, 1982.

54. John McCarron, "Study Charges City Gets Short End of Tax Break for Hilton," *Chicago Tribune*, Nov. 8, 1981; Raffaela Y. Nanetti, "Community Groups as Alternative Political Organizations in Chicago," photocopy, April 1983, pp. 21–26; interview with Jared Shlaes, president, Shlaes and Co., Chicago, July 7, 1984.

55. Stanley Ziemba and David Axelrod, "Hynes' Hilton Decision Avoids Political Fallout," *Chicago Tribune*, Dec. 9, 1981. Speaking for the City Club of Chicago, James Fuerst had proposed a "recapture" arrangement at the Hilton hearings. See "Report and Decision of Cook Co. Assessor on the Application of the City of Chicago for Class 7 Certification of the State-Wacker Area," Dec. 8, 1981, pp. 223–231.

56. William Juneau, "Hilton: Can't Build Without Tax Break," *Chicago Tribune*, Jan. 24, 1982; Stanley Ziemba, "Hilton Scraps N. Loop Project," *Chicago Tribune*, March 4, 1982.

57. Stanley Ziemba, "City Gets 3 North Loop Bids," *Chicago Tribune*, July 16, 1981; Ziemba, "City Gets Its N. Loop Act Together."

58. Stanley Ziemba, "Council O.K. Is Expected on Sole North Loop Bid," *Chicago Tribune*, Dec. 16, 1982; Charles Nicodemus, "Council O.K. of N. Loop Plan Urged," *Chicago Sun-Times*, Jan. 5, 1983.

59. Stanley Ziemba, "5th Group Offers North Loop Plan," *Chicago Tribune*, Jan. 23, 1985.

60. Thom Shanker and Stanley Ziemba, "North Loop Project Could Begin by '85," *Chicago Tribune*, June 21, 1984; interview with Glenn Steinberg, director, North Loop Planning, Chicago Department of Planning, Chicago, June 27, 1984.

61. Stanley Ziemba, "Chicago Theatre Gets a Reprieve," *Chicago Tribune*, Nov. 3, 1984.

62. Robert Davis, "Unveil City Home Loan Plan," *Chicago Tribune*, June 28, 1978; John McCarron, "City's Rehab Loan Plan Will Favor Smaller Buildings," *Chicago Tribune*, Dec. 10, 1981.

63. Stanley Ziemba, "Many Blacks, Suburbanites Got Low-Interest Mortgages," *Chicago Tribune*, Jan. 8, 1979; John McCarron, "Program Not Lending Itself to Aid of Poor Homes," *Chicago Tribune*, June 14, 1982.

64. Bonita Brodt, "Albany Park: Community Participation That Worked," *Chicago Tribune*, May 1, 1980; Stevenson Swanson, "Albany Park Mapping Its Revival," *Chicago Tribune*, Sept. 24, 1981; Bonita Brodt, "Albany Park Wants a Housing Court of Its Own," *Chicago Tribune*, Aug. 7, 1980; Bonita Brodt, "Lawrence Av. Shopping Strip Bounces Back with Loans," *Chicago Tribune*, July 12, 1979; "Financial Assistance to Businesses: LADCOR Networking," *TRUST Inc.* (Chicago), Feb. 16, 1984, pp. 4–6.

65. City of Chicago, "Chicago 1992 Comprehensive Plan," pp. 5–7. It is worth noting, also, that the neighborhood councils proposed in this document do not represent the same geographic subdivisions as the 16 "development areas" defined in the 1966 Comprehensive Plan.

66. John McCarron, "City Dressing Up Dingy Storefronts," *Chicago Tribune*, July 16, 1981; David Ibata, "New Vigor for Old Stores with a Pretty Face," *Chicago Tribune*, Aug. 21, 1983.

67. City of Chicago, "Chicago Works Together: 1984 Chicago Development Plan," report, May 1984.

68. Ed Zotti, "Q & A," *The Reader* (Chicago), March 2, 1984.

69. City support for Dearborn Park was discussed earlier in this chapter. The Presidential Towers project is discussed in John McCarron, "Presidential Towers Rise on Government Subsidies," *Chicago Tribune*, Dec. 18, 1983.

Chapter 7

1. Vernon Jarrett, "I Feel Wonderful About My City Again," *Chicago Sun-Times*, Sept. 21, 1983.

2. John H. Mollenkopf, *The Contested City* (Princeton, N.J.: Princeton University Press, 1983); Larry Bennett, Kathleen McCourt, Philip Nyden, and Gregory Squires, "Chicago's North Loop Redevelopment Project: A Growth Machine on Hold," in Scott

Cummings (ed.), *Business Elites and Urban Development* (Albany: State University of New York Press, 1987).

3. Harvey Molotch, "The City as a Growth Machine: Toward a Political Economy of Place," *American Journal of Sociology* 82 (Sept. 1976): 309–330.

4. David Smith and Patrick McGuigan, *Towards a Public Balance Sheet* (Washington, D.C.: National Center for Economic Alternatives, 1979).

5. M. W. Newman, "Behind the Facade: Isn't It Time for a More Human City?," *Chicago*, Jan. 1984, p. 153.

6. Derek Shearer, "Planning with a Political Face," *The Nation* 237 (Dec. 31, 1983–Jan. 7, 1984): 696.

7. Joshua Cohen and Joel Rogers, *On Democracy: Toward a Transformation of American Society* (New York: Penguin Books, 1983), p. 161.

8. Harvey Molotch and John Logan, "Tensions in the Growth Machine: Overcoming Resistance to Value-Free Development," *Social Problems* 31 (June 1984): 483–499; Todd Swanstrom, *The Crisis of Growth Politics: Cleveland, Kucinich, and the Promise of Urban Populism* (Philadelphia: Temple University Press, 1985).

9. City of Chicago, "Chicago Works Together: 1984 Chicago Development Plan," report, May 1984.

10. Edward Greer, *Big Steel: Black Politics and Corporate Power in Gary, Indiana* (New York: Monthly Review Press, 1979), pp. 12, 13.

11. "Growth Plans Need a Push," *Chicago Tribune*, April 9, 1984.

12. Commercial Club of Chicago, "Make No Little Plans: Jobs for Metropolitan Chicago," report, 1984, p. 6.

13. *Ibid.*, p. 8.

14. *Ibid.*, p. 24.

Index